INDIAN FOREIGN POLICY IN THE 21ST CENTURY

INDIAN FOREIGN POLICY IN THE 21ST CENTURY

DEEPAK YADAV

Kaveri Books
New Delhi-110 002

ISBN: 978-93-86463-01-2
First Published in 2017

Published by
Kaveri Books
4832/24, Ansari Road, Darya Ganj
New Delhi-110002 (India)
Tel: 011-23288140, 47072321
E-mail : info@kaveribooks.com
kaveribooks@gmail.com
Website: www.kaveribooks.com

Typeset at
Delta Book World, New Delhi - 110 002

PRINTED IN INDIA

Dedicated to

My Wife Anisha

and kids

Khushi, Anushri and Aadvik

ACKNOWLEDGEMENTS

I would like to express my gratitude to the many people who saw me through this book; to all those who provided support, talked things over, read, wrote, offered comments, allowed me to quote their remarks and assisted in the editing, proofreading and design.

The most credit for this book goes to the Principal of Kalindi College, University of Delhi, Dr. Anula Maurya mam who has always been so kind to me.

I would like to thank my colleagues at Department of Political Science, Kalindi College for their valuable support and suggestions.

Dr. Sudhir Singh sir has always encouraged me to raise the bar in academic excellence. My friends who have been providing their constant help in writing this book included Devendra Pratap, Vinay Singh, Rajiv Dubey, Avdhesh Yadav, Jaswant Singh Negi, Rishiji, Minakshiji, Pushpaji.

I would like to express my gratitude to Rakeshji and Abhishekji for enabling me to publish this book.

I also want to thank the library staff of JNU, Delhi University, IDSA and Teen Murti Library for providing useful materials for this book.

It is the family where child learns first lession of his life. Dear Mummy and Papa, it is because of you I exist in this world. My elder brother Keval Bhaiya deserves the most credits, who always encouraged me to pursue higher education. My other family members, who are close to my heart includes Bhabhi, Chandan, Pooja, Suraj, Archana, Rajan, Sneha, Snehil.

Above all I want to thank my wife Anisha and my kids Khushi, Anushri and Aadvik who supported and encouraged me in spite of all the time it took me away from them. It was a long and difficult journey for them.

Last but not the least, I beg forgiveness of all those who have been with me over the course of the years and whose names I have failed to mention.

Dr. Deepak Yadav

PREFACE

Even before independence, the Government of India maintained semi-autonomous diplomatic relations. After India gained independence from the United Kingdom in 1947, it soon joined the Commonwealth of Nations and strongly supported independence movements in other colonies, like the Indonesian National Revolution. The partition and various territorial disputes, particularly that over Kashmir, would strain its relations with Pakistan for years to come. During the Cold War, India adopted a foreign policy of not aligning itself with any major power bloc. However, India developed close ties with the Soviet Union and received extensive military support from it.

The end of the Cold War significantly affected India's foreign policy, as it did for much of the world. The country now seeks to strengthen its diplomatic and economic ties with the United States, the People's Republic of China, the European Union, Japan, Israel, Mexico and Brazil. India has also forged close ties with the member states of the Association of Southeast Asian Nations, the African Union, the Arab League and Iran. Though India continues to have a military relationship with Russia, Israel has emerged as India's second largest military partner while India has built a strong strategic partnership with the United States. The foreign policy of Narendra Modi indicated a shift towards focusing on the Asian region and, more broadly, trade deals.

Jawaharlal Nehru, India's first Prime Minister, promoted a strong personal role for the Prime Minister but a weak institutional structure. Nehru served concurrently as Prime Minister and Minister of External Affairs; he made all major foreign policy decisions himself after consulting with his advisers and then entrusted the conduct of international affairs to senior members of the Indian Foreign Service. He was the main founding fathers of the Panchsheel or the five principles of peaceful co-existence.

Unwittingly, the absence of an indigenous foreign policy tradition allowed the Indian freedom movement to evolve its external perspectives without external baggage. Jawaharlal Nehru, later India's first Prime Minister, and rightly acknowledged as the architect of India's foreign policy - whose essential parameters and guiding values have remained largely unaltered, already refused to choose between fascism and imperialism, and started saying what India's foreign policy would be. From the late 1920s on, he formulated the Congress stance on international issues, and the Congress party established a small foreign department in 1925.

As interim Prime Minister, Nehru, in 1946, articulated India's approach to the world, when he expostulated: "Our general policy is to avoid entanglement in power politics and not to join any group of powers as against any other group. We must be friends to both (blocs) and yet not join either." This is when in the prevailing Cold War between two heavily armed and hostile camps, each rival superpower stared saying that if you were not with them you were against them. It took courage and vision to retain the choice to judge each issue on its merits and on how it affected our enlightened self-interest, rather than that of an alliance. Having fought so hard for our freedom, we were not about to abdicate our independence of judgment to others. Incidentally, the term Non-Alignment was coined by V Krishna Menon in his speech at the UN in 1953; Nehru later used it during his speech in 1954 in Colombo.

The primary purpose of independent India's foreign policy was to help enable the domestic transformation of India from a poor and backward society into one which could offer her people their basic needs and an opportunity to achieve their potential. Nehru delineated the role that foreign policy could play in achieving this, by striving to create an external environment which would accelerate capital flows from abroad, increase the use of science and technology, help modernization of India's infrastructure, ensure energy security, facilitate development and import of hydrocarbon resources, and import of natural resources in which India was deficient. Today, too, India's principal foreign policy objectives remain a peaceful environment and strategic space and autonomy, so as to concentrate on our tasks of integration and nation building. This necessitates good relations with major powers and economies, and the neighbours.

Several factors – historical, civilizational, and cultural – that are innate to our people's genius, as well as current relevant ones like economic, technological, and demographic, lie behind our foreign policy consensus in shaping it. The quintessential strands of our foreign policy: peaceful co-existence, non-interference, peaceful resolution of disputes, non-alignment, anti-colonialism, anti-racism, multilateralism, pluralism, general and complete disarmament, opposition to all forms of terrorism, extremism and fundamentalism, pro-development, wider global cooperation in general, and South-South cooperation in particular, and so on, are moored in India's civilizational beliefs in peace, tolerance and One World. These have admirably stood the test of time. India, as an open, inclusive, and responsible member of the global community, believes that durable peace is only possible in a world in which all are equal stakeholders in prosperity, progress and happiness. We also propounded Panchasheela, the five principles of peaceful co-existence for international relations.

In the 1960s and 1970s India's international position among developed and developing countries faded in the course of wars with China and Pakistan, disputes with other countries in South Asia, and India's attempt to balance Pakistan's support from the United States and China by signing the Indo-Soviet Treaty of Friendship and Cooperation in August 1971. Although India obtained substantial Soviet military and economic aid, which helped to strengthen the nation, India's influence was undercut regionally and internationally by the perception that its friendship with the Soviet Union prevented a more forthright condemnation of the Soviet presence in Afghanistan. In the late 1980s, India improved relations with the United States, other developed countries, and China while continuing close ties with the Soviet Union. Relations with its South Asian neighbours, especially Pakistan, Sri Lanka, and Nepal, occupied much of the energies of the Ministry of External Affairs.

In the 1990s, India's economic problems and the demise of the bipolar world political system forced India to reassess its foreign policy and adjust its foreign relations. Previous policies proved inadequate to cope with the serious domestic and international problems facing India. The end of the Cold War gutted the core meaning of nonalignment and left Indian foreign policy without significant direction. The hard, pragmatic considerations of the early 1990s were still viewed within the nonaligned framework of the past, but the disintegration of the Soviet Union removed much of India's international leverage, for which relations with Russia and the other post-Soviet states could not compensate. After the dissolution of the Soviet Union, India improved its relations with the United States, Canada, France, Japan and Germany. In 1992, India established formal diplomatic relations with Israel and this relationship grew during the tenures of the Bharatiya Janata Party (BJP) government and the subsequent UPA (United Progressive Alliance) governments.

Even before he formally took charge of office Modi, Prime Minister elect, had made his maiden foreign policy statement by inviting all the heads of state/heads of government of India's neighbours and doing so he had undone his criticism as being a hardliner. Modi's swearing-in ceremony featured nearly all the SAARC leaders along with Navin Ramgoolam of Mauritius who holds an observer status at the grouping. Guests list included Afghanistan's Hamid Karzai, Bhutan's Tshering Tobgay, Maldives' Abdulla Yameen, Nepal's Sushil Koirala, Pakistan's Nawaz Sharif, Sri Lanka's Mahinda Rajapaksa, Mauritius's Navin Ramgoolam. As Bangladeshi Prime Minister Sheikh Hasina was travelling, parliamentary Speaker Shirin Sharmin Chaudhury came instead. Significantly Lobsang Sangay, the Prime Minister of Tibetan Government-in-Exile, was also spotted seating in the spectators gallery. The media reacted positively to this in response to their own criticism of his foreign policy.

From the very beginning the Modi led government made it ample clear that India would focus more and more on improving relations with ASEAN and other East Asian countries as per India's Look East policy which was formulated during PM Narasimha Rao's government in 1992 for better economic engagement with its eastern neighbours but successive government later successfully turned it into a tool for forging strategic partnership and security cooperation with countries in that region in general and Vietnam and Japan in particular. In her recent visit to Hanoi, Vietnam Sushma Swaraj has stressed on the need for an Act East Policy that she said should replace

India's over two decade-old Look East Policy emphasizing a more proactive role for India in this region.

I, hope this book will serve its purpose to researchers, academicians and the general readers who have interest in Indian foreign policy.

CONTENTS

ABBREVIATIONS

ABM	:	Anti Ballistic Missile
ASEAN	:	Association of South East Asian Nations
AYUSH	:	Ayurveda, Yoga, Unami, Siddha, Homeopathy
BASIC	:	Brazil, South Africa, India, China
BIMSTEC	:	Bay of Bengal Initiative for Multisectoral Technical and Economic Co-operation
BRICS	:	Brazil, Russia, India, China, South Africa
CARs	:	Central Asian Republics
CIS	:	Commonwealth of Independent States
CRA	:	Contingency Reserve Arrangement
CSTO	:	Collective Security Treaty Organization
CTBT	:	Comprehensive Test Ban Treaty
ECOSOC	:	Economic and Social Council
EEC	:	European Economic Community
EEU	:	Eurasian Economic Union
EURATOM	:	European Atomic Energy Community
IAEA	:	International Atomic Energy Agency
IMF	:	International Monetary Fund
IMU	:	Islamic Movement of Uzbekistan

ISAF	:	International Security Assistance Force
NAM	:	Non Aligned Movement
NATO	:	North Atlantic Treaty Organization
NCTC	:	National Counter Terrorism Centre
NIEO	:	New International Economic Order
NMD	:	National Missile Defence
NPT	:	Nuclear Proliferation Treaty
NSCN	:	National Socialist Council of Nagaland
NSG	:	Nuclear Supplier Group
OECD	:	Organization for Economic Cooperation and Development
PLA	:	People's Liberation Army
PRC	:	People's Republic of China
RAW	:	Research & Analysis Wing
RIC	:	Russia-India-China
SCO	:	Sanghai Corporation Organization
TAPI	:	Turkmenistan, Afghanistan, Pakistan, India
TMD	:	Theatre Missile Defence
TOI	:	Times of India
ULFA	:	United Liberation Front of Assam
UNCLOS	:	United Convention on the Law of the Sea
UNSC	:	United Nations Security Council
USSR	:	Union of Soviet Socialist Republics

1

INDIAN FOREIGN POLICY: CONTINUITY AND CHANGE UNDER MODI REGIME

Time and again Modi emphasized his believe on 21st century being the Asian century and also asked whether it would be the Indian century. China, Japan and India being the first, second and third largest Asian economy respectively are among the most likely candidate to lead the strategically important Asia in the later part of this century. But China's increasingly assertive postures in the region recent years have raised concerns in the respective quarters. It seems Modi's foreign policy is focused on improving bilateral relations to higher levels with strategically located Asian countries like Japan, Vietnam, and Australia without forging any formal security alliance in the Indo-Pacific region to avoid direct confrontation with China. India, due to its good relation with both Russia and United States, is often considered to be the swing state in the race for strategic dominance in Asia between the democratic alliance of Japan and US and China-Russia club on the other hand.

Prime Minister Narendra Modi's one year in the office has really galvanised the Ministry of External Affairs, and Delhi based think tanks and security experts are amazed with the speed at which these developments are taking place. His hosting of leaders from India's neighbourhood when he was sworn in, his highly effective visits to two of India's neighbours, Nepal and

Bhutan, his diplomatic dexterity at the BRICS (Brazil, Russia, India, China, and South Africa) summit in Brazil, and his watershed trip to Japan are coming to define his nimble foreign policy approach. Since his thumping electoral mandate, foreign dignitaries have made a beeline to call on him. Modi's foreign policy is currently focused on improving relations with neighbouring countries in South Asia, engaging the extended neighbourhood in Southeast Asia and the major global powers.[1] In pursuit of this, he has made official visits to Bhutan and Nepal and Japan within the first 100 days of his government. Sushma Swaraj has also made official visits to Dhaka, Bangladesh, Kathmandu, Nepal, Naypidaw, Myanmar, Singapore, Hanoi, Vietnam, Manama, Bahrain, Kabul, Afghanistan and Dushanbe, Tajikistan and, New York and Washington, D.C., United States.

On completion of the first 100 days of Modi government the External Affairs Ministry published a booklet called "*Fast Track Diplomacy*" show-casing the achievement made in the foreign policy arena. In her first media interaction the minister Sushma Swaraj said the catchphrase for her tenure was "fast-track diplomacy" and said it had three faces - *proactive, strong* and *sensitive.*[2] Since taking office the External Affairs Minister held round-table meeting with all Indian heads of missions to the SAARC region, ASEAN region and Middle East separately as a follow up measure to carry forward the leads gained by high profile visits and exchanges.

Modi's first foreign policy outlook were revealed during the run up for the Prime Ministerial candidature in his party in 2013 when he in a Network 18 program called "Think India, Dialogue Forum" had outlined the following points: Improving relations with immediate neighbours would be his priority as peace and tranquillity in South Asia is essential for realizing his development agenda. Significantly he pledged to introduce the concept of "*paradiplomacy*" in India where each states and cities would have liberty to forge special relation with countries or federal states or even cities of their interest. Bilateral trade going to dominate the relations with most countries except few important global powers with which India shares a strategic partnership.[3] Modi further responded to the many congratulatory messages and phone calls from most world leaders that he received in the aftermath of his historic election victory.

Even before he formally took charge of office Modi, Prime Minister elect, had made his maiden foreign policy statement by inviting all the heads of state/heads of government of India's neighbours and doing so he had undone his criticism as being a hardliner. Modi's swearing-in ceremony featured nearly all the SAARC leaders along with Navin Ramgoolam of Mauritius who holds an observer status at the grouping. Guests list included Afghanistan's Hamid Karzai, Bhutan's Tshering Tobgay, Maldives' Abdulla Yameen, Nepal's Sushil Koirala, Pakistan's Nawaz Sharif, Sri Lanka's Mahinda Rajapaksa, Mauritius's Navin Ramgoolam. As Bangladeshi Prime Minister Sheikh Hasina was travelling, parliamentary Speaker Shirin Sharmin Chaudhury came instead. Significantly Lobsang Sangay, the Prime Minister of Tibetan Government-in-Exile, was also spotted seating in the spectators gallery.[4] The media reacted positively to this in response to their own criticism of his foreign policy.[5]

Vajpayee was assertive in his conduct of foreign policy. Within three months of coming to power, his government conducted a string of nuclear tests, declared India to be a nuclear weapon state, and abandoned the decades-old policy of nuclear ambiguity. His government's relations with Pakistan were often tense; the two countries fought a near-war at Kargil in 1999 and tensions soared repeatedly over major terrorist attacks in India. Following a terrorist attack on India's parliament in 2001, the Vajpayee government ordered a massive, year-long mobilization of the security forces along the India-Pakistan border to push Pakistan to dismantle the anti-India terrorist network on its soil.[6]

MODI'S FIRST OFFICIAL VISIT TO BHUTAN

Prime Minister Narendra Modi chose Bhutan as his first foreign destination, placing regional co-operation before global co-operation. He had inaugurated the Supreme Court Complex in Bhutan and also promised help to Bhutan on IT and digital sector. During Modi's tour, both countries reaffirmed their commitment to extensive development cooperation and discussed ways to further enhance economicties.[7]

India and Bhutan reiterated their commitment to achieving the 10,000 MW target in hydropower cooperation and not to allow their territories to be used for interests "inimical" to each other. Modi inaugurated one of India's assistance projects - the building of the Supreme Court of Bhutan and laid foundation stone of the 600 MW Kholongchu Hydro-electric project, a joint venture between India and Bhutan. India also announced a number of measures and concessions including the exemption of Bhutan from any ban on export of milk powder, wheat, edible oil, pulses and non-basmati rice.

The two sides recalled the free trade arrangement between them and the expanding bilateral trade and its importance in further cementing their friendship. Prime Minister Narendra Modi also mooted the idea of an annual hill sports festival with India's northeastern states along with Bhutan and Nepal. Modi announced doubling of scholarships being provided to Bhutanese students in India which will now be worth Rs. 2 crore. India will also assist Bhutan set up a digital library which will provide access to Bhutanese youth to two million books and periodicals. Both India-Bhutan reaffirmed their commitment to extensive development cooperation and discussed ways to further enhance economic ties. Modi described Bhutan as a natural choice for his first visit abroad as the two countries shared a "special relationship'. 'The fact that the Prime Minister chose Bhutan as his first foreign destination assumes significance since China has lately intensified efforts to woo it and establish full- fledged diplomatic ties with Thimphu.[8]

MODI'S NEPAL VISIT

Nepal is seen as closest ally of India in South Asia. Indians and Nepalese share a common culture and terrain south of the Himalaya. Bound by languages and religions, marriage and mythology, the links of their civilizational contacts run through Lumbini to Bodh Gaya, Pashupatinath to Kashi Vishwanath, and Muktinath to Tirupati. At the people-to-people level, relations between India and Nepal are closer and more multifaceted than between India and any other country. Many partisans of Nepalese democracy also fought for India's freedom, for which they were jailed by the British, including Matrika Koirala, B.P. Koirala, and Man Mohan Adhikari, who became Prime Ministers of Nepal.

Relations between India and Nepal have traditionally been close since ancient times as a result of geographical location and common religious, linguistic and cultural identities that overlap the two countries. Independent India and Nepal initiated their special relationship with the 1950 Indo-Nepal Treaty of Peace and Friendship and accompanying letters that defined security relations between the two countries, and an agreement governing both bilateral trade and trade transiting Indian soil. The 1950 treaty and letters stated that "neither government shall tolerate any threat to the security of the other by a foreign aggressor" and obligated both sides "to inform each other of any serious friction or misunderstanding with any neighbouring state likely to cause any breach in the friendly relations subsisting between the two governments". These accords cemented a "special relationship" between India and Nepal that granted Nepal preferential economic treatment and provided Nepali in India the same economic and educational opportunities as Indian citizens. The Indo-Nepal border is open; Nepalese and Indian nationals may move freely across the border without passports or visas and may live and work in either country.

Charting a new course in bilateral relations, India and Nepal agreed Monday to "review, adjust and update" the 1950 Treaty of Peace and Friendship to "better reflect the current realities" and expand ties in "a forward looking manner". A joint press statement issued at the end of Modi's visit said the two Prime Ministers underlined the need to explore ways to enhance sub-regional cooperation, particularly in the areas of trade, transit, connectivity and hydropower. They said "high level visits are vital for greater momentum to the close and cordial ties" between the two countries. Modi invited Koirala to India at an early date and the latter "appreciated the enhanced focus and priority" given by the new Indian government on relations with neighbouring countries. He referred to Modi's invitation to the SAARC leaders to attend his swearing-in ceremony in May, saying "this provided a unique opportunity for meaningful dialogue at the political level as well as for advancing regional cooperation under the framework of SAARC".[10]

MODI AT BRICS SUMMIT

Modi in his maiden speech at the BRICS, a group of emerging economies comprising Brazil, Russia, India, China and South Africa, called for brotherhood among the member states citing *Vasudhaiva Kutumbakam,* an ancient India concept meaning the entire world is one family, to unitedly face the global challenges.

India together with its BRICS partner working toward launching of a financial institute rivalling the western dominated

World Bank and IMF which was first proposed during the New Delhi summit in 2012 by the then Indian Prime Minister Manmohan Singh. In the 6th BRICS Summit held on 14-26 July in Fortaleza, Brazil the group have agreed to establish the bank with a corpus of US$100 billion. The bank would be named the *New Development Bank* as suggested by the Indian side but Modi government has failed to bag the bank's headquarter for New Delhi which would be located in Shanghai, China.[11] However India succeeded in grabbing the opportunity to appoint first Indian president of the proposed bank.

The joint declaration was issued at the end of the Summit. "The New Development Bank shall have an initial authorized capital of US$ 100 billion. The initial subscribed capital shall be of US$ 50 billion, equally shared among founding members. The first chair of the Board of Governors shall be from Russia. The first chair of the Board of Directors shall be from Brazil. The first President of the Bank shall be from India. The headquarters of the Bank shall be located in Shanghai. The New Development Bank Africa Regional Centre shall be established in South Africa concurrently with the headquarters. We direct our Finance Ministers to work out the modalities for its operationalization".

"We are pleased to announce the signing of the Treaty for the establishment of the BRICS Contingent Reserve Arrangement (CRA) with an initial size of US$ 100 billion. This arrangement will have a positive precautionary effect, help countries forestall short-term liquidity pressures, promote further BRICS cooperation, strengthen the global financial safety net and complement existing international arrangements. We appreciate the work undertaken by our Finance Ministers and Central Bank Governors. The Agreement is a framework for the provision of liquidity through currency swaps in response to actual or potential short-term balance of payments pressures".

MODI' S JAPAN VISIT

Meticulous to a fault, the Japanese do not like sudden changes in programmes. Yet, when Prime Minister Narendra Modi announced a change in his itinerary in Japan, arriving a day early to travel to the heritage temple city of Kyoto, they were delighted. With that one stroke, Mr. Modi showed his desire to lift bilateral relations with Japan from a transactional one to something more holistic. "Amid all the B2B (business to business) and G2G (government to government) (interactions), he likes to find ways of establishing an H2H (heart to heart) relationship too," said someone who helped organise international visits of Mr. Modi when he was Gujarat Chief Minister.[12]

Instead of bumptiously enunciating a Modi doctrine in foreign policy, the Prime Minister is allowing his actions, including diplomatic successes and breaks, to define his approach. From the big bear hug with Japanese Prime Minister Shinzo Abe that symbolized the dawn of an India-Japan alliance to his scrapping of scheduled foreign secretary level talks with Pakistan after its high commissioner definately met Kashmiri secessionists, Modi has managed to put his stamp on foreign policy faster than any predecessor, other than Jawaharlal Nehru.[13] Indeed, as India's veto at the World Trade Organization talks in Geneva exemplified, Modi will even stand up to a powerful, rich nations' cabal when national interest is at stake.

Prime Minister Narendra Modi's maiden five-day visit to Japan saw the latter nation pledging financial support for building infrastructure in India. Sticking to his 'Make in India' slogan, Modi gave an open invitation to Japanese companies to consider India as a 'competitive low-cost manufacturing hub'. The meet also saw India-Japan relations being upgraded to the level of 'Special Strategic Global Partnership'. Inviting Japanese investors to 'Make in India', PM Modi said, "There is no better place than India for Japanese investors. India is one of the most competitive markets in the world."Addressing Japan's Nikkei Exchange, Modi said that India offers the three essential 'Ds' for businessmen to thrive namely– Democracy, Demography and Demand. "It is important for Japan to move to low cost hubs of manufacturing". Promising a conducive environment for investors, Modi said, "Foreign investors need a proper environment to grow in India. We are working towards improving ease of doing business in India". "There is no red tape but red carpet in India. We have eased off a lot of regulations", Modi sought to assure. We take a look at the ten take aways from PM Modi's visit.

i. Japan has promised to give $35 billion to India through public and private funding over the next 5 years for developmental projects, including building of smart cities and clean-up of river Ganges.
ii. Both sides have signed five pacts covering defence exchanges, cooperation in clean energy, roads and highways, healthcare and women while vowing to take their relationship from strategic partnership to a special strategic partnership.
iii. Japan has lifted the ban on six Indian entities including Hindustan Aeronautics Limited (HAL) which was imposed in the aftermath of 1998 nuclear tests.
iv. The two sides agreed to enhance their defence and strategic cooperation to a new level and also decided to speed up negotiations on a civil nuclear deal that could not be concluded now.
v. In Kyoto, a pact was signed under which Modi's Lok Sabha constituency Varanasi will be developed on the pattern of Kyoto 'smart city' with the help of Japan.
vi. Tokyo will help India in providing financial, technical and operational support to introduce Bullet trains, a project that Modi has been actively pursuing.

vii. Prime Minister Modi has asked NRIs to visit India at least once a year to boost tourism.

viii. Both sides have signed a MoU for cooperation in heritage conservation, city modernisation and cooperation in the fields of art, culture and academics.

ix. Both countries have decided to build a strong, deep and strategic relationship under the India-Japan Cooperation framework.

x. India has decided to set up a Special Management Team directly under the PMO to facilitate proposals from Japan.[14]

MEETING WITH RUSSIAN PRESIDENT PUTIN

Modi met the Russian President, Vladmir Putin on the side-lines of the 6th BRICS Summit in Fortaleza, Brazil in July 2014. During the meeting, Modi said that relations with Russia will continue to enjoy the priority that they always had in India's foreign policy. Modi, who had also met Putin in 2001 in Moscow, remarked, "Even a child in India, if asked to say who is India's best friend, will reply it is Russia because Russia has been with India in times of crisis".[15] The PM added that he looked forward to working with the Russian President to further deepen and broad-base the strategic partnership including in the areas of defence, nuclear energy, space, energy, trade and investment, people-to-people contacts and addressing regional and global challenges. The two leaders looked forward to their Annual Summit in Delhi in December 2014 as an opportunity to outline a bold vision and roadmap for their relationship in the years ahead, the Prime Minister invited President Vladimir Putin to visit Kudankulam Nuclear Power Plant during his trip. Putin congratulated Modi on his great victory in the recent elections. Modi said there was a need to look at a liberal visa regime, especially students going for studies.[16]

The two leaders looked forward to their Annual Summit in Delhi in December 2014 as an opportunity to outline a bold vision and road map for their relationship in the years ahead, the Prime Minister invited President Vladimir Putin to visit Kudankulam Nuclear Power Plant during his trip. Putin congratulated Modi on his great victory in the recent elections. Modi said there was a need to look at a liberal visa regime, especially students going for studies.

CHINESE PRESIDENT XI JINPING VISITS INDIA

Xi began his three-day trip of Indian Prime Minister Narendra Modi's 64th birthday, at Ahmedabad in Modi's home state of Gujarat – another first, since no Prime Minister has received a foreign leader anywhere but New Delhi. China is India's largest trading partner (although the trade deficit between the two countries has been widening), and trade and investment will undoubtedly be foremost on both leaders' minds. Beijing has already outlined plans to build two industrial parks, with multibillion dollar investments in both. There are also projects being discussed that will revamp India's vast but outdated railway network. Modi's recent visit to Japan was described as "successful" by the Indian media, with Japanese Prime Minister Shinzo Abe pledging $34 billion in investments to India and Indo-Japan ties receiving a significant boost. The personal warmth between Modi and Abe was also evident, and although Modi and Xi connected during the BRICS summit in Fortaleza, Brazil, earlier this year, it remains to be seen how that equation will progress this week.

India and China have signed 12 agreements in Delhi, one of which will see China investing $20 bn in India's infrastructure over five years. At a news conference with Chinese President Xi Jinping, India's PM Narendra Modi said "peace on the border" was important for progress. Talks came as India accused China of fresh territorial incursions in Ladakh. China is one of India's top trading partners but they vie for regional influence and dispute their border. Mr. Modi and Mr. Xi made separate statements at the end of their talks in Delhi on Thursday. Under the investment plans, China pledged to: Help bring India's ageing railway system up-to-date with high-speed links and upgraded railway stations. Set up industrial parks in Gujarat and Maharashtra. Give more market access to India to products, including pharmaceuticals and farm products. Both sides also focussed on increasing co-operation in trade, space exploration and civil nuclear energy.[17] Mr. Modi called for an early settlement on the disputed common border between the two countries and said the "true potential of our relations" would be realised when there was "peace in our relations and in the borders".

MODI' S MUCH AWAITED US VISIT

In 2005 during the Bush administration, US officials denied Modi a visa due to allegations that he failed to prevent the 2002 Gujarat riots (when he was chief minister of Gujarat). He was barred from entering the United States under a provision of the Immigration and Nationality Act[18] (the only person ever denied a visa to the U.S. under this provision). Following his 2014 election as the Prime Minister of India, however, President Obama invited him to visit the US and Modi reciprocated in September 2014. The five day trip included attending the sixty-ninth session of the United Nations General Assembly in New York and giving a talk in New York City's Madison Square Garden to an audience of over 18,000 (hosted by Miss America 2014, Nina Davuluri and PBS News Hour Weekend anchor Hari Sreenivasan).[19] While there, Modi also met with President Obama and several business leaders from the US.

The Obama administration reached an agreement with India on Tuesday on measures intended to accelerate that country's shift to renewable fuels, steps that officials say will reduce carbon emissions while helping India's new government extend electricity to all of its 1.2 billion citizens. The package, announced after talks between President Obama and visiting Indian Prime Minister Narendra Modi, also contained a modest step toward reducing global emissions of hydro fluoro carbons, industrial chemicals that act as a powerful greenhouse gas in the atmosphere. Indian officials formally agreed to engage in international discussions that the White House hopes will lead to a phase-out of the chemicals, known as HFCs.[20] Modi mostly talked about economic issues during a working dinner Monday night, including the importance of education and job training. Other topics included the threats from Ebola and the Islamic State.

The security agreements involved a US and Indian decision to take "joint and concerted efforts" against Pakistan-based militant groups, including the Lashkar-e-Taiba and Jamaatud-Dawa networks that have launched deadly attacks on Indian soil. Syed Akbaruddin, a spokesman for the Foreign Ministry, said the two sides would work together to dismantle havens of these networks and disrupt tactical and financial support to them, suggesting that the US would put pressure on India's rival neighbour Pakistan, whose once-close relations with Washington incensed Indian officials.

In a brief statement at the White House after the two-hour meeting, Mr. Modi said the US was an integral part of India's "Look East–Link West" policy, and mentioned enhanced cooperation in the Asian-Pacific region, which is in flux owing to China's rise and increasing military assertiveness. The shifting balance of power in Asia has driven the US to seek closer ties with India as a democratic bulwark against China. Modi's government has announced ambitious plans to modernize its military as India prepares to counter China and potential regional instability following a drawdown of US troops in Afghanistan. Among agreements, the US pledged to help India transform three of its cities into modern "smart cities" and agreed to help upgrade the water and sewage system.[21]

MODI'S SECOND US VISIT AND MEETING WITH CEOs AT SILICON VALLEY

Silicon Valley often hosts world leaders, but rarely gives them the rock-star reception that it did for Indian Prime Minister Narendra Modi. Seats for an 18,500-person where event took place, at the SAP Center in San Jose, disappeared within days and tens of thousands more could have sold. The Silicon Valley Indian community is especially abuzz. Companies such as Google, Facebook, and Tesla are rolling out the red carpet. Among the leaders of Fortune 500 companies attended at the dinner meeting with PM Modi at New York's Waldorf Astoria hotel were Lockheed Martin chairman Marillyn A Hewson, Ford Motor president Mark Fields, IBM CEO Ginni Rometty, Pepsi Co CEO Indra Nooyi, and Johnson & Johnson chairman Jorge Mesquita.

The euphoria arises partly because Indians here are still optimistic that Modi will transform India – after decades of economic stagnation under socialist governments. But his greater appeal to the tech community is that he is one of the world's few truly tech-savvy leaders. He has mastered social media and has more than 15 million followers on Twitter – second only to President Obama among world leaders. And Modi has declared his intent to build a Digital India: a knowledge economy that delivers key government services electronically, connects all parts of the country with high-speed internet networks, and ensures its populace is digitally literate.

CONCLUSION

Both limitations and possibilities lie ahead. A key advantage for India right now is that a number of countries see it as an opportunity and this moment as the right time to establish or expand relations with it. The high intensity of the government's external engagement might be attributable to its recognition of this fact and its desire to capitalize on the interest in India. While Modi's honeymoon period at home might have ended, this is not the case abroad. However, a question that lies ahead is: can the Modi government effectively seize the opportunity that this moment offers? For one, how long the honeymoon period will last will depend on India's performance, especially its economic performance. Thus, in one way a key foreign policy challenge for the Modi government will be an economic one, with foreign officials and investors asking the same question that Indian voters are: can it deliver on the promise of prosperity? The wooing will continue as long as the answer seems to be yes; if the government is not seen as meeting expectations, the whiming about India will start again, with countries exploring other options.

NOTES

1. Lakshmi, Rama. "Modi's speech in Nepal shows India is paying attention to its neighbours". *The Washington Post.*
2. PM Modi's 100 days: Sushma Swaraj talks tough on Pakistan, China and US. *The Economic Times.* (2014-09-09).
3. Aswathy (17 May 2014). "World leaders, media react to Narendra Modi led BJP's election victory" *Oneindia.in.*
4. Krishna Uppuluri (25 May 2014). "Narendra Modi's swearing in offers a new lease of life to SAARC". *Daily News and Analysis.*
5. "PM swearing-in: US media praises Modi for inviting all SAARC leaders". *Firstpost.* 27 May 2014.

6. Sudha Ramachandran (May 06, 2014) "Indian Foreign Policy Under Narendra Modi" *The Diplomat*see at http://thediplomat.com/2014/05/indian-foreign-policy-under-narendra-modi/.
7. "In Bhutan Narendra Modi vows to nurture ties". *The Hindu.*(June 15, 2014).
8. "Key points of PM Narendra Modi's Bhutan visit". *The Times of India,* (Jun 16, 2014).
9. Jayant Prasad "A new template for India-Nepal ties" *The Hindu, (*August 2, 2014).
10. Rakesh Sinha, Yubaraj Ghimire "2014 and beyond: India, Nepal agree to refresh 1950 treaty" Indian Express (August 4, 2014), see more at: http://indianexpress.com/article/world/neighbours/india-nepal-agree-to-review-adjust-update-1950-treaty/#sthash.NtuHNNax.dpuf
11. Press Trust of India (7 July 2014). "BRICS summit to be Modi's first multilateral meet". *Business Standard.*
12. Suhasini Haidar, "Foreign policy: Modi brings style to substance" *The Hindu,* (September 3, 2014).
13. Brahma Chellaney" Narendra Modi's imprint on foreign policy" *Live Mint* (Tue, Sep 02 2014). See at http://www.livemint.com/Opinion/Rx9Waq6uNG6yHJaSJMur TL/Narendra-Modis-imprint-on-foreign-policy.html
14. "Ten highlights of Modi's visit to Japan" *India Today.in* (Tokyo, September 3, 2014). see athttp://indiatoday.intoday.in/story/10-highlights-of-modi-visit-to-japan/1/380647.html.
15. "PM Modi meets Putin, invites him to visit Kudankulam power plant" *IndiaToday.in* New Delhi, (July 16, 2014).
16. Rishi Iyengar" What's at Stake in Xi Jinping's Visit to India" *Time* (Sept. 17, 2014).
17. "China's Xi Jinping signs landmark deals on India visit"*BBC,* (18 September 2014)

18. Mann, James (2 May 2014). "Why Narendra Modi Was Banned From the US". *Wall Street Journal.*

19. Sinha, Shreeya (September 27, 2014). "Indian Leader Narendra Modi, Once Unwelcome in US, Gets Rock Star Reception",*The New York Times.*

20. Joby Warrick (September 30) "Obama and Modi announce agreement on US-India efforts to fight global warming" *The Washington Post.* see at http://www.washingtonpost. com/ national/health-science/obama-modi-announce-modest-progress-in-joint-efforts-to-fight-global-warming/2014/09/ 30/c3e7464e-48aa-11e4-b72e-d60a 9229cc10_ story.html

21. Niharika Mandhana and William Mauldin "Indian Leader Modi Moves Closer to U.S. as Differences Persist" (September 30, 2014) *The Wall Street Journal.* see athttp:// online.wsj.com/articles/obama-narendra-modi-meet-at-white-house-in-first-formal-talks-1412089904.

2

INDIA'S ECONOMIC DIPLOMACY

Economic diplomacy is a form of diplomacy. Economic diplomacy is the use of the full spectrum economic tools of the state to achieve its national interest. Economic diplomacy includes all the economic activities, including export, import, investment, lending, aid, free trade agreements etc.[1] Economic diplomacy is concerned with economic policy issues, e.g. work of delegations at standard setting organizations such as World Trade Organization (WTO). Economic diplomats also monitor and report on economic policies in foreign countries and give the home government advice on how to best influence them. Economic diplomacy employs economic resources, either as rewards or sanctions, in pursuit of a particular foreign policy objective. This is sometimes called "economic statecraft".[2]

Economic diplomacy is traditionally defined as the decision-making, policy-making and advocating of the sending state-business interests. Economic diplomacy requires application of technical expertise that analyzes the effects of a country's (Receiving State) economic situation on its political climate and on the sending State's economic interests. The Sending State and Receiving State, foreign business leaders as well as government decision-makers work together on some of the most cutting-edge issues in foreign policy, such as technology, the environment, and HIV/AIDS, as well as in the more traditional areas of trade and finance. Versatility, flexibility, sound judgment and strong business skills are all needed in the execution of economic diplomacy.

According to Van Bergeij, Peter A. G. there are three main elements of economic diplomacy-

1. **Commercial diplomacy and NGO's**: The use of political influence and relationships to promote and/or influence international trade and investment, to improve on functioning of markets and/or to address market failures and to reduce costs and risks of cross border transactions (including property rights).
2. **Structural policies and bilateral trade and investment agreements**: The use of economic assets and relationships to increase the cost of conflict and to strengthen the mutual benefits of cooperation and politically stable relationships, i.e. to increase economic security.
3. **International organizations**: Ways to consolidate the right political climate and international political economic environment to facilitate and institute these objectives.[3]

INDIA'S ECONOMIC DIPLOMACY WITH MAJOR POWERS OF THE WORLD

India has engaged in economic diplomacy primarily through the use of trade and aid. For example, in order to build a stronger, more stable relationship with Bangladesh, India granted it an $800 million soft loan, and provided $200 million in aid.[4] India set up a development wing in its government in January 2012. The Development Partners Administration (DPA), is a primary way India uses economic diplomacy, in this case development aid, as a way to engage diplomatically. The DPA is building 50,000 housing units in Sri Lanka, a large transmission line in Puli Khumri, Afghanistan, and extends Lines of Credit projects globally, particularly in Africa. Economic diplomacy and the DPA are very important to Indian foreign policy. As the former Indian Foreign Secretary Lalit Mansingh stated: "The fact that the DPA division is located in the ministry of external affairs shows it is in sync with our foreign policy objectives ofobjectives of transforming India into a global player".[5]

While economic diplomacy has always been an integral part of India's foreign policy, it has received greater emphasis since the liberalization of the Indian economy in the 1990s. India's economic strategy during the first three decades of independence was largely based on import-substitution and license-raj, while its economic diplomacy focused on securing development assistance. This overall economic policy framework did not change even during Indira Gandhi's government. In 1970, a more stringent industrial licensing policy was adopted in the wake of decreasing foreign aid from major western donors and the devaluation of the rupee. Rising sentiments against the concentration of economic power within India also translated into more restrictive measures against big business by the Indian government.

Without much ado, a new trend is quietly transforming the nation's foreign policy – economic diplomacy. The reforms initiated in 1991 and some intensive recent efforts have begun to have an impact on our external relations that few could have visualized. Negotiation of liberal trading arrangements with key nations, large-scale national investments in the hydro carbon sectors of other countries, focus on developing transport infrastructure in the neighborhood, India's new role as an economic donor, and the focus on mega projects such as natural gas pipelines cutting across our borders have significantly transformed our foreign policy template.[6]

Globalization has radically transformed the contours of international economic relationships between countries, throwing up new challenges and complexities in the economic, social, political and cultural spheres. In this scenario of interconnectivity and interdependency, with an increasing number of players striving to influence the outcome of economic relationships, economic diplomacy has assumed immense significance and posed new challenges to diplomats around the world. With the ever increasing integration of markets, economies and cultures, the term 'diplomacy' itself has undergone an enormous change in connotation.[7] This transformation encompasses a widening and deepening of the dimensions of diplomacy, a gradual evolution of its modus operandi and a change in the role and nature of players involved in it. Terms like non-state diplomacy, corporate diplomacy, business diplomacy, NGO diplomacy and track two diplomacy have found their place in the lexicon of economic diplomacy.

INDO-US ECONOMIC RELATION

Despite being one of the pioneers and founding members of the Non-Aligned Movement of 1961, India developed a closer relationship with the Soviet Union during the Cold War. During that period, India's relatively cooperative strategic and military relations with Moscow and strong socialist policies had a distinctly adverse impact on its relations with the United States. After the dissolution of the Soviet Union in 1991, India began to review its foreign policy in a unipolar world, and took steps to develop closer ties with the European Union and the United States. Current Indian foreign policy is based on maintaining strategic autonomy to promote and safeguard national interests.[8]

The United States is one of India's largest direct investors. From 1991 to 2004, the stock of FDI inflow has increased from USD $11.3 million to $344.4 million, and totaling $4.13

billion. This is a compound rate increase of 57.5 percent annually. Indian direct investments abroad began in 1992, and Indian corporations and registered partnership firms are now allowed to invest in businesses up to 100 percent of their net worth. India's largest outgoing investments are in the manufacturing sector, which accounts for 54.8 percent of the country's foreign investments. The second largest are in non-financial services (software development), accounting for 35.4 percent of investments.

The US is one of India's largest trading partners. In 2011, the US exported $21.50 billion worth of goods to India, and imported $36.15 billion worth of Indian goods.[9] Major items imported from India include information technology services, textiles, machinery, gems and diamonds, chemicals, iron and steel products, coffee, tea, and other edible food products. Major American items imported by India include aircraft, fertilisers, computer hardware, scrap metal, and medical equipment.The United States is also India's largest investment partner, with a direct investment of $9 billion (accounting for 9 percent of total foreign investment). Americans have made notable foreign investments in the Asian country's power generation, telecommunications, ports, roads, petroleum exploration and processing, and mining industries.[10]

Trade and commerce form a crucial component of the rapidly expanding and multi-faceted relations between India and US. From a modest $ 5.6 billion in 1990, the bilateral trade in merchandise goods has increased to $ 66.9 billion in 2014 representing an impressive 1094.6 per cent growth in a span of 24 years. India's merchandise exports to the US grew by 8.1 per cent from $ 41.85 billion during the year 2013 to $ 45.23 billion during the year 2014. US exports of merchandise to India fell by one per cent from $ 21.84 billion during the year 2013 to $ 21.63 billion during the year 2014. India-US bilateral merchandise trade during the period January-December 2014 was $ 66.86 billion.

TRADE DURING THE YEAR, 2014

(I) MAJOR ITEMS OF EXPORT FROM INDIA TO US

Select major items with their percentage shares, are given below:

(a) Textiles (16.4 percent)
(b) Precious stones & metals (21percent)
(c) Pharmaceutical products (10.7 percent)
(d) Mineral Fuel, Oil (10.2 percent)
(e) Machinery (5.1 percent)
(f) Organic chemicals (5 percent)
(g) Electrical Machinery (3 percent)
(h) Lac, Gum, Resins (3 percent)

(II) MAJOR ITEMS OF EXPORT FROM US TO INDIA

Select major items with their percentage shares, are given below:

(a) Precious stones & metals (24.7 percent)
(b) Aircraft, spacecraft, Parts (13.6 percent)
(c) Machinery (9.7 percent)
(d) Electrical machinery (6.5 percent)
(e) Optical instruments & equipment (5.9 percent)
(f) Mineral Fuel, Oil etc (5.8 percent)
(g) Organic chemicals (3.3 percent)
(h) Plastic Products (3 percent)[11]

The bilateral cooperation is now broad-based and multi-sectoral, covering trade and investment, defence and security, education, science and technology, cyber security, high technology, civil nuclear energy, space technology and applications, clean energy, environment, agriculture and health. People to people interaction provide further vitality and strength to bilateral relationship.

INDO-ASEAN ECONOMIC DIPLOMACY

The Association of South-East Asian Nations (ASEAN) comprises of Indonesia, Singapore, Philippines, Malaysia, Brunei, Thailand, Cambodia, Lao PDR, Myanmar and Vietnam. India's focus on a strengthened and multi-faceted relationship with ASEAN is an outcome of the significant changes in the world's political and economic scenario since the early 1990s and India's own march towards economic liberalisation. India's search for economic space resulted in the 'Look East Policy'. The Look East Policy has today matured into a dynamic and action oriented 'Act East Policy'. PM at the 12th ASEAN India Summit and the 9th East Asia Summit held in Nay Pyi Taw, Myanmar, in November, 2014, formally enunciated the Act East Policy.

Apart from ASEAN, India has taken other policy initiatives in the region that involve some members of ASEAN like BIMSTEC, MGC etc. India is also an active participant in several regional forums like the Asia-Europe Meeting (ASEM), East Asia Summit (EAS), ASEAN Regional Forum (ARF), ASEAN Defence Ministers' Meeting+(ADMM+) and Expanded ASEAN Maritime Forum (EAMF).

India's relationship with ASEAN is a key pillar of our foreign policy and the foundation of our Act East Policy. The up-gradation of the relationship into a Strategic Partnership in 2012 was a natural progression to the ground covered since India became a Sectoral Partner of the ASEAN in 1992, Dialogue Partner in 1996 and Summit Level Partner in 2002. There are, in total, 30 Dialogue Mechanisms between India and ASEAN, cutting across various sectors.

Commemorative Summit: In 2012, ASEAN and India commemorated 20 years of dialogue partnership and 10 years of Summit level partnership with ASEAN with a Commemorative Summit in New Delhi under the theme 'ASEAN-India Partnership for Peace and Shared Prosperity' on 20-21 December 2012. The Commemorative Summit attended by the Leaders from all the 10 ASEAN countries endorsed elevating the partnership to a 'Strategic Partnership'. The Leaders also adopted the 'ASEAN-India Vision Statement', which charts the future of ASEAN-India cooperation. Two major events that were organized in 2012 in the run-up to the Commemorative Summit included the 2nd ASEAN-India Car Rally and Shipping Expedition of INS Sudarshini to ASEAN countries.

25th anniversary of ASEAN-India relations: India and ASEAN would observe 25 years of their Dialogue Partnership, 15 years of Summit Level interaction and 5 years of Strategic Partnership in 2017 by undertaking a wide range of activities, both in India and through our Missions in ASEAN Member States, including a Commemorative Summit on the theme "Shared Values, Common Destiny".

ASEAN-India Centre (AIC): At the Commemorative Summit held in 2012, the Heads of the Government recommended establishment of ASEAN-India Centre (AIC) to undertake policy research, advocacy and networking activities with organizations and think-tanks in India and ASEAN, with the aim to promote the ASEAN-India Strategic Partnership. The AIC has been serving as a resource centre for ASEAN Member States and India since its establishment in 2013, for strengthening ASEAN-India strategic partnership and promoting India-ASEAN dialogue and cooperation in the areas of mutual interests.

AIC has provided some very valuable inputs to policy makers in India and ASEAN on implementation of ASEAN-India connectivity by organising seminars, roundtables etc. AIC also organizes workshops, seminars and conferences on various cross-cutting issues relevant to ASEAN-India strategic partnership. It undertakes regular networking activities with relevant public/ private agencies, organizations and think-tanks in India and ASEAN and EAS countries, with the aim of providing up-to-date information, data resources and sustained interaction, for promoting ASEAN-India Strategic Partnership.

Plans of Action: As a reflection of the interest of ASEAN and India to intensify their engagement, the ASEAN-India Partnership for Peace, Progress and Shared Prosperity, which sets out the roadmap for long-term ASEAN-India engagement, was signed at the 3rd ASEAN-India Summit in 2004 in Vientiane. A Plan of Action (POA) for the period 2004-2010 was also developed to implement the Partnership. Most of the paras of the 2nd POA (2010-15) have been implemented. The 3rd POA (2016-20) was adopted by the ASEAN-India Foreign Ministers Meeting held in August 2015.

ASEAN and India have finalised a list of priority areas for the period of 2016-2018, which would contribute towards successful implementation of the 2016-2020 Plan of Action. 54 out of 130 activities identified in the 3rd Plan of Action have been already implemented.

Security cooperation: The main forum for ASEAN security dialogue is the ASEAN Regional Forum (ARF). India has been attending annual meetings of this forum since 1996 and has actively participated in its various activities. The ASEAN Defence Ministers' Meeting (ADMM) is the highest defence consultative and cooperative mechanism in ASEAN. The ADMM+brings together Defence Ministers from the 10 ASEAN nations plus

Australia, China, India, Japan, New Zealand, Republic of Korea, Russia, and the United States on a biannual basis. Defense Minister attended the 3rd ADMM Plus held from 4-5 November 2015 in Kuala Lumpur. Expanded ASEAN Maritime Forum (EAMF) is an avenue for track 1.5 diplomacy focusing on cross cutting maritime issues of common concern. India participated in the 4th EAMF held in Manado, Indonesia on 10-11 September 2015.

Trade and Investment: India-ASEAN trade and investment relations have been growing steadily, with ASEAN being India's fourth largest trading partner. The annual trade between India and ASEAN stood at approximately US$ 76.53 billion in 2014-15. It declined to US$ 65.04 billion in 2015-16 essentially due to declining commodity prices amidst a general slowing down of the global economy. Investment flows are also substantial both ways, with ASEAN accounting for approximately 12.5 per cent of investment flows into India since 2000. FDI inflows into India from ASEAN between April 2000 to May 2016 was about US$49.40 billion, while FDI outflows from India to ASEAN countries, from April 2007 to March 2015, as per data maintained by DEA, was about US$38.672 billion.

The ASEAN-India Free Trade Area has been completed with the entering into force of the ASEAN-India Agreements on Trade in Service and Investments on 1 July 2015.

ASEAN and India have been also working on enhancing private sector engagement. ASEAN India-Business Council (AIBC) was set up in March 2003 in Kuala Lumpur as a forum to bring key private sector players from India and the ASEAN countries on a single platform for business networking and sharing of ideas.

AIBC organized the ASEAN-India Business Leadership Conclave 2016 on 21 July 2016 in Kuala Lumpur, Malaysia.

Connectivity: ASEAN-India connectivity is a matter of strategic priority for India as also the ASEAN countries. In 2013, India became the third dialogue partner of ASEAN to initiate an ASEAN Connectivity Coordinating Committee-India Meeting. While India has made considerable progress in implementing the India-Myanmar-Thailand Trilateral Highway and the Kaladan Multi-modal Project, issues related to increasing the maritime and air connectivity between ASEAN and India and transforming the corridors of connectivity into economic corridors are under discussion. A possible extension to India-Myanmar-Thailand Trilateral Highway to Cambodia, Lao PDR and Viet Nam is also under consideration. A consensus on finalising the proposed protocol of the India-Myanmar-Thailand Motor Vehicle Agreement (IMT MVA) has been reached. This agreement will have a critical role in realizing seamless movement of passenger, personal and cargo vehicles along roads linking India, Myanmar and Thailand. PM announced a Line of Credit of US$ 1 billion to promote projects that support physical and digital connectivity between India and ASEAN and a Project Development Fund with a corpus of Rs. 500 crores to develop manufacturing hubs in CLMV countries at the 13th ASEAN India Summit held in Malaysia in November 2015.

Funds: ASEAN Multilateral Division offers project-based financial assistance to ASEAN countries. Financial assistance has been provided to ASEAN countries in following forms:

ASEAN-India Cooperation Fund: At the 7th ASEAN-India Summit in 2009, India announced a contribution of US$ 50 million to the ASEAN-India Fund, to support implementation of the ASEAN-India Plan of Action 2010-15, which envisages cooperation in a range of sectors in the political, economic and socio-cultural spheres for deepening and intensifying ASEAN-India cooperation. Projects worth approximately US$ 47 million are under various stages of implementation or processing. In order to take the development and capacity building initiatives forward, PM has proposed enhancing the ASEAN-India Fund with an additional grant of US$ 50 million at the 14th ASEAN India Summit in Vientiane in September 2016.

ASEAN-India S&T Development Fund (AISTDF): At the 6th ASEAN-India Summit in November 2007 in Singapore, India announced the setting up of an ASEAN-India Science & Technology Development Fund with a US$ 1 million contribution from India to promote joint collaborative R&D research projects in Science & Technology. This Fund become operational in 2009-10 and expenditure began to be incurred from FY 2010-11. This fund has been enlarged to US$5 million from 2016-17. Projects worth US$ 0.67 million are already under implementation.

ASEAN-India Green Fund: At the 6th ASEAN-India Summit on 21 November 2007 in Singapore, India announced the setting up of an ASEAN-India Green Fund with an initial contribution of US$ 5 million from India to support collaboration activities relating to environment and climate change. Some of the areas identified for collaboration under the Fund are climate change, energy efficiency, clean technologies, renewable energy, biodiversity conservation and environmental education. Project worth US$ 1.97 million covered under this Fund are currently at the implementation stage.

ASEAN-India Projects: India has been cooperating with ASEAN by way of implementation of various projects in the fields of Agriculture, Science & Technology, Space, Environment & Climate Change, Human Resource Development, Capacity Building, New and Renewable Energy, Tourism, People-to-People contacts and Connectivity etc.

Programmes and projects totalling over US$ 48 million

have been proposed since September 2011 till date to ASEAN through the ASEAN Secretariat and are under various stages of processing. Some of the prominent projects, which are either ongoing or in the final stages of approval are as follows:

Space Project envisaging establishment of a Tracking, Data Reception/Data Processing Station in Ho Chi Minh City, Vietnam and upgradation of Telemetry Tracking and Command Station in Biak, Indonesia; Setting up of Centres of Excellence in Software Development & Training in CLMV countries are some of the major projects under implementation.

Apart from the above projects, India has been supporting ASEAN specially CLMV countries under the Initiatives for ASEAN Integration, which include projects on Training of English Language for Law Enforcement Officers in CLMV countries and Training of professionals dealing with capital markets in CLMV by National Institute of Securities Management Mumbai. To boost People-to-people Interaction with ASEAN, India has been organising various programme including Training Programme for ASEAN diplomats, Exchange of Parliamentarians, Participation of ASEAN students in the National Children's Science Congress, ASEAN-India Network of Think Tanks, ASEAN-India Eminent Persons Lecture Series etc. India is establishing four Centres of Excellence in Software Development & Training (CESDT) in CLMV countries, including the setting up of an IT Resource cum Study Centre at CDAC, Noida consisting of 1 existing Lab and 1 new Lab as well as the development of 12 e-learning courses in six identified areas.

The Mekong-Ganga Cooperation (MGC) is an initiative by six countries – India and five ASEAN countries, namely, Cambodia, Lao PDR, Myanmar, Thailand and Vietnam for cooperation in tourism, culture, education, as well as transport and communications. It was launched in 2000 at Vientiane, Lao PDR. Both the Ganga and the Mekong are civilizational rivers, and the MGC initiative aims to facilitate closer contacts among the people inhabiting these two major river basins. The MGC is also indicative of the cultural and commercial linkages among the member countries of the MGC down the centuries. The 1st MGC Ministerial Meeting was held in Vientiane from November 9-13, 2000. It issued the Vientiane Declaration on MGC covering cooperation in the 4 traditional areas. The 2nd MGC Ministerial Meeting was held in Hanoi on July 28, 2001, and adopted the Hanoi Programme of Action (HPA), a detailed Work Programme for six years (July 2001 to July 2007), providing specific actions for cooperation, in the 4 traditional areas. The 3rd MGC Ministerial Meeting was held in Phnom Penh on June 20, 2003 and provided additional political impetus to the MGC initiative. It adopted the Phnom Penh Roadmap. On the margins of the ASEAN Summit in Cebu, the Philippines, in January 2007, Thailand, the then chairman of the MGC, handed over chairmanship to India on January 12, 2007. The 5th MGC Ministerial Meeting was held at Manila, Philippines on August 1, 2007, and was chaired by India. Thereafter, the MGC Ministerial Meetings remained pending for 5 years from 2007-2012 and India hosted the 6th MGC Ministerial Meeting on September 4, 2012. To provide a fresh impetus to the MGC initiative, the 7th MGC Ministerial Meeting was held on July 24, 2016 and saw the participation of the Foreign Ministers of all participating countries.

In the field of agriculture, India and ASEAN have projects such as Exchange of Farmers, ASEAN-India Fellowships for Higher Agricultural Education in India and ASEAN, Exchange of Agriculture Scientists, Empowerment of ASEAN-Indian Women through Cooperatives etc. In the S&T field, there are projects such as ASEAN-India Collaborative Project on S&T

for Combating Malaria, ASEAN-India Programme on Quality Systems in Manufacturing, ASEAN-India Collaborative R&D Project on Mari culture, Bio-mining and Bioremediation Technologies etc.

Delhi Dialogue: India has an annual Track 1.5 event Delhi Dialogue, for discussing politico-security and economic issues between ASEAN and India. Since 2009, India has had eight editions of this event. The 8th edition of Delhi Dialogue was hosted by the MEA in partnership with IDSA, FICCI and other selected Indian and ASEAN partners on 17-19 February 2016 in New Delhi. DD VIII had 'ASEAN-India Relations: A New Paradigm' as its theme and included an Inaugural Business Session, a Ministerial Session, and an Academic Session.

Mission to ASEAN: India has set up a separate Mission to ASEAN and the EAS in Jakarta in April 2015 with a dedicated Ambassador to strengthen engagement with ASEAN and ASEAN-centric processes.[12]

ASEAN Studies Centre: Inaugurated on 8 August 2016, it will function from the Indian Council of Social Science and Research-North Eastern Regional Centre located in the North-Eastern Hill University (NEHU) in Shillong. The Centre is proposed to serve all the stakeholders in the North-eastern region and ASEAN by facilitating ASEAN-India research projects, studies, workshops and related activities.

NOTES

1. Moons, Selwyn and Van Bergeijk, Peter A. G., *Economic Diplomacy and Economic Security*, New Frontiers for Economic Diplomacy, pp. 37-54.
2. R. Saner, L. Yiu, *International Economic Diplomacy: Mutations in Post-modern Times*, Discussion Papers in Diplomacy, Netherlands Institute of International Relations.

3. Van Bergeij, Peter A. G., (2009) "Economic Diplomacy and the Geography of International Trade", Edward Elgar Publishing, North Hampton.
4. Bose, PratimRanjan, "Economic Diplomacy, Indian Style", *The Hindu Business Line*, 28 March 2013.
5. Roche, Elizabeth, "India goes from aid beneficiary to donor", Ministry of External Affairs, Government of India, July 1, 2012.
6. C.Raja Mohan, "India's economic diplomacy", *The Hindu*,Thursday, Aug 14, 2003.
7. Nirupama M Rao, (2011) in the book *"Economic Diplomacy: India's Experience"* Kishan S Rana, and Bipul Chatterjee, (eds).
8. US Ambassador Nirupama Rao on "Indian Foreign Policy in the 21st Century: Challenges and Opportunities" see athttps://www.indianembassy.org/archives_details.php?nid=1743
9. Foreign Trade Census, Govt. of India, see athttp://www.census.gov/foreign-trade/balance/c5330.html#2007
10. India-US Trade Relations, Indian Embassy in US, seeathttps://www.indianembassy.org/indusrel/trade.ht
11. *Embassy of India* at DC, USA, for detail kindly see https://www.indianembassy.org/pages.php?id=42.
12. Indo-ASEAN Relations at https://www.mea.gov.in/aseanindia/20-years.htm

3

INDIA AND BRICS: A NEW WORLD ORDER

BRICS is the acronym for an association of five major emerging national economies: Brazil, Russia, India, China, and South Africa. The grouping was originally known as "BRIC" before the inclusion of South Africa in 2010. The BRICS members are all developing or newly industrialized countries, but they are distinguished by their large, fast-growing economies and significant influence on regional and global affairs; all five are G-20 members. As of 2014, the five BRICS countries represent almost 3 billion people which is 40 per cent of the world population, with a combined nominal GDP of US$16.039 trillion (20 per cent world GDP) and an estimated US$4 trillion in combined foreign reserves. As of 2014, the BRICS nations represented 18 percent of the world economy.

The acronym was coined by Jim O'Neill in a 2001 paper entitled "*Building Better Global Economic BRICs*". The acronym has come into widespread use as a symbol of the apparent shift in global economic power away from the developed G7 economies towards the developing world.Projections on the future power of the BRIC economies vary widely. Some sources suggest that they might overtake the G7 economies by 2027. More modestly, Goldman Sachs has argued that, although the four BRIC countries are developing rapidly, it was only by 2050 that their combined economies could eclipse the combined economies of the current richest countries of the world.[1]

In 2010, however, while the four BRIC countries accounted for over a quarter of the world's land area and more than 40 per cent of the world's population,they accounted for only one-quarter of the world gross national income.[2] According to a paper published in 2005, Mexico and South Korea were the only other countries comparable to the BRICs, but their economies were excluded initially because they were considered already more developed, as they were already members of the OECD.

South Africa was subsequently successful in joining the bloc, despite the fact that economists at the Reuters 2011 Investment Outlook Summit dismissed the prospects of South African success. Jim O'Neill, for example, told the summit that South Africa, at a population of under 50 million people, was just too small an economy to join the BRIC ranks. However, after the BRIC countries formed a political organization among themselves, they later expanded to include South Africa, becoming the BRICS.[3]

The BRIC grouping's first formal summit, also held in Yekaterinburg, commenced on 16 June 2009, with LuizInácio Lula da Silva, Dmitry Medvedev, Manmohan Singh, and Hu Jintao, the respective leaders of Brazil, Russia, India and China, all attending. The Summit's focus was on means of improving the global economic situation and reforming financial institutions, and discussed how the four countries could better co-operate in the future.[4] There was further discussion of ways that developing countries, such as the BRIC members, could become more involved in global affairs.

In the aftermath of the Yekaterinburg summit, the BRIC nations announced the need for a new global reserve currency, which would have to be "diversified, stable and predictable". Although the statement that was released did not directly criticise the perceived "dominance" of the US dollar – something that Russia had criticised in the past – it did spark a fall in the value of the dollar against other major currencies.

FIRST BRIC SUMMIT

The inaugural BRIC summit took place in Yekaterinburg, Russia on June 16, 2009 The four heads of government from the BRIC countries attended. The BRIC leaders called for increased economic reform, demanding a "greater voice and representation in international financial institutions, and their heads and senior leadership should be appointed through an open, transparent and merit-based selection process".

They urged the international community to push for comprehensive results of the Doha Round. Amongst the important issues discussed were United Nations reform. "We reiterate the importance we attach to the status of India and Brazil in international affairs, and understand and support their aspirations to play a greater role in the United Nations." Regarding the 2007–2008 world food price crisis, the leaders issued a joint statement on global food security, calling for "action by all governments and the relevant international agencies"; and reaffirmed "their commitment to contribute to the efforts to overcome the global food crisis".

SECOND BRIC SUMMIT

The 2010 BRIC summit took place in Brasília, Brazil on April 16, 2010. This was the second BRIC summit after Yekaterinburg in 2009. The meeting took place between the four heads of government from the BRIC states following bilateral meetings in the prior days. A few months before the Summit, the Indian Foreign Minister, SM Krishna, met President Lula in Brasília, where he stressed for the need to accelerate relations between the three countries. He also emphasized India's commitment to IBSA as a symbol of "the spirit of South-South cooperation."

Days prior to the official summit, bilateral meetings also took place between Brazil and India, as well as between Brazil and China. India and China also agreed to work together instead of competitively signaling there is enough room for the both to grow together. The two also agreed to give greater market access to each other's products to boost trade. Additionally, between April 13 to 16 other meetings and forums took place such as: the IBSA/BRIC Business Forum; meeting of development banks and commercial banks meeting; a think-tank seminar; a cooperatives forum; and a meeting of representatives on strategy and security.

The leaders discussed various current issues including the Iran and nuclear weapons, development, the furtherance of the BRIC (and IBSA that was occurring at the same time) as an international body, the global economic situation at the time, reform of financial institutions, the financial G20, and cooperation and issues related to global governance.

However, China explicitly stated the Chinese Yuan was not discussed. Despite coming under heavy pressure to let their currency appreciate the Chinese appeared to be standing their ground. Despite the refusal to discuss this the currency fell. The day before the summit Brazil expressed "affinity" with China towards the Iranian nuclear issue. Foreign Minister of Brazil, Celso Amorim, said "Our impression... is that the effectiveness of sanctions is debatable." He added that President Lula had brought up the same with the Indian Prime Minister Singh. In the same vein, the IBSA talk preceding the summit called for further talk on the Iranian issue.

Chinese Premier Hu Jintao showed China's willingness to be a positive partner in global development when he showed China's meteoric rise in saying: "The scale and complexity of the challenges that we face in the course of development are unmatched anywhere else in the world and have been rarely seen in human history. We must make persistent efforts for a long time to come. The Chinese people suffered so much in modern history, and we therefore value peace, stability, harmony and freedom more than anything else. A prosperous and growing China dedicated to peace and cooperation is willing and able to make new and even greater contribution to mankind's pursuit of peace and development.

India took the initiative to call for improving the importance of the BRIC and IBSA groups. Indian PM Singh also called for closer cooperation in the fields of energy and food security, as well as tapping into the potential of other sectors such as trade and investment, science and technology and infrastructure. He added that pooling together the experiences of each can lead to more inclusive growth. "We are four large countries with abundant resources, large populations and diverse societies. We aspire for rapid growth for ourselves and for an external environment that is conducive to our development goals. Our people expect us to work together so as to bring the benefits of inclusive social and economic development to them. Our grouping includes two of the largest energy producers and two of the largest consumers in the world. We can cooperate in both upstream and downstream areas, and in the development of new fuels and clean energy technologies."

THIRD BRICS SUMMIT

The 2011 BRICS summit took place in Sanya on the island of Hainan, China, on 14 April 2011. This was the third BRICS summit since 2009. The meeting took place between the five heads of state/heads of government from the BRICS states following bilateral meetings in the prior days.

On 13 April, prior to the heads of state meeting, economic delegations met for discussions. China was lobbied by the other leaders to import not only commodities but also value added products and other commodities such as oil, soybeans and iron ore. Indian Trade Minister Anand Sharma said that China's Commerce Minister Chen Deming had assured the other leaders that his country would make it a priority to import more value-added products from the other four countries. Russia's Deputy Economic Development Minister Oleg Fomichev also said that China pledged to set up high-technology projects in cooperation with Russia so as to "not just importing our resources and exporting industrial goods."[6]

Brazil and India also pressed China to buy such goods as Brazilian aircraft and Indian pharmaceuticals; the two countries also complained about the artificially undervalued yuan that they claimed was undermining their exports. South Africa wanted to process iron ore and other raw materials within the country before exporting them to China. However, at the heads of government summit China's currency valuation was not on the agenda.

All five countries also continued their calls for reform of global monetary and financial institutions. They also pledged greater cooperation amongst themselves. All five countries also called for an early conclusion to deadlocked talks an anti-terror law under UN auspices that would curtail funding for illegal groups that partake in violence against countries and deny their supporters access to funds, arms, and safe havens. A joint statement read: "We reiterate our strong condemnation of terrorism in all its forms and manifestations and stress that there can be no justification, whatsoever, for any acts of terrorism. In this context, we urge early conclusion of negotiations in the UN General Assembly of the Comprehensive Convention on International Terrorism and its adoption by all member states." The heads of government at the summit said that the UN's role was central in coordinating international action against what they labeled terrorism within the framework of the UN Charter and in accordance with principles and norms of international law.

All BRICS countries called for "comprehensive reform of the UN, including its Security Council." China said it would endorse the aspirations of India, Brazil and South Africa for permanent membership of the UNSC. Coincidentally, the five countries are all now members of the Security Council, China and Russia as permanent members and the other three non-permanent.[7]

FOURTH BRICS SUMMIT

The 2012 BRICS summit was the fourth annual BRICS summit, an international relations conference attended by the heads of state or heads of government of the five member states Brazil, Russia, India, China and South Africa. The Summit was held at Taj Mahal Hotel in New Delhi, India on 29 March 2012 and began at 10:00 Indian Standard Time. This is the first time that India has hosted a BRICS summit. The theme of the summit was "BRICS Partnership for Global Stability, Security and Prosperity".

The main agenda for the summit was the creation of a new development bank. The idea for setting up such a bank was put forward by India, as a sign of firming the power of the group and increasing its influence in global decision-making; Sudhir Vyas, a senior Indian official, said that the idea for a BRICS bank had been "in the air for some time. The aims of the bank would include: funding development and infrastructure projects in developing and least developed countries, lending, in the long term, during global financial crises such as the Eurozone crisis; and issuing convertible debt, which could be bought by the central banks of all the member states and hence act as a vessel for risk-sharing.[8]

Economic experts which predicted several beneficent effects of such a bank. Such a bank would allow successful implementation of regional development projects, with increased efficiency and transparency. Brazilian Trade Minister Fernando Pimentel said that the bank "would be a very powerful financial tool to improve trade opportunities, and may be a major step to support the EU to overcome its financial crisis.

In the Delhi Declaration at the end of the summit, the BRICS announced the setting up of the bank, described as a "BRICS-led South-South Development Bank." The finance ministers of the member states were directed to conduct feasibility studies of the initiative and to submit their reports at the next BRICS summit. Pimentel said that the proposed bank was not meant as a sign of abandonment of existing global financial institutions, but that it was a response to current economic necessities. Vyas commented that the BRICS would determine the capital structure and that the initiative would take some time to get started.[9]

FIFTH BRICS SUMMIT

The 2013 BRICS summit was the fifth annual BRICS summit, an international relations conference attended by the head of states or heads of government of the five member states Brazil, Russia, India, China and South Africa. The Summit was held in Durban, South Africa in 2013. This completed the first cycle of BRICS summits. Host President Jacob Zuma said of the summit that it could address South Africa's economic problems, such as high unemployment. He added: "BRICS provides an opportunity for South Africa to promote its competitiveness. It is an opportunity to move further in our drive to promote economic growth and confront the challenge of poverty, inequality and unemployment that afflicts our country."

Daniel Twining of the German Marshall Fund said: "Ironically it may be the cleavages within the BRICS grouping that more accurately hint at the future of the global order: tensions between China and Brazil on trade, India on security, and Russia on status highlight the difficulty Beijing will have in staking its claim to global leadership. "The media suggested the bank was way to bypass the IMF and the World Bank.[10]

SIXTH BRICS SUMMIT

The 6th BRICS summit was the sixth annual diplomatic meeting of the BRICS, a grouping of major emerging economies that includes Brazil, Russia, India, China and South Africa. It was hosted by Brazil, as the first host country of the current five-year summit cycle; the host city was Fortaleza. Argentine President Cristina Kirchner was a special guest of the summit. Though Brazil hosted a four-member BRIC summit in April 2010, 2014 marked its first full BRICS summit; the 2010 summit in Brasília did not officially include South Africa, who were only invited as guests in a prelude to full membership, which they achieved in December 2010. Most importantly, the New Development Bank was officially inaugurated.

At the end of the Sixth BRICS Summit in Fortaleza, Brazil on July 16, 2014, the leaders of the BRICS countries announced the "Fortaleza Action Plan." This plan is in the context of the Fortaleza Declaration, where the leaders reinforced their position that BRICS would be an international force in challenging the neo-liberal policies of the Washington Consensus. Touching on areas of major destabilization in the world – from Syria to Sudan and from Ukraine to Iraq – the leaders spelt out the need for new paths to peace and for strengthening the United

Nations to resolve the outstanding questions of war and insecurity.[10]

The most daring aspect of the Fortaleza Declaration was the announcement of a new financial architecture to intervene in relation to the international tensions that have arisen since the Federal Reserve Bank of the United States announced the monetary policy of Quantitative Easing. This policy allows a central bank, like the Federal Reserve System, to purchase government or other securities from the market with the goal of lowering interest rates and increasing the available money supply. The BRICS summit announced two new pillars in a new financial architecture that is to be anchored with the headquarters of the New Development Bank in Shanghai, China.

The Fortaleza Action Plan and the outcomes of this summit represented a major step in breaking the Exorbitant Privilege of the US dollar as a the dominant international currency. Along with the formal establishment of the New Development Bank (NDB), the leaders announced the launch of a Contingency Reserve Arrangement (CRA), which in 2013 was approved to receive a $100 billion fund to combat currency crises. The first president of the Bank will be from India, the inaugural Chairman of the Board of directors will come from Brazil and the inaugural chairman of the Board of Governors will be Russian. It was stressed in the Fortaleza proclamations that the BRICS Bank would be organized on the basis of equality unlike the current IMF and World Bank where the leader of the IMF is always a European and the head of the World Bank is always a US citizen. The proposal for the BRICS bank had been announced at the BRICS summit in New Delhi in 2012 and at the summit in Durban in 2013 the plan for the CRA was also outlined. The long term goal of the CRA will be to provide emergency cash to BRICS countries faced with short term credit crisis or balance of payments problems. Ultimately, in the context of the present currency wars, the CRA will replace the International Monetary Fund (IMF) as the provider of resources for BRICS members and other poor societies when there is balance of payment difficulties.

NEW DEVELOPMENT BANK

The creation of the BRICS bank came after there had been failed efforts to change the structure of the International Monetary Fund and the World Bank. The NDB will begin with US$50 billion, divided equally between the five countries, with an initial amount of US$10 billion in cash put in over seven years and $40 billion in guarantees. The BRICS bank is scheduled to start lending in 2016. In order to be a platform for the poorer nations, the BRICS bank will open its membership to other countries other than the five BRICS members. In simple terms, the New Development Bank will challenge the role of the World Bank in the current international system. However, the nature of the challenge will be very dependent on whether the popular anti-globalization forces in BRICS will become dominant over those forces within the BRICS that support the neo-liberal economic policies of the Washington Consensus. The BRICS bank is emerging at a moment when the failures of the strategies of global capital are destroying human beings and the planet earth with citizens all over the world looking for social and political formations that can accelerate inclusive sustainable transformations.

SEVENTH BRICS SUMMIT

Russian President Vladimir Putin said at Ufa that the coming together of the BRICS, SCO and EEU can provide a "powerful economic breakthrough". However, the bigger picture is instead of being 'merely' economic or political, the BRICS are waltzing to strategic, long-term ties.Unlike previous meetings that were focussed on laying the groundwork for partnership among the five members, the seventh BRICS summit at Ufa marks the milestone where the BRICS signalled their intention to shift the world's centre of gravity away from the West.

Because the acronym has its origins in the world of finance, many observers view the BRICS as an economic grouping. When the BRICS stock markets were on fire, finance gurus talked them up to the sky. But since nothing grows to the sky and these economies are not performing up to expectations, the BRICS are being written off. Also, the western media often refers to the complete lack of homogeneity in the BRICS as if racial similarity was a precondition for unity. It also never fails to mention the India-China rivalry and border tensions that stand in the way of a true union. But the BRICS group is not only an economic entity. It has expanded into the political arena so that the economy was just one of the agendas – among several – at Ufa.

The wide-ranging, punitive and illegal economic sanctions slapped by the West against Russia have given Moscow and Beijing the Goldilocks moment – not too early, not too late, but the perfect opportunity – to pitch BRICS, the Shanghai Cooperation Organisation (SCO) and the Eurasian Economic Union (EEU) as the core of a new international order.That economic sanctions are a really harebrained scheme is now being realised by the hotheads who imposed them. Sanctions haven't burned Moscow but they are hurting Europeans, who were already reeling under joblessness and faced tough future prospects. Sadly for them, Russia is leading the BRICS towards an alternative ecosystem as an insurance against western economic blackmail.

NO MORE LOAN SHARKS

The BRICS now have the answer to the American loan sharks, the World Bank and the International Monetary Fund (IMF), which have been responsible for the economic enslavement of a number of developing countries. With its HQ in the financial powerhouse of Shanghai, the New Development Bank (NDB) has just held its first board meeting and will soon be lending internationally.

The NDB and the China-led Asian Infrastructure Investment Bank – in which all BRICS countries are founding members – will break the monopoly of the World Bank and IMF and could make their functioning more transparent. "It will motivate the IMF and the World Bank to function more normatively, democratically and efficiently, in order to promote the reform of international financial system as well as democratisation of international relations," said China's official newspaper Global Times in an article titled "BRICS cooperation helps to build new international framework".

So the next time American and British intelligence agents, embedded within the IMF or World Bank as "consultants" – want to sabotage the economy of a free-minded developing country or assassinate a nationalist leader or an honest bureaucrat, the chances are they will be asked to stand down by the bankers. Competition – like money – talks in a language everyone understands.

BYE-BYE SANCTIONS

The NDB a.k.a. BRICS Bank, will start off with a capital of $50 billion which will be hiked to $100 billion in two years. Headed by India's K.V. Kamath, the bank is just what the doctor ordered for large Russian enterprises such as state oil company Rosneft, private gas producer Novatek and Russia's biggest bank Sber bank, that are impacted by sanctions.

However, according to Kamath, the NDB should not be viewed as a tool to help sanctions-hit companies but said the bank would look at requests from Russian companies. "We are not looking at it in that context at all," he told Reuters.

Guess what, Kamath or not, Russian firms will be queuing up at the NDB.

HELLENIC HELLHOLE VS ORDER IN THE URALS

Success has a lot to with public perception. The eastern nations are the ones supposed to be divided and squabbling, but for weeks the world has been witnessing the westerners slug it out in an ugly family drama gone viral. While BRICS leaders attending their summits appear to walk with the bearing of conquerors, European politicians are battling furious public protests.

At Ufa in the Urals, as the leaders of the BRICS calmly presented their drafts for a new world order, in the Hellenic Hellhole that is Greece, overbearing and overfed Germans were shoving austerity down the throats of hungry Greeks reeling under 50 per cent youth unemployment.

Such perceptions can directly impact financial flows, which tend to gravitate towards markets and economies that are secure and stable. Where would you like to keep your hard earned millions – in turbulent Europe, racially divided America or the comparatively calmer BRICS?

EIGHTS BRICS SUMMIT

The eighth BRICS summit was held in Goa from 15 to 16 October 2016. The summit concluded with adaptation of Goa Declaration. The two day summit was attended by the Prime Minister Narendra Modi, Chinese President Xi Jinping, Russian President Vladimir Putin, Brazilian President Michel Temer and South African President Jacob Zuma. The theme for the summit was "Building Responsive, Inclusive and Collective Solutions". Key Highlights of Goa Declaration BRICS nations condemns terrorism in all its forms and stressed that there can be no justification for such acts. International terrorism, especially the Islamic State (IS) is an unprecedented threat to international peace and security. BRICS nations reaffirmed the commitment to increase effectiveness of the UN counter terrorism framework. Need for adaptation of Comprehensive Convention on International Terrorism (CCIT) in the UN General Assembly. Urgent need to reforms of the United Nations, including UN Security Council, to increase representation of developing countries. Resolution of civil war in Syria, in accordance with the "legitimate aspirations of the people of Syria" and action against UN-designated terrorist groups like IS and Jabhat al-Nusra. All nations must counter radicalism and block sources of financing international terrorism, dismantling terrorist bases and countering misuse of the Internet including social media. Appreciated progress in implementation of Strategy for BRICS Economic Partnership and emphasise importance of BRICS Roadmap for Trade, Economic and Investment Cooperation until 2020. Welcomed adoption of 2030 Agenda for Sustainable Development and its Sustainable Development Goals. Reiterated determination to use all policy tools to achieve the goal of sustainable and inclusive growth. The ninth BRICS Summit will be hosted by China in 2017. Besides, first-ever BRICS-BIMSTEC Outreach Summit was also held on side-lines of 2016 BRICS Summit. Leaders from both forums planned to jointly explore possibilities of expanding ties between them on issues such as terrorism, economy, trade and connectivity. BIMSTEC stands for Bay of Bengal Initiative for Multi-Sectoral Technical and Economic Cooperation. BIMSTEC member countries are Bangladesh, India, Myanmar, Sri Lanka, Thailand, Bhutan and Nepal.

CONCLUSION

There is no question that this institution will pose as a rival to the Bretton Woods Institutions. The bigger danger for the dollar is the reality that other emerging states that want to break from the conditional ties of the IMF can benefit from the NDB and CRA. The BRICS states make up more than a quarter of the Global GDP and holds less than 11 per cent of the voting rights in the IMF. The United States holds over 16.8 per cent of the voting power in the IMF and along with the countries of Britain, France, Germany and Italy control over 34 per cent of the vote of the IMF. After the crash of Wall Street in 2008 there were efforts by the BRICS group to restructure the World Bank and the IMF to increase the influence of China and other BRICS societies. Wall Street could not countenance this restructuring because the dominance of the Bretton Woods Institutions ensured the military management of the international system in so far as the poorer countries of the world had to keep their reserves in dollars and the US could finance its expenditures from the hard earned savings of other peoples. The BRICS formation will now give the poorer societies a greater say in the international financial order. In this, the BRICS societies will be sure that Washington will not take these developments sitting down.

NOTES

1. O'Neill, Jim (30 November 2001). *Building Better Global Economic BRICs,* Global Economics Paper No: 66. Goldman Sachs.
2. Jim O'Neill; Dominic Wilson; RoopaPurushothaman; Anna Stupnytska (1 December 2005). *How Solid are the BRICs?* (Global Economics Paper No: 134). Goldman Sachs Economic Research.
3. "World Economic Outlook". *IMF.* April 2013.
4. "Emerging Economies Meet in Russia" *New York Times,* on 2009-06-16.
5. "Front Page: India pitches for greater IBSA, BRIC role". *The Hindu,* on 2010-04-16.

6. Samanta, Pranab Dhal, "BRICS calls for UNSC reforms", *Indian Express*, 15 Apr 2011.
7. "Countries of BRICS refuse dollars". *Forex.us.* 27 April 2011.
8. "Brics summit of emerging nations to explore bank plan". BBC. 29 March 2012.
9. Business Economy: BRICS for collective action to deal with EU debt crisis. *The Hindu* (28 March 2012).
10. "Brics eye infrastructure funding through new development bank". *The Guardian.* 28 March 2013.
11. Simha, Rakesh Krishnan, *Russia and India Report*, "Five takeaways from the BRICS summit"16 July 2015.
12. http://currentaffairs.gktoday.in/8th-brics-summit-concludes-goa-10201636488.html

4

EUROPEAN UNION-INDIA AND THE MULTIPOLAR WORLD ORDER

The European Economic Community (EEC) was set up in 1957 under the Treaty of Rome. Prime Minister Jawaharlal Nehru was not very positive at the formations of EEC and argued that the EEC would further divide the cold war divisions, widen the gap between rich and poor countries. He saw no relevancy of EEC to India and called it as a "Rich Men's Club" from which he did not expect a great deal.[1]

India and Europe are linked by half a century of common values that unites the two regions as the world's largest democratic state and the largest confederation of democracies respectively. Both modern India and Europe are built on ancient cultures based on similar linguistic and cultural roots, with trading contracts dating back more than 2300 years. As in most of Europe, free elections have been regularly in India, as one of the few stable democracies in the South for the last six decades in stark contrast to Latin America, China, and the Arab and African regions, with the Indian democracy having more voters than the European Union has residents. Indian governments have frequently been longer lasting and stable than those of Italy and the Fourth French Republic. There is an extensive freedom of speech and press, the army remains a non-political entity and the judiciary is predominantly independent in India. India is thus one of the few developing countries to remain both a secular state and a democracy since independence, with the exception of the short period of emergency rule in 1975-77.[2]

Despite having negative sentiments towards EEC, India was the first country outside the European community to establish the diplomatic relation with it in 1962 by opening an embassy in Brussels. For a decade (1963-73), Indian efforts focused on securing better market access for India major exports and alleviation of its chronic trade deficit with the EEC, which was largest it had amongst all its trading partners. This was dealt with on a product byproduct basis by the conclusion of annual agreements on the suspension in whole or in part of the custom duty. Though the EEC introduced the General System of Preferences (GSP) in 1971, India felt that the GSP was not structured to solve the specific problems created for India by its loss of preferential access to the British Market. Many of India's main exports, including jute, coir, cotton and textile and tobacco were either excluded from the scheme or else subject to special arrangements.

With the United Kingdom's entry in to EEC in 1973, the enlarged community had to decide on the arrangements to be concluded with the developing countries of the commonwealth. The EEC was in no position to take the burden of financial aid to countries as populous as India. Under the joint declaration of intent, annexed to the UK's Treaty of Accession (1973) the EEC agreed to examine with the Asian Commonwealth countries" such problems as many arise in the field of trade with a view to seek appropriate solutions". India was the first country to take advantage of this offer. However, member states even with those with past colonial conventions with India had no real interest in alleviating India's difficulties. India was perceived as "Britain's baby" and it was up to British to act in its favour.[3]

With the end of the Cold War, the EEC (which became EU in 1993) no longer had to look at India through the lens of Cold war equations. Moreover, India was becoming progressively more interesting economically to the EU. Its policy of liberalization and privatization in 1991 was taken positively by the EU. The policy of privatization, with constant high economic growth rate, acquiring of nuclear weapons in 1998, steadily improvement of relations with USA, all led to recognition of India as a potential global player by the EU. In the post-cold war era, India pursued a pragmatic foreign policy, shed most of the ideological baggage, and accorded greater priority to the west as a market, source of technology and FDI.[4]

The institutional architecture between India and EU is now quite multilayered. Apart from the joint commission and sub-commissions, troika ministerial meetings have been held since 1982. Other institutional mechanisms include senior officials meetings, meetings between the European commission and Indian planners, bilateral meetings in the margins of multilateral forums, working group of specialists (on the subjects like export control, terrorism exports, and consular affairs) the EU-India Round Table, The EU India Energy Panel, Security Dialogue Group, Macro-Economic dialogue on financial cooperation, Dialogue on Human Rights, Dialogue on cooperation in Science and Technology.[5]

SUMMIT MEETINGS: THE BEGINNING OF INSTITUTIONALIZED RELATIONSHIP

The EU-India relations became institutionalized with the staring of summit meetings which first took place in Lisbon, Portugal on 28th June, 2000. In this meeting both agreed to build a new strategic partnership founded on shared values and aspirations characterized by enhanced and multifaceted cooperation. Also, the joint declaration of the first summit gave the new concept of strategic partnership oriented towards 21st century.

The Second summit meeting between EU and India took place in New Delhi on 23rd November, 2001. This meeting saw a tacit understanding of India's point of view on the issue of cross border terrorism. The 9/11 attacks on US had forced EU to rethink on their point of view on terrorism. Now, EU came to approve the point that Pakistan sponsored terrorism is not only threat to India but to the whole world.

Among the summit meetings, Fifth Summit meeting is considered to be a landmark which was held in The Hague, Netherlands on 8th Nov. 2004. In this meeting EU endorsed India as a "Strategic Partner" showing growing importance of India in the European continents. The EU had strategic partnership with only five other countries (USA, Canada, Russia, Japan and China) and now India joined the elite club.

The next Summit meeting between the top EU and Indian leadership took place in New Delhi on September 7, 2005. A political declaration on EU-India Strategic Partnership provided the executive summary and a joint action plan the fine print. Setting a broad political agenda for future Indo-European cooperation on top of trade and aid, Brussels and New Delhi pledged to strengthen dialogue and consultation, especially in mutual forums, jointly foster democracy, human rights, and cultural diversity, promote global disarmament and non-proliferation, to combat terrorism organized crime and drug trafficking, and identity areas of cooperation in peacekeeping, conflict resolution and post-conflict assistance. Among other steps, both sides further agreed to upgrade their existing dialogue on migration and consular issues, increase cultural cooperation, stimulate more educational and academic exchanges and intensify contacts between parliamentarians as well as civil society.

The Eight Summits between EU and India took place in New Delhi on 30th November 2007, co-chaired by our Prime Minister and Portuguese Prime Minister who then held the rotating presidency of European Union. EU and India reaffirmed their commitment to a rule-based multilateral trading system and to deeper level of bilateral relations. The successful and timely outcome of the Doha Development Agenda (DDA) multilateral trade negotiations remains the foremost trade policy priority of the two sides. The leaders noted that bilateral trade and investment between India and EU has been growing steadily and reflects the strengthening of bilateral economic ties and welcomed the progress achieved in the first few rounds of negotiations on the India-EU trade and investment agreement and reaffirmed commitment to further intensify negotiations.[6]

The Ninth Summit between EU and India was held in Marseille, France on 29th September, 2008. The summit, inter-alia, reviewed India-EU Joint Action Plan of 2005 and issued a revised plan extending the strategic partnership to new areas; took note of the signature of India-EU horizontal Civil Aviation Agreement signed on 28th September; 2003; issued a Joint Work Programme (JWP) for cooperation in Energy, Clean Development and Climate change, and adopted a target of Euros100 billion for bilateral trade in the next five years. The JWP envisages cooperation on, among others, clean coal technology, energy efficiency, fusion energy research and renewable energy as also conclusion of fusion energy research cooperation agreement between EURATOM and India.

The Ninth meeting also adopted a joint communiqué. Prime Minister also attended the India-EU Business summit titled. 'New Synergies for Partnership' which was held on 30th September 2008 in Paris. The two revised Joint Action Plan (JAP) signed during the last summit Marseilles and reaffirmed their commitment to expanding and diversifying economic and trade ties. Both India and EU agreed to double bilateral trade to $ 145 billion in another five years at the last summit in Marsilles. The revised JAP in September, 2008 titled "Global Patterns for Global Challenges", added forty odd items to the hundred odd items already contained in the original JAP.[7]

The 10th India-EU Summit took place on 6th November, 2009 in New Delhi which decided to put the negotiations for a Free Trade Agreement (FTA) on the fast track and wanted to rap it by 2010. EU was the largest trading partner of India accounting for about 77 billion in trade in goods and services in 2008. The EU accounts for 21 per cent of India's total exports and 16 per cent of India's total imports. It has been biggest investor in India with a cumulative volume of about 10 billion since 2000.

It can be remembered that both India and EU launched negotiations in 2007 for an Free Trade Agreement, but the negotiations are still dragging due to differences over differences over intellectual property rights and the EU's negotiating stance to link trade with climate change and other extraneous issues like child labour, high rate of tariffs, signing on CTBT and NPT etc.

The Tenth India-European Union Summit which held in New Delhi on the November, 2009.The meeting was chaired by Prime Minister of India Dr. Manmohan Singh and the EU was represented by Fredrik Reinfeldt, the Prime Minister of Sweden, in his capacity as president of the council of the European Union and Jose Manuel Barroso, the President of the European Commission.

The leaders of both countries called for strengthening the relations between the two with the spirit of "strategic partnership". They emphasized that our strategic partnership is rooted in our shared values of democracy, rule of law, respect for human rights, and fundamental freedom. They also assured each other to strengthen effective multilateral systems like WTO, UN as key players in tackling climate change like global challenges. In the same context they also drew the importance and need to pursue the reform of the main UN bodies, among them the General Assembly, ECOSOC, and the Security Council with a view to enhancing the representativeness, transparency and the effectiveness of the system.

In the Summit, India and EU also recognized the importance of tackling the problem of climate change and regarded it as the most challenging task in front of global community. They reaffirmed the provisions and principles of the United Nations Framework on Climate Change (UNFCC). EU recognizes the position of countries like India and respects the concept of "common but differentiated responsibilities" and "respective capabilities".

EU's policy towards the issue of climate change have been different and serious-vis-à-vis other developed countries. This is the one area where EU has arguably been fairly consistent in following its own script and trying to lead by example. Backed by a broad popular consensus on the irreversible effects of the global warming, the EU can claim to remain the driving force within the industrialized world for a binding, universal regime to reduce greenhouse gas emission. As a country particularly vulnerable to global warming because of its reliance on the annual monsoon and the Himalayan glaciers watering its densely populated great riparian basins, India has been considered a crucial partner and potentially in this effort.[8]

The EU hopes of Indian support for a comprehensive new climate change agreement received a severe blow in the Copenhagen. In the final phase of nearly collapsed conference, New Delhi settled instead for the vague and non-binding "Copenhagen Accord" negotiated between the United States and the four BASIC countries.[9] This sobering experience led to much soul-searching in the European capitals and a less ambitions EU approach to the follow up conference in Cancun. The 2011 Durban conference, however, with the end of first commitment period of the Kyoto Protocol looming and no replacement in sight, raw a major realignment of positions, which brought the EU back into the driver's seat.[10]

The leaders of the both countries also discussed the energy security issues without which effective implementation of Kyoto protocol and meeting the target of UNFCC is not possible. The leaders welcomed the launch of International Partnership for Energy Efficiency Cooperation (IPEEC) in May 2009 at the G8+5 Energy Ministerial meeting in Rome and looked forward for the close cooperation between EU-India cooperation in the framework of IPEEC. They also welcomed the ongoing establishment of the International Renewable Energy Agency (IRENA) to which both parties adhere and will join efforts for a rapid transition towards the wide spread and sustainable use of the renewable energy worldwide. Apart from this they also discussed issues like terrorism, food security, ongoing FTA, WTO, disarmament etc.

The 11th EU-India Summit was held in Brussels on December 10, 2010. The EU was represented by European Council President Merman Van Rompuy and by European Commission President Jose Manuel Barroso. Whereas, India was led by Manmohan Singh and assisted by Anand Sharma and Shiv Shankar Menon. The leaders, emphasized that EU and India, which share common values relating to democracy rule of law, civil liberties and respect for human rights, agreed to reinforce their strategic partnership for their mutual benefit in all areas and to better contribute to the resolutions of the challenges of the 21st century. They discussed bilateral regional and global issues of common interest and concern.

In the joint statement of 11th EU-India Summit, leaders of the both sides recognized the value of an ambitions and balanced Broad Based Trade and Investment Agreement (BBTIA) which will bring the significant economic benefits to both sides and further strengthen the bilateral economic relationship. Leaders welcomed the business summit held in the margins of the summit and also welcomed increasing cooperation in the field of security and defense. They agreed to pursue EU-India dialogue and cooperation in this area, including in the context of counter-privacy naval operations and more broadly in support of the UNSC resolutions. EU and India condemned terrorism in all its forms and manifestations and reaffirmed their united stance in combating threats to international peace and security caused by terrorist acts wherever they take place. Leaders also welcomed the EU-India joint declaration on International Terrorism.[11]

The 12th India-EU Summit was held in New Delhi on 10th February, 2012. EU was represented by Herman Van Rompuy, President of the European Council and Jose Manual Durao Barroso, President of the European Commission. The leaders expressed satisfaction at the deepening comprehensive bilateral ties. India and EU, as long-standing strategic partners, are committed to working together with a balanced and result-oriented approach, bearing in mind each side, respective development priorities, based on common shared values, relating to democracy, rule of law, civil liberties, fundamental freedoms and respect to human rights.

Recalling their joint declaration on international terrorism, adopted at the provisions summit in December 2010, leaders welcomed the holding of the India-EU joint working group on Counter Terrorism in New Delhi in January 2012. Both sides recognized the importance of the activities of the UN Counter Terrorism Committee (CTC) of which India is the chair and concluding negotiations on the Comprehensive Convention on International Terrorism (CCIT) at the earliest. Leaders also discussed for enhancing cooperation on anti-piracy efforts and their division to have such exchanges on a regular basis. They expressed satisfaction on working on cyber security and cybercrimes. They looked forward to an expeditious finalization of the Joint Report on the Results of the India-EU joint work programme on energy, Clean Development and Climate Change and reaffirmed their commitment to strengthening cooperation in these areas. Both leaders expressed satisfaction on the progress in finalizing ISRO-ESA Agreement for cooperation on Earth Observation and Climate change. Leaders called for progress and finalization of an agreement between India and the European Atomic Energy Community for R&D Cooperation in the peaceful uses of nuclear energy.[12]

On the regional issues, leaders reiterated their commitment to assisting Afghanistan to become a stable, democratic nation free of terrorism and experience as NATO/ISAF prepares to complete withdrawal from Afghanistan by the end of 2014. They stressed that a stable and democratic Pakistan is in the interest of entire region. They recalled their views that terrorism cannot be justified on any grounds and stressed that perpetrators of the November, 2008 Mumbai attacks should be brought to justice expeditiously. They recognized that close cooperation among the countries of South Asia is crucial for the development of the region and to continue with the consultation and cooperation between SAARC and the EU.

EU-INDIA: AREAS OF COMMON CONCERNS

India's democratic political system valuable in its own rights has now become an asset for her. Like a ship with many water tight compartments, India is relatively immune to the kinds of large-scale, extremist or totalitarian movements that have shook other nations. India's cultural influence has grown fast due to Bollywood movies, classical music and yoga.[13] With the acquiring of Nuclear technology in 1998, India has become a 'nuclear weapon state, increasing its prestige and status world over.

In the military–political arena, India shares a common interest with other major powers including EU. Some of the common issues include – preventing of spread of weapons of mass destruction and terrorism, in fostering maritime security stabilization of weak states, and coping with health hazards and pandemics. India will continue to strongly favour the development of multilateral regimes to regulate international trade and politics.[14] In 2007, the EU, along with several other major world powers gained official observer status in the SAARC which reflects the keen EU interest in the SAARC experiment.

TERRORISM AND DISARMAMENTS

India has been a victim of state sponsored terrorism for a long time but despite recognition by the EU and its members states dislike for Pakistan misadventure in Kargil (1999), Europe did not support Indian characterizations of Pakistan either a 'failed state' or an 'epicenter of terrorism'. But 9/11 attack on US forced EU to rethink its decisions on terrorism. At the second EU-India summit (2001), the issue of terrorist attack on parliament was taken very seriously. The London Bus bombing and Spain tube train attack and later Glasgow Airport conspiracy has woken the EU to understand and support India's point of view on terrorism. After US banned several Pakistan terrorist organizations Brussels followed the suit and declared several terrorist outfits as terrorist organizations in April 2004.

Both sides have recognized that terrorism constitutes one of the most serious threats to international peace and security. India and EU has established contents between counter Terrorism coordinators for blocking access to terrorist financing and cooperate in fighting against money laundering. Both sides have established an EU-India security dialogue on global and regional security issues, disarmament and non-proliferation.

CLIMATE CHANGE

EU has taken more serious action to solve the irreversible problem of climate change viz-a-viz other developed countries like US. Both India and EU have launched an EU-India Initiative on Clean Development and Climate Change with the aim of promoting cleaner technologies and their use. Although EU has some reservations regarding reduction of green house gases by developed countries, it acknowledge the principle of "common but differentiated responsibilities" that represents the cornerstone of New Delhi's multilateral climate policy.[15]

EFFECTIVE MULTI-LATERISM

The Brussel's philosophy to lean on the new global heavy weights with efforts to shape the multilateral agenda. The European security strategy calls for strategic partnership with Japan, China, Canada, and India, in addition to the special ties with US and Russia. The 2008 update is less precise in pointing out the EU's collaborators of choice, but the additional strategic partnerships concluded to date –Brazil, South Africa, Mexico and South Korea-give a general idea of the selection criteria –a political leadership role in their region, an economy large enough to matter to Europe, the adherence to the same goods and values, with China being the more obvious exception in this category.

Both, India and EU have shown a common belief in the fundamental importance of multilateralism and in the essential role of the UN for maintaining international peace and security, promoting the economic and social advancement of all people and meeting global treaty and challenges. They believe that international institutions like UN, IMF, World Bank, WTO should work independently and autonomously without coming under pressure from any power of the day.

FOSTERING MARITIME SECURITY

The safety of heavy vessels at high seas has become a major concern world over. Indian Ocean falls at the major international trade route and number of ships being hijacked by pirates at Gulf of Eden and adjoining areas have enhanced the role of Indian Navy. In 2007, the EU along with several other major powers gained official status in SAARC and during the meeting issue of piracy was came up for discussion. EU is ready to play a constructive role with Indian Navy for the safe passage of commercial ships.

The importance of the Indian Ocean in India's strategic thinking is driven by the constants of geography and also the imperatives of globalization and economic cooperation. Over 97 per cent of India's trade by volume and 75 percent of its trade by value is sea-born. The safety and security of sea lanes and energy supply chains through the Indian Ocean especially passing through the Strait of Bab-el-Mandeb, Strait of Hormuz, Strait of Malacca and the areas around the cape of Good Hope is very crucial for India's economic and strategic point of view. Also, India's Maritime security Doctrine puts Indian Ocean region on its top of operations and interests.

COOPERATION IN NUCLEAR ENERGY

Since 1998, when India conduced its five nuclear tests at Pokharan, EU and India have traveled a long route to reach at a peaceful cooperation in nuclear energy. India is now a partner International Thermonuclear Experimental Reactor (ITER) project which began in 1985. ITER began as a collaboration between the European Union (Through EURATOM), USA,

USSR and Japan. On June 28, 2005 it was officially declare that ITER will be built in the EU in Southern France. Construction of ITER complex began in 2008.

At the ITER meeting at Jeju, South Korea, the six non-host partners will now contribute 6/11th of the total cost a little over half while EU will put in the rest. On 6th December 2005 India joined as the 7th participating member of ITER with other members like China, EU, Japan, Korea, Russia and US. This project involves a Tokamak fusion reactor that should be capable to produce 500 MW thermal power. India already has several fusion research projects underway including experimental Tokamak devices like ADITYA and SST-1.

Although, India is not the signatory of CTBT and NPT but EU agreed to cooperate with India in the field of peaceful nuclear energy due to its past impeccable record of non-proliferation and being a responsible power. EU and NSG also approved the Indo-US nuclear deal between India and US, which is unofficially acknowledges India as a nuclear power state.[16]

The Galilio programme, a joint European Commission and European Space Agency Initiative is based on constellation of 30 satellites orbiting at an altitude of 24000 km which is similar to US global positioning system (GPS) and the Russian GLONASS. India has signed up to the 30 satellites land work space navigation project in September 2005.

DEMOCRACY AS A COMMON THREAD

The belief that their common values as well as their growing statutures would predestine Europe and India for much closer ties is expressed in the EU's initial strategic partnership proposal of June 2004. It outlined four main areas of closer cooperation – political bilateral and multilateral cooperation with an emphasis on transnational security treats; enhanced economic and sartorial cooperation; development and closer cultural ties and promotion of people to people exchanges.

EU and India believe in 'shared values and beliefs' and the "common commitment to democracy, pluralism, human rights and the rule of law" that the Strategic Partnership Declaration of 2005 heralds. India generally does not aspire to advocate democracy and human rights abroad. It may see its own democratic credentials as important elements of the 'soft power' it can project it in South Asia and beyond, and may hope to attract and inspire others but it does not believe in lending direct support to pro-democratic movements berating other governments over their human rights records.[17]

GROWING ECONOMIC COOPERATION

The presence of a large numbers of English speaking Indians, growing economic power, sophisticated and modern legal, banking, and commercial infrastructure, presence of highly qualified technical and professional personnel, secular nature of polity along with free press, independent judiciary are some of the important drives of Indo-EU trade and economic cooperation.

In the recent years, India's exports with EU have increased from about $8.8 billion in 1996-97 to about $46 billion in 2010-11. Similarly, India imported commodities worth US$44 billion in the same year from EU. There imports were only worth $10.6 billion in 1996-97. Due to global economic slowdown, bilateral trade declined to about $74 billion in 2009-10, with $36 million in exports and $38 billion in imports. India is major trading partners in the EU are Germany, UK, France, Belgium, Italy, Netherlands, Spain and Sweden. In 2007-08, these eight countries accounted for about 89 per cent of the trade with the EU. The remaining 19 countries accounted for only 11 percent of total trade with the EU.[18]

EU-INDIA DIVERGENT VIEWS

Despite having shared views on many international and regional issues, there are some areas where both EU and India's interests seems to be on odds. There are basic differences in both perceptions and interests between India and EU in many fields including trade, development, climate change, globalization, humanitarian intervention etc. Some of the major disagreement areas are as follow:

1) Although both EU and India are on same side to reform UN and other global multilateral institutions like WTO, IMF, World Bank but there is difference in nature of reform. India has complaint about over representation of Europe in UN Security Council which reflects the colonial and post-World War II world order and not the 21st century reality. Although, EU has sympathetic view on India's claim to be permanent member of UNSC but it is not in favor of radical reform in the UN and clearly do not want to leave its privileged position. New Delhi also protests against over domination of US and EU on international financial institutions like IMF, World Bank etc.
2) Indian products face considerable market access problems due to sanitary and physto-santiary related EU legislations. Agricultural products from India face considerable delays at custom offices in Europe causing considerable loss to the traders.
3) EU countries always complaint Indian government for not opening up economy for foreign investments and considerably high rate of taxes and excise duty. On the other hand India complains EU for its rising standards, cumbersome and complex rules and procedures, and frequent use of trade-defence instruments.
4) India is concerned with EU's anti dumping action against Indian products especially in areas like textiles, electronics, chemicals, pharmaceutical products and herbal ayurveda

products. India is also opposed to the quality certification norms proposed by EU for exporting Basmati to EU region.

5) WTO is another forum where differences persist between India & EU. India is against withdrawal of subsidies to the farmers from developing countries. There are also divergent opinions between the two on environment and Singapore issues at WTO.

6) There is a clear disparity in matter of trade engagement of various EU members with non-EU member countries such as India. For instance, UK is the close trading partner of India followed by France, Germany and Italy. As the result apart from big four of EU, other countries will hardly show any interest in India related matters.

7) EU lacks a coherent and all agreed foreign and defence policy which is proving to be biggest hurdle while dealing countries outside EU. Individual country diplomacy is more successful than the EU's policy as a whole.

8) India is opposed of any humanitarian intervention without the prior permission of the UN. The blatant NATO attacks on Kosovo, Libya, Iraq have brought countries like India, Russia and China to speak up against US led unipolarity in which EU is playing the role of junior partner.

9) EU is imposing number of non-tariff barriers via use of child labour (especially in the carpet industry) and not opening up their market for the stronger Indian services sector. EU is also imposing quantitative restrictions, import licencing mandatory testing, lengthy custom procedures etc.

CONCLUSION

India being the largest functioning democracy of the world whereas EU region is called the 'mother of democracy', both regions are destined to be natural allies. Despite the ongoing economic crisis in the EU region, it still dominates the Indian trade with India becoming a key destination for research and development, outsourcing of manufacturing process, and with the reservoir of scientific talent to foster inventions, the relation between EU and India is destined to grow. The worsening demographic profile of with an ageing population of EU will provide an unique opportunity to Indians especially to skilled migrants. The worst economic depression phase is over for EU and their economy is showing signal of recovery. With these positive treads, EU and India are going to become two important poles of multilateralism in international policies in the times to come.

NOTES

1. Kohli, Atul (ed), (2001) "The Success of India's Democracy" (Cambridge: Cambridge University Press).
2. Frank Biermann and Hans-Dieter Sohn, (2004) "Europe and Multipolar Global Governance: India and East Asia as New Parteners?" Amsterdam, pp. 17-20. See at www. globgov.org/ images/docs/wp-10.
3. R. Abhyankar, "India and European Union: A Parternship for all Reasons", *India Quarterly,* vol. 65, No. 4, 2009.
4. Rajendra K. Jain, "India's Relations with the European Union" in the book, "*Handbook of India's International Relations*" by David Scott (ed): Routldege, London & New York, 2011, p. 225.
5. Ibid. pp. 224-227.
6. *India-EU, Global Parterns for Global Challenges: The EU-India Action Plan,* 29th Sept; 2008, see at www.eeas. europa.eu.
7. Ibid. pp.17-20.
8. Sunil Khilnani, "Bridging Identities: India as a Positive Power?" In the book "*Through a Billion Voices: India's Role in Multipolar World*", (London, Foresight, 2010) pp. 13-17.

9. Praful Bidwai, "Foulding UP the Air" *Frontline*, 27(2), January 16, 2010.
10. Bernd vou Muenchow–Pohl, "India and Europe in a Multipolar World", Carnegie Paper, May, 2012. See at www.carnegieeurope.eu/publications/?fa=48038 EU-India Summit: Joint Statement, Brussels, 10 December, 2010. See at www.conslium.europa.eu/uedocs/cms_data/docs/press data/EN/toraff/118404.pdf.
11. EU-India Summit: Joint Statement, Brussels, 10 December, 2010. See at www.conslium.europa.eu/uedocs/cms_data/docs/pressdata/EN/toraff/118404.pdf.
12. India-EU Joint Statement,10th February, 2012,New Delhi. see at www.eeas.europa.eu/india/sum02_12/docs/2012 0210_joint_statement_en.pdf.
13. Cohen, Stephen, P. "*Emerging Power: India*", Oxford University Press, London, 2008 p.300.
14. Rajendra Kr. Jain, op. cit. p.227.
15. ConnieHedegaard, "Climate Change: India a Constructive Force at Durban" *Economic Times*, January 9, 2012.
16. Richard Gowan and Sushant Singh, "Atlas of Indo-European Strategy", *The Mint*, December 19, 2010.
17. Christian Wagner, "India's Soft Power: Prospects and Limitations", *India Quarterly*, 66(4), 2010, pp. 333-342.
18. Gulshan Sachdeva, "EU-India Economic Ties: Strengthening the Core of the Strategic Partnership" in the book Luis Peral and Vijay Sakhuja (eds) "The EU-India Partnership: Time to Go Strategic" (The European Union Institute for Security Studies, Paris, 2012), p.41.

5

INDIAN MARITIME DIPLOMACY AND THE SOUTH CHINA SEA

The South China Sea is a marginal sea that is part of the Pacific Ocean, encompassing an area from the Karimata and Malacca Straits to the Strait of Taiwan of around 3,500,000 square kilometers (1,400,000sq.miles). The area's importance largely results from one-third of the world's shipping sailing through its waters and that it is believed to hold huge oil and gas reserves beneath its seabed. The minute South China Sea Islands, collectively an archipelago, number in the hundreds. The sea and its mostly uninhabited islands are subject to competing claims of sovereignty by several countries. These claims are also reflected in the variety of names used for the islands and the sea.

The risk of conflict in the South China Sea is significant. China, Taiwan, Vietnam, Malaysia, Brunei, and the Philippines have competing territorial and jurisdictional claims, particularly over rights to exploit the region's possibly extensive reserves of oil and gas. Freedom of navigation in the region is also a contentious issue, especially between the United States and China over the right of U.S. military vessels to operate in China's two-hundred-mile Exclusive Economic Zone (EEZ). These tensions are shaping—and being shaped by—rising apprehensions about the growth of China's military power and its regional intentions. China has embarked on a substantial modernization of its maritime paramilitary forces as well as naval capabilities to enforce its sovereignty and jurisdiction claims by force if necessary. At the same time, it is developing capabilities that would put U.S. forces in the region at risk in a conflict, thus potentially denying access to the U.S. Navy in the western Pacific.[1]

China has backed its expansive claims with island-building and naval patrols. The US says it does not take sides in territorial disputes, but has sent military ships and planes near disputed islands, calling them "freedom of navigation" operations to ensure access to key shipping and air routes. Both sides have accused each other of "militarizing" the South China Sea. There are fears that the area is becoming a flashpoint, with potentially serious global consequences.

Vietnam hotly disputes China's historical account, saying China had never claimed sovereignty over the islands before the 1940s. Vietnam says it has actively ruled over both the Paracels and the Spratlys since the 17th century - and has the documents to prove it. The other major claimant in the area is the Philippines, which invokes its geographical proximity to the Spratly Islands as the main basis of its claim for part of the grouping. Both the Philippines and China lay claim to the Scarborough Shoal (known as Huangyan Island in China) - a little more than 100 miles (160 km) from the Philippines and 500 miles from China. Malaysia and Brunei also lay claim to territory in the South China Sea that they say falls within their economic exclusion zones, as defined by UNCLOS - the United Nations Convention on the Law of the Sea. Brunei does not claim any of the disputed islands, but Malaysia claims a small number of islands in the Spratlys.[2]

The South China Sea is an extremely significant body of water in a geopolitical sense. It is the second most used sea lane in the world, while in terms of world annual merchant fleet tonnage, over 50 per cent passes through the Strait of Malacca, the Sunda Strait, and the Lombok Strait. Over 1.6 million m^3 (10 million barrels) of crude oil a day are shipped through the Strait of Malacca, where there are regular reports of piracy, but much less frequently than before the mid-20th century. The region has proven oil reserves of around 1.2km^3 (7.7 billion barrels), with an estimate of 4.5km^3 (28 billion barrels) in total. Natural gas reserves are estimated to total around 7,500km^3 (266 trillion cubic feet). A 2013 report by the US Energy Information Administration raised the total estimated oil reserves to 11 billion barrels. In 2014 China began to drill for oil in waters disputed with Vietnam.[3] According to studies made by the Department of Environment and Natural Resources, Philippines, this body of water holds one third of the entire world's marine biodiversity, thereby making it a very important area for the ecosystem. However the fish stocks in the area are depleted and countries are using fishing bans as a means of asserting their sovereignty claims.[4]

In September 2011, shortly after China and Vietnam had signed an agreement seeking to contain a dispute over the South China Sea, India's state-run explorer, Oil and Natural Gas Corporation (ONGC) said that its overseas investment arm ONGC, Videsh Limited had signed a three-year deal with Petro Vietnam for developing long-term cooperation in the oil sector and that it had accepted Vietnam's offer of exploration in certain specified blocks in the South China Sea. In response, Chinese Foreign Ministry spokesperson Jiang Yu issued a protest. The spokesman of the Ministry of External Affairs of the Government of India responded by saying that "The Chinese had concerns but we are going by what the Vietnamese authorities have told us and have conveyed this to the Chinese."[5] The Indo-Vietnamese deal was also denounced by the Chinese state-run newspaper Global Times.

The United States could be drawn into a China-Philippines conflict because of its 1951 Mutual Defense Treaty with the Philippines. The treaty states, "Each Party recognizes that an armed attack in the Pacific Area on either of the Parties would be dangerous to its own peace and safety and declares that it would act to meet the common dangers in accordance with its constitutional processes." American officials insist that Washington does not take sides in the territorial dispute in the South China Sea and refuse to comment on how the United States might respond to Chinese aggression in contested waters. Nevertheless, an apparent gap exists between American views of US obligations and Manila's expectations. In mid-June 2011, a Filipino presidential spokesperson stated that in the event of armed conflict with China, Manila expected the United States would come to its aid. Statements by senior US officials may have inadvertently led Manila to conclude that the United States would provide military assistance if China attacked Filipino forces in the disputed Spratly Islands.

THE AWARD OF ARBITRATION TRIBUNAL IN THE HAGUE ON SOUTH CHINA SEA DISPUTE

In January 2013, the Philippines formally initiated arbitration proceedings against China's claim on the territories within the "nine-dash line" that includes Spratly Islands, which it said is unlawful under the United Nations Convention on the Law of the Sea (UNCLOS) convention.[6]

Philippines v. China (also known as The South China Sea Arbitration) were an arbitration case brought by the Republic of the Philippines under the arbitration provisions of the United Nations Convention on the Law of the Sea (UNCLOS). Against the People's Republic of China concerning certain issues in the South China Sea including the legality of China's "nine-dotted line" claim over the South China Sea under the

UNCLOS. On 19 February 2013, China officially refused to participate in the arbitration because, according to China, its 2006 declaration under article 298covers the disputes brought by the Philippines and that this case concerns sovereignty, thus it deems the arbitral tribunal formed for the case has no jurisdiction over the issue.[7] On 7 December 2014, a position paper was published by China to elaborate its position. On 29 October 2015, the arbitral tribunal ruled that it has jurisdiction over the case, taking up seven of the 15 submissions made by the Philippines.

On July 12, 2016, the Permanent Court of Arbitration published an arbitration award by the tribunal which it states is final and binding as set out in the Convention. Conclusions expressed in the award included the following:

Regarding the "Nine-Dash Line" and China's claim in the maritime areas of the South China Sea.

The [UNCLOS] Convention defines the scope of maritime entitlements in the South China Sea, which may not extend beyond the limits imposed therein. China's claims to historic rights, or other sovereign rights or jurisdiction, with respect to the maritime areas of the South China Sea encompassed by the relevant part of the 'nine-dash line' are contrary to the Convention and without lawful effect to the extent that they exceed the geographic and substantive limits of China's maritime entitlements under the Convention. The Convention superseded any historic rights or other sovereign rights or jurisdiction in excess of the limits imposed therein.[8]

Regarding the status of features as above/below water at high tide features:

(a) Scarborough Shoal,

(b) Cuarteron Reef,

(c) Fiery Cross Reef,

(d) Johnson Reef,
(e) McKennan Reef,
(f) Gaven Reef (North).

Low-tide elevations:

(a) Hughes Reef,
(b) Gaven Reef (South),
(c) Subi Reef,
(d) Mischief Reef,
(e) Second Thomas Shoal.

Hughes Reef lies within 12 nautical miles of the high-tide features on McKennan Reef and Sin Cowe Island, Gaven Reef (South) lies within 12 nautical miles of the high-tide features at Gaven Reef (North) and Namyit Island, and that Subi Reef lies within 12 nautical miles of the high-tide feature of Sandy Cay on the reefs to the west of Thitu.[9]

Regarding the status of features as rocks/islands

Scarborough Shoal contains, within the meaning of Article 121(1) of the Convention, naturally formed areas of land, surrounded by water, which are above water at high tide. However, under Article 121(3) of the Convention, the high-tide features at Scarborough Shoal are rocks that cannot sustain human habitation or economic life of their own and accordingly shall have no exclusive economic zone or continental shelf.

Johnson Reef, Cuarteron Reef, and Fiery Cross Reef contain, within the meaning of Article 121(1) of the Convention, naturally formed areas of land, surrounded by water, which are above water at high tide. However, for purposes of Article 121(3) of the Convention, the high-tide features at Johnson Reef, Cuarteron Reef, and Fiery Cross Reef are rocks that cannot sustain human habitation or economic life of their own and accordingly shall have no exclusive economic zone or continental shelf.

The high-tide features at Gaven Reef (North) and McKennan Reef are rocks that cannot sustain human habitation or economic life of their own and accordingly shall have no exclusive economic zone or continental shelf.[10] Mischief Reef and Second Thomas Shoal are both low-tide elevations that generate no maritime zones of their own [and] that none of the high-tide features in the Spratly Islands are capable of sustaining human habitation or an economic life of their own within the meaning of those terms in Article 121(3) of the Convention. All of the high-tide features in the Spratly Islands are therefore legally rocks for purposes of Article 121(3) and do not generate entitlements to an exclusive economic zone or continental shelf. There is, accordingly, no possible entitlement by China to any maritime zone in the area of either Mischief Reef or Second Thomas Shoal and no jurisdictional obstacle to the tribunal's consideration of the Philippines'.[11]

Both Mischief Reef and Second Thomas Shoal are located within 200 nautical miles of the Philippines' coast on the island of Palawan and are located in an area that is not overlapped by the entitlements generated by any maritime feature claimed by China. It follows, therefore, that, as between the Philippines and China, Mischief Reef and Second Thomas Shoal form part of the exclusive economic zone and continental shelf of the Philippines.[12]

Regarding alleged interference with the Philippines' sovereign rights in its EEZ and continental shelf-

China has, through the operation of its marine surveillance vessels with respect to M/V Veritas Voyager on 1 to 2 March 2011 breached Article 77 of the Convention with respect to the Philippines' sovereign rights over the non-living resources of its continental shelf in the area of Reed Bank [and] that China has, by promulgating its 2012 moratorium on fishing in the South

China Sea, without exception for areas of the South China Sea falling within the exclusive economic zone of the Philippines and without limiting the moratorium to Chinese flagged vessels, breached Article 56 of the Convention with respect to the Philippines' sovereign rights over the living resources of its exclusive economic zone.[13]

Regarding alleged failure to prevent Chinese nationals from exploiting the Philippines' living resources

China has, through the operation of its marine surveillance vessels in tolerating and failing to exercise due diligence to prevent fishing by Chinese flagged vessels at Mischief Reef and Second Thomas Shoal in May 2013, failed to exhibit due regard for the Philippines' sovereign rights with respect to fisheries in its exclusive economic zone. Accordingly, China has breached its obligations under Article 58(3) of the Convention.[14]

Regarding China's actions in respect of traditional fishing at Scarborough

China has, through the operation of its official vessels at Scarborough Shoal from May 2012 onwards, unlawfully prevented Filipino fishermen from engaging in traditional fishing at Scarborough Shoal.

Regarding alleged failure to protect and preserve the Marine

China has, through its toleration and protection of, and failure to prevent Chinese fishing vessels engaging in harmful harvesting activities of endangered species at Scarborough Shoal, Second Thomas Shoal and other features in the Spratly Islands, breached Articles 192 and 194(5) of the Convention. China has, through its island-building activities at Cuarteron Reef, Fiery Cross Reef, Gaven Reef (North), Johnson Reef, Hughes Reef, Subi Reef and Mischief Reef, breached Articles 192, 194(1), 194(5), 197, 123, and 206 of the Convention.[15]

Regarding occupation and construction activities on Mischief Reef

China has, through its construction of installations and artificial islands at Mischief Reef without the authorisation of the Philippines, breached Articles 60 and 80 of the Convention with respect to the Philippines' sovereign rights in its exclusive economic zone and continental shelf, as a low-tide elevation; Mischief Reef is not capable of appropriation.

Regarding operation of law enforcement vessels in a dangerous manner

China has, by virtue of the conduct of Chinese law enforcement vessels in the vicinity of Scarborough Shoal, created serious risk of collision and danger to Philippine vessels and personnel. The Tribunal finds China to have violated Rules 2, 6, 7, 8, 15, and 16 of the COLREGS and, as a consequence, to be in breach of Article 94 of the Convention.

Regarding aggravation or extension of the dispute between the parties

China has in the course of these proceedings aggravated and extended the disputes between the Parties through its dredging, artificial island-building, and construction activities [in several particulars itemized in the award].[16]

Regarding the future conduct of the parties

Both Parties are obliged to comply with the Convention, including its provisions regarding the resolution of disputes, and to respect the rights and freedoms of other States under the Convention. Neither Party contests this.[17]

INDIA AND SOUTH CHINA SEA DISPUTE

The verdict by the Permanent Court of Arbitration (PCA) rejecting China's ownership claims to 80 percent of the South

China Sea (an area almost the size of India) was greeted with much satisfaction and glee in New Delhi. This was the first time that the entire basis of China's "historical claims" (for example, the "nine-dash line") was ruled to be invalid under international law by an international tribunal. The ruling not only has important implications for countries with unresolved territorial disputes with China but also impinges on India's relations with Japan, the United States, ASEAN countries, and the international order. Coming as it did close on the heels of Beijing's successful blocking–citing legal procedures—of New Delhi's bids to gain entry into the Nuclear Suppliers Group (NSG) and to have the Pakistani terrorist Masood Azhar banned by the United Nations Security Council (UNSC), the verdict was seen as a "damning indictment" of China's flouting of the United Nations Convention on the Law of the Sea (UNCLOS) and Security Council resolutions against terrorism that Beijing had itself signed and supported

While India isn't party to the South China Sea dispute, two aspects of the recent developments might interest New Delhi. First, irrespective of the claims and counter-claims by the United States and China, it is clear that Beijing operates from a position of strength in the South China Sea, wherein it has physical control over critical islands in the region. China has shown the US and its allies that what matters in a maritime territorial dispute is the actual 'possession' of the islands, and as long as the PLA exercises military control over the features, it will exploit their location to support broader territorial claims. For New Delhi, which has been concerned about the security of its trade-flows and energy interests in the South China Sea, however, Beijing's placement of missiles points to a sober reality. As the disputed islands are militarized, it could imperil freedom of navigation, making Beijing the main arbiter of the accepted range of 'legitimate' operations in the South China Sea.

Second, China's exertion of authority over areas of maritime interest is mostly through indirect means. In the immediate aftermath of the new radar installations in the Spratly's and deployment of missiles on Woody Island, it looks increasingly likely that Beijing would impose an Air Defense Identification Zone (ADIZ) in the South China Sea, ensuring the PLA's dominance over the surrounding air-space and seas. At present, the likelihood of Chinese aggression occurring outside the disputed maritime spaces in Southeast Asia looks remote. Yet, there is no discounting Chinese maritime assertion in other areas where Beijing might have strategic interests – including critical spaces in the Indian Ocean. For Indian observers, it is useful to extrapolate known Chinese positions in the IOR, to assess Beijing's likely strategic behavior after the PLA has established a foothold in critical Indian Ocean states. Could the PLA, for instance, play a role in assisting Sri Lanka, Pakistan or Maldives in securing vital sea and air pockets in the Indian Ocean? What could the implications of such a move be for India? As a key security provider in the Indian Ocean, New Delhi appreciates the need for greater stability in the region.

The Indian government's official reaction was prompt and measured, with the Ministry of External Affairs (MEA) issuing a statement on the day of the award that called on all parties to show the "utmost respect" for the UNCLOS. By stressing that "India supports freedom of navigation and over-flight, and unimpeded commerce, based on the principles of international law, as reflected notably in the UNCLOS," the MEA statement was seen as chiding China. Emphasizing India's specific national interest in the issue, it added: "States should resolve disputes through peaceful means without threat or use of force and exercise self-restraint in the conduct of activities that could complicate or escalate disputes affecting peace and stability." The demand for "utmost respect," the assertion of India's vital interest in maintaining "freedom of navigation and over flight rights under UNCLOS" and aversion to "activities that complicate or escalate disputes"–all implied strong criticism of Beijing's intention to reject the tribunal's verdict and continue as before.[19]

CONCLUSION

Minister of external affairs Sushma Swaraj while answering the questions in Rajya Sabha has expressed that "Government has seen such a report. Government's position on this issue and the ruling is clear. The authority of Annex VII Tribunal and its award is recognized in Part XV of the UNCLOS itself. India's own record in this regard is well known. India supports freedom of navigation and over flight, and unimpeded commerce, based on the principles of international law, as reflected notably in the UNCLOS. India believes that States should resolve disputes through peaceful means without threat or use of force and exercise self-restraint in the conduct of activities that could complicate or escalate disputes affecting peace and stability. As a State Party to the UNCLOS, India urges all parties to show utmost respect for the UNCLOS, which establishes the international legal order of the seas and oceans."

The ruling should give India greater maneuverability to act as a balancing power or as a possible counter weight to China in the Indo-Pacific. Given China's bases (Djibouti and Gwadar) and increasing naval forays in the Indian Ocean, the Indian Navy wants to stake out a presence in the South China Sea, mainly to counter China's in the Indian Ocean. Not only that, the court ruling's denunciation of Xi Jinping's South China Sea policy raises questions about his judgment and leadership and could weaken Xi's hold on power at the next Party congress. In addition, it could unravel Xi's ambitious Maritime Silk Road through the Indian Ocean–another net gain for India.

South China Sea is a major waterway and over US$ 5 trillion trade passes through the sea lanes in this region. Over 55 per cent of India's trade passes through South China Sea. Peace and stability in the region is of great significance to India. India undertakes various activities, including cooperation in oil and gas sector, with littoral states of South China Sea. India supports freedom of navigation and over flight, and unimpeded commerce, based on the principles of international law, as reflected notably in the UNCLOS. India believes that States should resolve disputes through peaceful means without threat or use of force and exercise self-restraint in the conduct of activities that could complicate or escalate disputes affecting peace and stability. As a State Party to the UNCLOS, India urges all parties to show utmost respect for the UNCLOS, which establishes the international legal order of the seas and oceans.

NOTES

1. Bonnie S. Glaser, "*Armed Clash in the South China Sea*", Council on Foreign Relations. See http://www.cfr.org/asia-and-pacific/armed-clash-south-china-sea/p27883.
2. "Why is the South China Sea contentious?" *BBC*,12 July 2016.
3. Johnson, Keith *"How Do You Say 'Drill, Baby, Drill' in Chinese?"* www.foreignpolicy.com. AFP, (5 May 2014).
4. Schearf, Daniel. "S. China Sea Dispute Blamed Partly on Depleted Fish Stocks." *VOA*, May 16, 2012.
5. Ananth Krishnan. "China warns India on South China Sea exploration projects". *The Hindu.*
6. Beech, Hannah,"China's Global Reputation Hinges on Upcoming South China Sea Court Decision". TIME, (11 July 2016).
7. Shicun Wu and Keyuan Zou (2016). Arbitration Concerning the South China Sea: Philippines versus China. Routledge. pp. 18-23.

8. "Award" *of Permanent Court of Arbitration (PCA),12 July 2016.*
9. PCA Award, Section VI (B) (5)(d)(384), p.174.
10. PCA Award, Section VI(C)(5)(f)(646), p.259-260.
11. PCA Award, Section VI(C)(5)(f)(647), p.260
12. PCA Award, Section VI(C)(5)(f)(646), p.259-260.
13. PCA Award, Section VII(A)(5)(c)(716), p.286.
14. PCA Award, Section VII(B)(5)(d)(757), p.297.
15. PCA Award, Section VII(D)(5)(e)(993), p.397.
16. PCA Award, Section VIII(E)(4)(1181), p.464.
17. PCA Award, Section IX(D)(1201), p.469.
18. Abhijit Singh, "India and the South China Sea Dispute: Recent Developments have Operational Implications for India" *The Diplomat,* March 01, 2016.
19. Mohan Malik, "India's Response to the South China Sea Verdict" *The American Interest,* 22 July, 2016.

6

INDO-CHINA RELATIONS: PROBLEMS AND PROSPECTS

Historically, India and China have had relations for more than 2,000 years, but the modern relationship began in 1950 when India was among the first countries to end formal ties with the Republic of China and recognize the PRC as the legitimate government of Mainland China. China and India are the two most populous countries and fastest growing major economies in the world. The resultant growth in China and India's international diplomatic and economic influence has also increased the significance of their bilateral relationship. China and India are two of the world's oldest civilizations and have co-existed in peace for millennia. Cultural and economic relations between China and India date back to ancient times.[1] The Silk Road not only served as a major trade route between India and China, but is also credited for facilitating the spread of Buddhism from India to East Asia.[2] During the 19th century, China's growing opium trade with the British Raj triggered the First and Second Opium Wars. During World War II, India and China played a crucial role in halting the progress of Imperial Japan.

Relations between contemporary China and India have been characterized by border disputes, resulting in three major military conflicts – the Sino-Indian War of 1962, the Chola incident in 1967, and the 1987 Sino-Indian skirmish. However, since the late 1980s, both countries have successfully attempted to reignite diplomatic and economic ties.[3] In 2008, China emerged as India's largest trading partner and the two countries have also attempted to extend their strategic and military relations.[4]

Despite growing economic and strategic ties, there are several hurdles for India and the PRC to overcome in order to establish favorable relations. Though bilateral trade has continuously grown, India faces massive trade imbalance heavily in favor of China.The two countries have failed to resolve their long-standing border dispute and Indian media outlets have repeatedly reported Chinese military incursions into Indian territory.[5] Both nations have steadily established heavy military infrastructure along border areas.[6] Additionally, India remains wary about China's strong strategic bilateral relations with Pakistan, while China has expressed concerns about Indian military and economic activities in the disputed South China Sea.

KEY ASPECTS OF CHINESE PRESIDENT XI JINXING'S VISIT TO INDIA

Unlike his predecessors Jiang Zemin and Hu Jintao, Xi and his wife Peng Liyuan have shown remarkable flexibility and were at ease during the Sabarmati River side events. It is said that both Jiang and Hu were very stiff during their interactions not only with domestic actors but with foreign leaders as well. Hu is also known never to have publicly interacted with children. In contrast was a recent photo of Xi meeting his mother on her birthday. During the Sabarmati trip, Xi displayed flexibility by squatting at the Mahatma's floor, trying his hand at charkha, sitting along with Peng on a jhoola, etc.

China and India interactions indicated the tough bargaining at Hyderabad House and both Modi and Xi expressed strong opinions on economic, territorial dispute and other issues. While China was the first to reach out to Modi after his elections –

reflected in Premier Li Keqiang's phone call in May, foreign minister Wang Yi's visit in June and the BRICS interaction on July 14 – China's diplomatic initiatives faced a challenge as Maritime Silk Road was not endorsed; Bangladesh-India-China Myanmar Economic corridor was conditionally accepted provided it ensures "peaceful, stable and cooperative environment". India also did not receive $100-300 billion from China in investments.[8]

The pronouncements of their intent to deepen ties with India as China's "strategic choice" along with promise to make "greater efforts" to resolve boundary issue is a welcome move. For, President Xi, the Chinese and Indian "dreams" are inter-connected and mutually compatible. Equally positive voice came from the Indian leadership for rejecting the relevance of "containment" idea in favour of "cooperation" that could bring more gains instead. The overall message was; time for confronting and containing each other is over and the wisdom should lay in cooperation and benefiting from achievements for the common good. Two clear signs were visible; (a) the "strategic partnership" launched in 2005 was yielding enduring results in a broad spectrum, (b) leadership has gained higher level of confidence.[9]

POLITICAL RELATIONS

On 1 April, 1950, India became the first non-socialistbloc country to establish diplomatic relations with the People's Republic of China. Prime Minister Nehru visited China in October 1954. While, the India-China border conflict in 1962 was a serious setback to ties, Prime Minister Rajiv Gandhi's landmark visit in 1988 began a phase of improvement in bilateral relations. In 1993, the signing of an Agreement on the Maintenance of Peace and Tranquility along the Line of Actual Control (LAC) on the India-China Border Areas during Prime

Minister Narasimha Rao's visit reflected the growing stability and substance in bilateral ties.

Cumulative outcomes of nine key visits in recent times have been transformational for our ties. These were that of Prime Minister Vajpayee (2003), of Premier Wen Jiabao (2005 & 2010), of President Hu Jintao (2006), of Prime Minister Manmohan Singh (2008 and 2013), of Premier Li Keqiang (2013), of President Xi Jinping (2014), of Prime Minister Narendra Modi (2015) and of President Pranab Mukherjee (2016).

During Prime Minister Vajpayee's visit, the two sides signed a Declaration on Principles for Relations and Comprehensive Cooperation and also mutually decided to appoint Special Representatives (SRs) to explore the framework of a boundary settlement from the political perspective. During the April 2005 visit of Premier Wen Jiabao, the two sides established a Strategic and Cooperative Partnership for Peace and Prosperity, while the signing of an agreement on Political Parameters and Guiding Principles, signalled the successful conclusion of the first phase of SR Talks. During Chinese President Hu Jintao's visit to India in November 2006, the two sides issued a Joint Declaration containing a ten-pronged strategy to intensify cooperation. Prime Minister Manmohan Singh visited China in January 2008. A joint document titled "A Shared Vision for the 21st Century" was issued during the visit. When Chinese Premier Wen Jiabao visited India in December 2010, the two sides jointly set a bilateral trade target of US$ 100 billion for 2015.

Li Keqiang, Premier of the State Council of the People's Republic of China paid a State visit to India (Delhi-Mumbai) from 19-21 May 2013. During this visit, the two sides signed eight agreements and released a Joint Statement. Some of the significant proposals included in the Joint Statement were the decisions to designate 2014 as the Year of Friendly Exchanges between India and China and hold the first High Level Media Forum.

Former Prime Minister Manmohan Singh paid an official visit to China from 22-24 October 2013. Agreements relating to border, trans-border Rivers, establishing service centers for servicing power equipment in India, road transport and Nalanda University were signed. Also signed were three agreements establishing sister-city partnership between Delhi-Beijing, Kolkata-Kunming and Bangalore-Chengdu.

Vice-President Hon'ble Hamid Ansari paid a visit to China on 26-20 June 2014. During the visit the Vice President met with President Xi Jinping, held talks with Vice President Liu Yuanchao, attended events to mark the 60th anniversary of'Panchsheel', and visited Xian in Shaanxi Province. Three agreements related to industrial parks, training of public officials, and exchange of flood season data on the Yarlung Zangbu River were signed. The two Vice-Presidents also jointly released the English and Chinese versions of the Encyclopedia of India-China Cultural Contacts.

Chinese President Xi Jinping paid a state visit to India from 17 to 19 September 2014. During the visit, President Xi Jinping met with President Pranab Mukherjee and held talks with Narendra Modi, Prime Minister of India. A total of 16 agreements were signed during the visit in various sectors including, commerce & trade, railways, space-cooperation, pharmaceuticals, audio-visual co-production, culture, establishment of industrial parks, sister-city arrangements etc. The two sides also signed a MoU to open an additional route for Kailash Mansarovar Yatra through Nathu La. The Chinese side agreed to establish two Chinese Industrial Parks in India and expressed their intention to enhance Chinese investment in India.

PRIME MINISTER'S VISIT TO CHINA (MAY 2015)

Prime Minister Narendra Modi visited China from May 14-16, the visit was rich in symbolism and substance and it opened up a new chapter in India-China relations. For the first time, Chinese President Xi Jinping travelled outside Beijing to receive a foreign leader, in Xi'an in his home province of Shaanxi. President Xi also accompanied Prime Minister to the Big Wild Goose Pagoda and organized a grand welcome ceremony at the Xi'an city wall. Premier Li Keqiang joined Prime Minister at the Yoga-Taichi performance in Beijing on 15 May with the world heritage site of Temple of Heaven as the backdrop, the first ever such event, which highlighted the cultural connectivity between the two countries.

There were 24 agreements signed on the government-to-government side, 26 MoUs on the business-to-business side and two joint statements,including one on climate change. The fact that India and China could come up with over 50 outcome documents in just eight months reveals the huge potential that exists between our two countries, as well as the efforts that we have made to elevate our partnership. The inter-governmental agreements covered, as Premier Li said, areas from the heaven to the earth! They included such diverse fields as space cooperation, earthquake engineering, ocean sciences, mining,railways, skill development, education, culture, Yoga, tourism and many more.The strength of our economic partnership could be gauged from the business events in Shanghai. Prime Minister interacted with 21 CEOs of leading Chinese companies and over 40 prominent Indian CEOs attended the Business Forum along with their counterparts from China. The 26 business understandings worth over US$ 22 billion signed at the Forum covered such varied sectors as industrial parks, renewable energy, thermal energy, telecommunication, steel, capital goods, IT and media. Besides, there was a clear consensus among the leaders of the two countries on correcting the existing imbalance in the bilateral trade and injecting sustainability into it. With this in mind, they agreed to establish a high-powered task force that will go into issues relating to the trade deficit as well as expansion of economic engagement.

There was, moreover, an action-oriented accord on broad-basing the bilateral partnership, as could be seen from the range of agreements signed and in the establishment of new dialogue mechanisms, such as the one between the DRC and the NITI Aayog and the Think Tanks' Forum, besides a bilateral consultative mechanism on WTO negotiations. Three new institutions were launched in partnership, the Centre for Gandhian and Indian Studies in Shanghai, Yoga College in Kunming, and National Institute for Skill Development and Entrepreneurship in Ahemdabad.

Both sides decided to establish new Consulates in each other's country, in Chengdu and Chennai and to expand our interactions at the sub-national level. Two agreements signed – one on cooperation between the Indian Ministry of External Affairs and the International Department of the Central Committee of the CPC and another on the establishment of a State/Provincial Leaders' Forum – reflect this understanding. Prime Minister Modi and Premier Li addressed the opening session of the new Forum in Beijing on 15 May, which is a significant initiative, considering that this is the first time that India has established such a dialogue mechanism with any country. A number of sister-city and sister-state relations agreements between: Karnataka and Sichuan, Chennai and Chongqing, Hyderabad and Qingdao, Aurangabad and Dunhuang were also signed.

Prime Minister also announced the extension of the e-visa facility to Chinese nationals wishing to travel to India. Prime

Minister addressed university students at the Tsinghua University and also gave a speech at the reception hosted by the Indian community in Shanghai, the largest ever gathering of the community in the region. The visit also went on to deliver a message to the international community on cooperation between India and China. There was agreement among the leaders that our relationship is poised to play a defining role in the 21st century in Asia and beyond, with the recognition that the simultaneous re-emergence of India and China as two major powers would have a profound impact on the course of this century. The Joint Statement has a separate section on "shaping the regional and global agenda" where India and China, as two major poles in the global architecture, agree to cooperate on a host of issues ranging from WTO, climate change and terrorism to regional organizations.

President Pranab Mukherjee made a state visit to China from May 24 to 27, 2016. Hon'ble President visited Guangdong and met with Secretary of the provincial committee of the Chinese Communist Party of Guangdong Hu Chunhua & Governor of the Guangdong Zhu Xiaodan. In Guangzhou, President addressed a large assembly of the Indian community and also visited the HualinTemple. In Beijing he met with Chinese President Xi Jinping, Premier Li Keqiang, Chairman of the National People's Congress Zhang Dejiang. Vice President Li Yuanchao joined a reception hosted in honour of President by the Chinese People's Association for Friendship with Foreign Countries. President delivered a keynote address at the prestigious Peking University and attended a Round Table between Vice Chancellors and Heads of institutions of higher learning of the two countries. Ten MoUs providing for enhanced faculty and student exchanges as well as collaboration in research and innovation were concluded between the higher education institutions of the two countries.

INDIA-CHINA ECONOMIC RELATIONS

India-China economic relations constitute an important element of the strategic and cooperative partnership between the two countries. Several institutional mechanisms have been established for enhancing and strengthening economic cooperation between the two countries. Besides the India-China Joint Economic Group on Economic Relations and Trade, Science and Technology (JEG) and the India-China Strategic and Economic Dialogue (SED), a Financial Dialogue has also been instituted since 2006.

India-China Financial Dialogue: In accordance with the MoU signed during Chinese Premier Wen Jiabao's visit to India in April 2005, the two sides have since successfully held eight Financial Dialogues in April 2006, December 2007, January 2009, September 2010, November 2011, September 2013, December 2014 and August 2016 respectively. The Eight India-China Financial Dialogue was held on August 19th in Beijing. During this Dialogue, the two sides held in-depth discussions on new challenges facing the global economy, macro-economic situations and policies in India and China, progress on structural reforms in both countries, cooperation under multilateral frameworks as well as bilateral financial cooperation. A Joint Statement was signed at the end of the Dialogue. The Ninth India-China Financial Dialogue is scheduled to be held in India.

Banking Links: Many Indian banks have established their presence in mainland China in the last few years. State Bank of India (Shanghai and Tianjin), Canara Bank (Shanghai), Bank of Baroda (Guangzhou), Bank of India (Shenzhen), Axis Bank (Shanghai) and ICICI (Shanghai) have branch offices in China. At present, the State Bank of India is the only Indian bank to have authorization to conduct local currency (RMB) business at its branch in Shanghai. Besides, the following representative offices of Indian banks are also operating in mainland China:

Punjab National Bank, (Shanghai),Union Bank of India (Shanghai and Beijing Bank of India (Beijing), Union Bank of India (Beijing) and Indian Overseas Bank (Guangzhou).

More Indian banks are planning to upgrade their Representative Offices in China to branch offices and existing branch offices are applying for RMB license.

In early 2011, Industrial and Commercial Bank of China (ICBC) secured a license to start banking operations in India. ICBC inaugurated their Mumbai branch on September 15, 2011. This marked the opening of the first branch of a mainland Chinese bank in India.

Various government institutions and agencies from the two countries have also been interacting with each other for furthering cooperation in the areas such as taxation, auditing, human resource development and employment, health, urban and rural development and tourism. There is a close exchange and interaction between the economic think tanks and scholars as well.

CULTURAL RELATIONS BETWEEN INDIA AND CHINA

Our exchanges continued during the days of our struggle for self-governance. In early 20th century, Nobel laureate Rabindranath Tagore visited China twice, in 1924 and in 1929. Since 1911, Chinese scholars and intellectuals have been visiting and revisiting Tagore's life, works and philosophy. Dr. Dwarkanath Kotnis, whose mortal remains rest in the North China Martyrs' Memorial Cemetery in Hebei Province, sacrificed his life in the service of the Chinese people during the Sino-Japanese war. A part of the 1938 medical team of five Indian doctors, he stayed on in China working in mobile clinics to treat wounded soldiers. He was eventually appointed as Director of the Dr. Bethune International Peace Hospital built by the Eighth Route Army.

Both India and China began their journey of independent governance almost at the same time, India in 1947 and the People's Republic of China in 1949. In 1955, the first Indian cultural delegation headed by then Deputy Minister of External Affairs A. K. Chanda visited China which was warmly received by the Chinese leaders and people during their tour. In the 1960s and 1970s Bollywood movies such as *Do Bigha Zameen, Awara* and *Sree 420* of Raj Kapoor and *Noorie* struck an emotional chord in the hearts and minds of the Chinese people. Even today, people on the street hum the tunes of the songs of these films. Movies like *3 Idiots* and *The Life of Pi* have been well received in recent times.

Since 1988 both countries are bringing their people together through structured Cultural Exchange Programmes. The latest CEP signed in October 2013 during the visit of then Prime Minister Manmohan Singh's to China, provides for cooperation in a gamut of cultural fields including exchanges of visits of performing artists, officials, writers, archivists and archaeologists, organizing cultural festivals, film festivals and exchanges in the field of mass media, youth affairs and sports.

In 2003, Prime Minister Vajpayee had committed to build an Indian style Buddhist temple in Luoyang, Henan province and President Pratibha Devi Singh Patil inaugurated the temple during her visit to China in May 2010. In February 2007, the Xuanzang memorial was inaugurated at Nalanda. In June 2008, joint stamps were released, one stamp depicting the Mahabodhi temple at Bodhgaya and the other depicting the White Horse temple at Luoyang. A Centre for Indian studies was set up in Peking University in 2003. Chairs of Indian Studies/Hindi have also been established in Shenzhen University, Jinan University, Fudan University, Guangdong University and in Shanghai International Studies University. The 60th anniversary of the establishment of India-China diplomatic relations was celebrated with much fanfare in both countries in 2010. In March 2012, during President Hu Jintao's visit to India for the BRICS Summit, leaders of both sides decided to celebrate 2012 as the "The Year of Friendship and Co-operation" and both countries resolved to further strengthen cultural exchanges between our peoples.

Exchange of Youth delegation between Indian and China has been continuing since 2007. During the visit of Chinese President Hu Jintao to India in November 2006, the two sides had agreed to launch a five year programme for mutual exchange of youth delegation. In this context, the China had invited five hundred youth from India over the next five years. Later, during the visit Chinese Premier Wen Jiabao to India in December 2010, the two sides agreed to continue youth exchange activities in next five years. Further, as part of the "Year of India-China Exchanges-2011", China also invited 500 Indian youth to visit China within the year 2011. Reciprocal visits were also paid by the Chinese side each year. During the visit of President Xi to India in September 2014 the two sides recognizing the significance of youth exchanges in increasing mutual understanding, the two sides agreed to continue with the annual exchange of 200 youth from 2015 to 2019.

During the visit of Prime Minister Manmohan Singh and Premier Li Keqiang in 2013 the leaders designated 2014 as the Year of Friendly Exchanges between India and China. To mark this special year, Glimpses of India Festival was organized across several cities of China through 2014 showcasing Indian performing arts, exhibitions of modern Indian arts, depictions of Buddhism links between the two countries, food and film festivals. As part of the festival Kalashetra, Kathak Kendra Troupe, Sangeet Natak Akademi and a Bollywood Troupe from Indian Council for Cultural Relations visited China. Sangeet Natak Akademi performed at the Reception Marking the 60th

Anniversary of the Five Principles of Peaceful Coexistence at the Great Hall of People. Food Festivals were also organised in cities like Beijing, Qingdao, Shanghai, Hong Kong to give the local people a taste of authentic Indian cuisine. Yoga Festivals were organized in the month of July, 2014 in Beijing, Shanghai and Dali in partnership with Department of AYUSH, Government of India. Buddhist Art Exhibitions were organized in cities like Hong Kong, Shanghai and Chengdu. Indian Film Festivals were also organized in cities like Beijing, Hangzhou, Guangzhou, Qingdao, Hong Kong and Xi'an in partnership with Ministry of Information & Broadcasting.

During the visit of Chinese Premier Wen Jiabao to India in December 2010, the leaders of India and China agreed on a project involving compilation of an Encyclopedia of India-China Cultural Contacts. The Encyclopedia of India-China Cultural Contacts was released in both English and Chinese versions during Hon'ble Vice President of India's visit to China on June 30, 2014 in Beijing. The Encyclopedia features over 700 entries, encapsulating the rich history of contacts and exchanges between the two countries in the trade, economic, literary, cultural and philosophical spheres.

Prime Minister Narendra Modi paid a three day state visit to China from May 14th to 16th 2015. Prior to the visit, Prime Minister launched his own 'Weibo' handle to connect withthe Chinese people. The details of the visit were first shared with the public via this Weibo handle, and the handle has since become immensely popular among Chinese netizens. The Prime Minister's visit was rich in symbolism, reflecting the growing closeness between India and China. For the first time, President Xi Jinping travelled outside Beijing to receive a foreign leader in Xi'an, in his home province of Shaanxi. President Xi also accompanied Prime Minister to the Big Wild Goose Pagoda–itself asymbol of the shared legacy of our two great civilizations and organized a grand welcome ceremony at the Xi'an city wall. Premier Li Keqiang joined Prime Minister at the Yoga-Taichi performance with the world heritage site of Temple of Heaven as the backdrop, the first ever such event, which highlighted the cultural connectivity between the two countries. The two leaders even clicked a 'selfie' which went viral with over 33 million hits on the Weibo. There were 24 agreements signed on the government-to-government side, 26 MoUs on the business-to-business side and two joint statements, including one on climate change Expanding people-to-people exchanges and cultural contacts figured as a major theme of the visit. Prime Minister's visit to the Great Wild Goose Pagoda, joined by President Xi, and his attendance at the Yoga-Taichi event along with Premier Li exemplified the importance that our leaders attach to tapping the shared cultural heritage. Moreover, three new institutions: the Centre for Gandhian and Indian Studies in Shanghai, Yoga College in Kunming, and National Institute for Skill Development and Entrepreneurship in Ahmedabad were launched.

On December 11, 2014, the 193 member UNGA approved by consensus with a record 177 co-sponsoring countries including China a resolution to establish 21st June as "International Day of Yoga". In its resolution, the UNGA recognized that Yoga providesa holistic approach to health and well-being and wider dissemination of informationabout the benefits of practicing Yoga for the health of the world population. Embassy of India Beijing and Consulates at Shanghai, Guangzhou and Hong Kong celebrated the First International Day of Yoga today on 21st June, 2015 in China. The event was celebrated in more than 14 cities of China including Beijing, Shanghai, Tianjin, Qingdao, Hong Kong, Macau, Guangzhou, Chengdu, Kunming, Xiamen, Wuxi, Hangzhou,Wenzhou and Changzhou in which thousands of people participated enthusiastically. Several Chinese celebrities including musician Siqin Gaoli, actors Wang Baoqiang, Du Yiheng, and snooker champion Ding Junhui gave personal video endorsement messages, congratulating on the occasion of International Day of Yoga and inviting people to participate in the event.[11] Both India and China have vibrant cultures and vibrant people. Buddhism, Xuan Zhang, Tagore, Dr. Kotnis, Nalanda, Yoga and Cinema are only symbols of our long tradition of exchanges. They are testimonies of our shared heritage. The momentum has been set and the pace can only increase in the 21st century.

SCIENCE & TECHNOLOGY COOPERATION

As civilizations with historical legacy of scientific and technological achievements spanning centuries, India and China have been engaged in pursuit of scientific and technological achievements and innovations, both individually as well as bilaterally and multilaterally. There have been contacts between Indian and Chinese scientists on issues of scientific interest much before the formalized agreement for cooperation in the field of science and technology was inked between the two countries in December, 1988 during the visit of former Prime Minister Rajiv Gandhi to China.

(A) JOINT COMMITTEE ON SCIENTIFIC AND TECHNOLOGICAL COOPERATION

The Agreement on cooperation in the field of Science and Technology is the umbrella agreement, within the framework of which, various agreements/MoUs between organizations/ scientific bodies of both countries have been signed and are being implemented. It envisages exchange of scientists, exchange of scientific and technical information and documentation, organization of bilateral scientific and technical seminars and conferences, joint identification of scientific and technical problems as well as formulation and implementation of joint research programs etc. The Agreement specifies establishment of a mechanism of India-China Joint Committee on Scientific and Technological cooperation to plan, coordinate, monitor and facilitate cooperation in the above fields. The Joint Committee, has, so far met six times as per schedule given below:

First Session	New Delhi	30-31 March,1989
Second Session	Beijing	22-24 July, 1991
Third Session	New Delhi	19-20 April, 1993
Fourth Session	Beijing	26 May, 1999
Fifth Session	New Delhi	8 February, 2002
Sixth Session	Beijing	10 September 2013

During the 3rd Joint Committee Meeting, the following 8 priority areas of cooperation were identified:

1. Laser;
2. Materials and Earth Sciences;
3. Space and Remote Sensing;
4. Agriculture and Fisheries
5. Chemical Engineering with emphasis on Engineering Plastics;
6. Medicine particularly devices, instrumentation and Traditional Medicine;
7. Biotechnology;
8. Electronics.

During the subsequent Joint Committee Meetings, the following additional priority areas of cooperation were identified:

(i) Biotechnology;

(ii) Medical science and technology;

(iii) Material Science and Technology including advanced materials;

(iv) Earth Sciences, including natural disaster reduction;
(v) Chemical science and technology;
(vi) Aeronautics;
(vii) Electronic Hardware and Information Technology, including Software Development;
(viii) High energy physics;
(ix) Astronomy and astrophysics;
(x) Natural Disaster Mitigation.

At the 6th Joint Working Committee Meeting, which was the first meeting in 11 years, the two sides decided to cooperate in (i) mitigation of earthquakes and natural disasters, (ii) astronomy and astrophysics, (iii) research on climate change,and, (iv) traditional knowledge and medicine.

(B) JOINT FORESTRY COOPERATION WORKING GROUP

An Agreement on Forestry Cooperation between the Ministry of Environment & Forests of India and State Forestry Administration of China was signed in November, 2006. The agreement envisages eight areas of cooperation including development and utilization of forest resources. Till date, three meetings of the Joint Forestry Working Group have been held, the last one was held in February, 2012.

NOTES

1. Backus, Maria. *Ancient China.* Lorenz Educational Press, 2002.pp23.
2. Williams, Barbara. *World War Two.* Twenty-First Century Books, 2004, p.45.
3. Lancaster, John (12 April 2005). "India, China Hoping to 'Reshape the World Order' Together". *The Washington Post.*
4. "India-China trade surpasses target", *The Hindu,* 27 January 2011.

5. *Wall Street Journal*, June 24, 2009.
6. "China-Pakistan military links upset India", *Financial Times*, November 27 2009.
7. "China warns India on South China Sea exploration projects", *The Hindu*, 15 September 2011.
8. Srikanth Kondapalli "Narendra Modi and Xi Jinping: Building a Closer Developmental Partnership"22 September 2014 see at http://www.ipcs.org/article/india-the-world/narendra-modi-and-xi-jinping-building-a-closer-developmental-partnership-4669.html
9. P. Stobdan "India-China Relations: Scenario 2014" (December 30, 2013), see athttp://www.idsa.in/idsacomments/IndiaChinaRelationsScenario2014_pstobdan_301213.html
10. India-China Bilateral Relations athttp://www.indianembassy.org.cn/DynamicContent.aspx?MenuId=97&SubMenuId=0
11. *ibid.*

7

INDIA-RUSSIA-CHINA TRIANGLE: MYTH OR REALITY

The emerging triangle between Russia-India-China is being closely watched in the strategic and academic quarters of the West and the three countries involved. This idea was mooted by the then Russian Prime Minister Yevgeny Primakov at a time when India has been internationally isolated after its May 1998, nuclear tests. This was also the time when Russia was facing intense pressure from the West on the issue of human rights violation in Chechnya and on the establishment of true democratic system in Russia. The third component of the triangle China, was already on the hit list of the US led West due to its ideological commitment to Marxism. The Thiamin massacre incident had made China almost untouchable internationally. China has also been facing constant pressure from the West on the issues of Taiwan and Tibet.

Aware of the circumstances in which all three countries found themselves and the power aspirations which all these shared; Primakov gave a call to unite in the face of unnecessary intervention of the West in their internal matters. However, no triangular relation can take off and be sustained if each had problem with the other.

To analyze the possibility of this triangle actually materializing it is, therefore, important to study the kind of relation these states share with each other. The disintegration of the Soviet Union created fresh opportunities for qualitatively different nation to develop between China and the successor Soviet states, especially Russia. The triangle can only be understood in this context. Thereafter the article focuses on the kind of relation is developing between Russia and India and China and India. An analysis of the bilateral relations would indicate the possibilities of this triangle actually materializing. The last section of the article briefly highlights the implication this triangle will have on India.

THE RUSSIA-CHINA RELATIONS

Soviet Union and China were bound to each other as comrades resolutely devoted to working class and peasant revolutions. Soviet Union's assistance under the Stalin regime to Mao's revolution endeared the two, who after the success of the 1949 Chinese revolution, presented themselves as the impenetrable and expanding socialist world of the early 1950s. The comradeship however began to drift apart on several counts and there were many reasons that soured Soviet-China relations. Both wanted to establish their credentials as true Marxists. Gradually the two drifted away from each other though, these two countries belonged to the same idea bloc but there were strong difference between them. Khrushchev's de-Stalinization campaigns were amongst the first signs of discord. Chairman Mao opposed CPSU's new ideological formulations like peaceful co-existence and non-antagonistic contradictions between imperialism and socialism. Concepts used by Soviets for the third world like non-capitalist path of development and policy of support to the 'national bourgeois' were similarly opposed. The real issue behind the ideological discord was however, leadership and hegemony over the international communist movement and relations with the newly emerging countries of Asia and Africa. (Chenoy, April 2005: 11).[1]

The Chinese and Russians had disagreements on internal matters as well. Chinese wanted assistance from the Soviets on their nuclear programme which was denied by the Soviets. The Chinese and Soviet became competitors in the space technology; Chinese needed more economic assistance for their modernization programmes that the over stretched Soviet Union failed to provide. Soviets were critical of several Chinese policies including the Cultural Revolution; Chinese called the Soviets revisionists', an insult to those who believed themselves to be Marxists. (Gorbachev,1987: 10-12).[2]

However, the tense relationship of two communist giants eased with the rise of Gorbachev as the Secretary General of CPSU in 1985. He made epoch making changes in the Soviet history by introducing 'Perestroika' and 'Glasnost'. Some have described him in Soviet history as 'reformer in hurry'. In the realm of international relations he introduced 'New Thinking' which stressed on a deidoelogised foreign policy.

In the words of Gorbachev, 'New Thinking' stood for –

> "We need normal international conditions for our internal progress. But we want a world free of war, without arms races, nuclear weapons and violence, not only because this is an optimal condition for our internal development." (Gorbachev, 1987: 10-12).[3]

Under the slogan of 'New Thinking' Gorbachev's foreign policy was based on shared moral and ethical principles to solve global problems rather than on Marxist-Leninist concept of irreconcilable conflict between capitalism and communism. The historic meeting between Deng and Gorbachev lead to resolution of many outstanding problems between the two. The border dispute was resolved by demarcating the Usuri River; trade was opened up and threat perceptions to a large extent eliminated.

While relations were improving between the two countries, the Soviet Union itself collapsed in December 1991. It was a historical event of global significance. Relations between the two neighbours, Russia and China could not therefore, escape the global effects of this historical event. (Imam, 2001:97-100).[4]

The bubble of "Common European Home" and "One World from Vancouver to Vladivostok" busted very soon. Disillusioned Russia turned her face towards the Third World, and Asia which had been a natural ally of the erstwhile Soviet Union again got prominence among the policy makers. So in the changed circumstances and policies countries like China, India, Iran got the top priority in Russian foreign policy list.

Soon, Andrei Kozyrev (pro-West Foreign Minister) was replaced by an academician Yevgeny Primakov (pro-Third World) as Russia's new foreign minister who tried to balance between the East and the West. In December 1998, he made an official visit to India. Primakov visited India at the time when India was internationally isolated after conducting five nuclear tests a few months back. He proposed to formulate a triangle between three major Eurasian countries Russia-China-India to counter US hegemony and unilateralism in the world politics. According to him 'Russia favours the creation of a Moscow-Beijing-Delhi triangle and also it would be a good idea.' (SWB/SU/3416 B/5, December 22, 1998).[5]

While in 1998 US loomed over the world as the sole super power ready to take unilateral action anywhere, there were some developments taking place to fill the geopolitical vacuum left behind by the collapse of USSR. Primakov visited India at a time when the later was internationally isolated for conducting nuclear tests few months back. This visit by one of the world's major powers did not just create a diplomatic opening for India. By talking of a "strategic triangle", Primakov underlined the importance of India in the global affairs. (Patnaik, April 2005:3-10).[6]

RUSSIA-INDIA RELATIONS

The legacy of strong mutually beneficial relations between Soviet Union and India weighed heavily on Indian expectations in developing relations with new Russia. Global events brought India and Soviet Union together in the fifties when the Cold War dominated international relations. India had identified itself with the Soviet Union World view just as Pakistan had with that of the USA. The general understanding was Indo-Soviet friendship being time tested; Indo-Russian equation would not dramatically alter in times to come. End of Soviet Union, however, altered the international scenario completely. It heralded the end of the confrontational bloc politics and end of the Cold War era and the weakening of ideologies. Free from ideological compulsion new Russia had new options. (Shams-ud-din, 2001: 1).[7]

After prolong dilly dallying and rescheduling his visit since 1992, Yeltsin finally arrived in New Delhi only in January 1993. President Yeltsin's belated visit to India in January 1993 was aimed to reassure New Delhi that Russia was not cold-shouldering India. Indian Prime Minister P. V. Narsimha Rao visited Moscow in 1994; during high visit President Yeltsin remarked that "there was no difference at all between the two countries on international and bilateral issues". The document signed during his visit promised for joint action by both countries against terrorism. The document supported all forms of cooperation, investment, joint enterprise, creation of conditions for economic initiative development of scientific technical cooperation, peaceful atom, cosmos, and laser technology. (Chenoy, 2005: 11-26).[8]

Between 1992-96, India imported defense equipments worth $3.5 billion from Russia. Indian military and defence orders now sustain many defence industries in Russia, especially in St. Petersburg and Irkutsk which would otherwise have faced closure at the time of transition in the Russian economy. India is the only country with which Russia has a long term programme of military-technical cooperation, which was signed in 1994. The Soviet era Treaty of Friendship, Peace and Cooperation was renewed for another 10 years, during the then Defence Minister Mulayam Singh Yadav's visit to Moscow in December 2000. (Chenoy, 2001: 183-184).[9] Russian spokesmen stated that Russian Indian military cooperation would touch $4.5 billion in 2000 and $6.5 billion in the end of 2005.

In February 2006, India and Russia also set up a Joint Study Group to examine ways to increase trade to US$10 billion by 2010 and to study feasibility of a Comprehensive Economic Co-operation Agreement (CECA). The group finalized its report after its fourth meeting in Moscow in July 2007. It has been agreed that a Joint Task Force would monitor the implementation of the recommendation made in the Joint Study Group Report, including considering CECA. The second BRIC summit was held in Brasília in April 2010. India and Russia agreed to jointly study a Comprehensive Economic Co-operation Agreement with Belarus-Kazakhstan with the aim of boosting trade ties and achieving the ambitious trade target of $20 billion by 2015. Prime Minister Manmohan Singh stated in speech given during President Putin's 2012 visit to India, "Our bilateral trade has grown by over 30 per cent this year. There is still untapped potential in areas such as pharmaceuticals, fertilisers, mining, steel, information technology, civil aviation, telecommunications, infrastructure, food processing, innovation and services, which we will work to exploit".

The crucial and the most time testing moment in Indo-Russian relations came in May 1998, when India conducted five nuclear tests in Pokhran, Rajasthan and most of the influential countries imposed economic and many other kinds of sanctions on India. Although Russia agreed with the West and USA that

India should sign on CTBT and NPT and ratify as soon as possible, but Russia opposed any kind of economic sanction against India. Tremendous pressure was exerted by the USA led West on Russia to scrap all its agreements in nuclear cooperation with India and also stop technical support to India's two nuclear reactors under construction with Russian assistance at Kudnakulam, Tamilnadu. But Russia stood up to the Indian expectations and refused to comply with US dictates. (Boquerat and Frederic, 2004:132-140).[10]

Russia has constantly supported India's point of view on the issue of Kashmir in various international forums. It has also promised India to using veto power in UNSC if India would be pressurized on the issue of Kashmir. As the reciprocal gesture India also always supported Russian stand on the Chechnya issue and criticized the West for interfering in Russia's internal matters on the pretext of addressing human rights violations.

India and Russia set up a joint working group on Afghanistan. As on many other issues their stance on this issue was similar. Together they made it possible for the Northern Alliance to keep afloat, and thereby a counterforce against the Taliban was available when the American attack on Afghanistan took place. Their joint proposal of resistance also mooted by General Musharraf and virtually endorsed by the USA prevented the sneaking in of Taliban elements in the interim government formed subsequently in Afghanistan under the leadership of Hamid Karzai. (Dutt, 2003: 18-19).[11]

Russia is one of the states which promised to support for India for a permanent seat in the UN Security Council, and thus has demonstrated to the Indian foreign policy establishment its loyalty to Indian position and its understanding of India's strategic aspirations globally.

Another important land mark in the development of Indo-

Russian ties was Prime Minister Primakov's visit at the end of 1998. The visit sparked off a debate following his references to an Indo-China-Russia strategic triangle. He remarked that "Russo-Indian relations are perhaps unique in diplomatic history of the past fifty years. Their strength has been tested by many turns and twists in the two countries political life and during the profound transformation of international system". He also rightly noted that cooperation between the two countries rests on a long established bread public consensus in both countries regarding the priority of Russian-Indian cooperation as a factor promoting national interests. (Wishnik, 2001)[12]

On March 22, 1999 India and Russia signed an agreement to train Indian defence personnel in key Russian defence establishments for maintaining advanced defence equipments. The 44,500 tones Kiev class Admiral Gorshkov aircraft carrier has been purchased by India from Russia. The Mig-29K Fulcrum aircrafts stand a better chance to be operated from this aircraft carrier. Up gradation of MiG-29 Fighters, construction of 3 Kirvak class frigates for the Indian Navy, modernization for T-72 MBT, procurement of T-90s MBTs, for the Indian army and antiballistic missiles systems were discussed (Wishnik, 2001).[13]

INDIA-CHINA RELATIONS

The history of India-China, interaction is almost as old as the two civilizations themselves. This centuries old relationship has been peaceful, mutually enriching, both materially and spiritually and is possibly unparallel in human history. It is generally believed that the contacts between India and China began as early as the time of Christ although there is as yet no definite record to establish. Trade and commerce flourished between them via the Silk Road, as also cultural contacts. One of the most significant aspects of the ancient contacts was the establishment of Buddhism in China. The Chinese responded with great enthusiasm to the arrival of Buddhist missionaries and thereafter initiated a number of moves to bring Indian Buddhist monks and scholars to help teach, explain and establish Buddhism firmly in China. This turnaround in their political loyalties and their radicalization came about with the work of Gadar Party in China and indeed, in retrospect, the Gadar movement figures in the history of Indo-China relations as a notable chapter of revolutionary comradeship. (Bakshi, 2000: 168-170).[14]

Relation with China was to figure prominently in independent India. In a notable essay "A Foreign Policy for India" in September 1927, Nehru wrote:

> In developing our foreign policy we shall naturally first cultivate friendly relations with the countries of East which have so much in common with us. Nepal will be our neighbour and friend, with China and Japan, Indonesia, Afghanistan and Central Asia we shall have the closest contact. (Nehru, 1927: p. 361).[15]

Nehru greeted the birth of communist China in October 1949 with great pomp. India was the first among non-communist countries to recognize the People's Republic of China. In a rare gesture, India displayed excessive zeal in promoting its membership in the UN". (Shambaugh, 1927: p. 361).[16]

The historic agreement between Prime Minister Jawaharlal Nehru and his Chinese counterpart Zhou Enlai in April 1954 was named as Panchsheel (five principles of peaceful co-existence). This formed bedrock for India and China to conduct bilateral relations with each-other. Panchsheel contained following five principles:

1. Mutual respect for each other's territorial integrity and sovereignty;
2. Mutual non-aggression;

3. Mutual non-interference in each other's affairs;
4. Equality and mutual benefit; and
5. Peaceful co-existence.

The sunshine period in Indo-China relations disappeared behind the dark cloud with the border clashes in October 1962, which ultimately spread in to a full-fledged war in which India suffered a crushing defeat. The opposition parties dubbed him a 'soaring idealist' incapable of defending the country's honour. Nehru's faith that a socialist China will never attack a 'non-aligned' India and his faith in non-aligned policy as a pathway to national security proved illusory.[17] Post-Nehru era has been relatively smooth and peaceful for China and India relations. Without being guided by passion and idealism Indira Gandhi, unlike her father endeavored to lend a component of 'hard realism' to Indian foreign policy. For instance, India's role in dismemberment of Pakistan in 1971, its first ever nuclear blast in May 1974, and later merging of Sikkim reinforced the premise that she was a practitioner of power politics. After 14 years of gap in 1976, K.R. Narayanan was accredited India's ambassador to Beijing, a pragmatic step towards normalizing Indo-China relations. (Li, 2000: 253-269).[18]

Sino-India relations entered a new' phase with the Prime Minister Rajiv Gandhi's path breaking visit to Beijing in December 1988. Also both countries agreed to concentrate on expanding bilateral cooperation in non-conventional field, as was evident from the signing of several agreements on scientific and technical cooperation, and on educational and cultural exchange programmes. (Jiali, 2003:214-257).[19]

The year 1998 came as the turnings point when India conducted five nuclear tests on May 15th and 17th at Pokhran, Rajasthan. China's initial reaction was mild. Its acerbic rebuff resulted from the fact that the Indian government justified these tests by pinpointing China as a 'potential threat' to Indian security. China's response shifted radically after the publication by The New York Times on May, 13 of a letter from PM Vajpayee to US President Bill Clinton and other world leaders. The Chinese government brushed aside the Indian accusation saying that it was "utterly groundless" if analyzed in pragmatic terms, this was an unwarranted and provocative act on India's part resulting in unnecessary tensions with China.

At the same time, a number of other factors facilitated a rapid improvement in the bilateral relationship. First, Beijing was conscious that India's nuclear arsenal would not threaten China for some time to come. Secondly the rise of radical Islam in Pakistan with which China has cultivated very close relations for decades, the increasing number of Xinjiang fighters taking refuge in poorly governed regions of Pakistan. Third, the Kosovo conflict in the spring of 1999 gave India-China a golden opportunity to condemn together NATO's intervention in Yugoslavia. There are several issues of national and international importance on which both India-China still have their own apprehensions.

I) PAKISTAN FACTOR

The Sino-Pakistan security and strategic nexus has remained a central issue in India-China relations ever since Beijing and Islamabad signed a historic border agreement in March 1963, ceding a chunk of Pakistan occupied Kashmir to China. China also assisted Pakistan, in its nuclear and missile building programmes, which were designed to help Pakistan to keep its option, open. Following an agreement signed between the two countries in September 1986, China also sold two mini nuclear research reactors to Pakistan in 1989 and 1990 and also promised to assist Pakistan's nuclear energy programmes. (Subramanyam, 1989, 23-28).[20]

II) CLOSE CHINA-MYANMAR RELATIONSHIP

Another area of serious concern is the close China-Myanmar relations which has far reaching implications. Of particular concern for India is the fact that the Coco Island base is situated merely 30 nautical from the Andaman Islands giving China a strategic presence in the Indian Ocean. The objective behind improving the Burma Road would also be security one, aimed at facilitating quick-movement of men and material between Yunan and the Indian Ocean. The Chinese are also believed to have assisted in the construction of a 50 meter-radar antenna on the Coco Islands.

III) TIBET ISSUE

The Tibet issue has been one of the major constraints in Indo-China relations ever since Tibet was forcibly occupied by China in 1950 and declared an integral part of its territory. India argues that she has given refuge to Dalai Lama and thousands of Tibetan refugees on humanitarian ground, but China criticizes India of providing secessionist movement in Tibet and intervening China's internal matters. A further controversy was sparked off between New Delhi and Beijing when Karmapa Lama, a Buddhist monk, fled to India in early 2000 and was given a status of a Tibetan refugee by the Indian government. The Indian government ignored Chinese sensitivity over the Karmapa episode. The real problem with China is that it regards Tibet as are edifice of unity. (Boqerat and Grare, 2004: 29-41).[21]

IV) ARUNACHAL PRADESH AND SIKKIM ISSUE

Although China has formally recognized recently Sikkim as the part of India, but on Arunachal Pradesh its stand is ambiguous. During Vajpayee visit to China in June 2003, India termed Tibet an autonomous region of PRC. India has also gained in return, by signing the accord on opening trade through

Sikkim (Nathula pass). The Nathula Pass was officially closed in 1975, after Sikkim became the part of India.

V) ECONOMIC APPREHENSIONS

In the early 1990s with a positive mood and thinking in the leadership of both countries they signed a much awaited trade agreement on avoidance of double taxes in each -other's country to boost the flow of goods and products on the basis of mutual benefit. On the trade front there has been a boost from $ 265 million in 1991 to $ 3.6 billion in 2001. According to some policy analysts, what are worrying Indian business circles is that the flooding of domestic markets by cheap Chinese goods. Their fear is rooted in the belief that all varieties of Chinese products are at unbeatable price and quality wise in international markets. That is why large and medium size business houses in India are raising a hue and cry over the 'dumping syndrome".

RUSSIA-INDIA-CHINA EMERGING TRIANGLE

During his visit in December 1998, the former Russian Prime Minister Yevgeny Primakov, proposed a Russia-India-China strategic triangle, which envisaged closer strategic cooperation. He said that "If we succeed in establishing a strategic triangle, it will be very good ... a lot depend in the region on the policies perused by India, China and Russia. Further, this proposal was made in the framework of partnership between the three countries that could bring about greater stability not just in the region but the world."

The immediate response from Beijing on the proposed triangle was positive. The spokesperson of Chinese foreign ministry dubbed it as 'very positive thought' and 'would help in containing growing unilateralism in international politics'. India's response was cautious and rather lukewarm because she did not want to send wrong signals to the West by joining in bloc politics. In his speech then Prime Minister Vajpayee said 'Russia is a longstanding partner of India with which we have traditionally enjoyed friendly relations. At the same time, India is working on normalizing its relations with China'. Due to this cold response from India, speaking to the media Primakov explained that his earlier words on the possibility of forming a triangle between Russia-China-India were not official proposal. He said "I wanted to say that such partnership could reliably stabilize the situation in the region and in the world". (SWB/SU/3417 B/4, December 23, 1998)[22]

The multi-ethnic and multi-cultural societies of Russia, India, and China have faced increasing pressure from the forces that seek to destroy their pluralistic societies. In India infiltration in Kargil was the culmination of years of infiltrations and terrorist activities. The terrorists have also attacked the highest symbol of Indian democracy, the parliament. Russia's long bleeding problem of Chechnya has been further aggravated with the Western and US media and human right group's intervention on the name of human rights violations. China is facing potential threat of secession in its Xinjiang province by Islamic extremists who are engaged with continuous low level warfare with Chinese authorities. There is growing feeling among the three countries that US alone should not set the agenda of global war against terror. The experience of Iraq also shows that the US polices can leave a bigger mess in the region, the effect of which has to be borne by neighbouring countries. (Jingji, 2000: 187-188).[23]

At broader level India, Russia and China agree that the world should be a multipolar one. China felt the pressures from the West after the Thiamin square massacre, the US relentless support to Taiwan and threat perception of China despite of years of normalization of US-Chinese relations, US sale of F-

16s to Taiwan and promised Theater Missile Defense (TMD), forced Chinese to reconsider relations with the USA. With the development of National Missile Defence (NMD), US will get cutting edge on strategic position vis-a-vis Russia and China. Russia, with its huge nuclear arsenal, could live with the US NMD. From Chinese perspective, however, the same system could immediately render China's minimalist nuclear relations form obsolete. (Yi, 2000:121-130).[24]

There are other interested players in the region, foremost and most influential being the USA. Due to presence of petroleum and hydrocarbons, the 'great game' in Central Asia has been revived. Russia, China, USA are the major players in this game and competing for lion's share in the Central Asian natural resources. India, though a marginal player in this game is trying to reduce her dependence on Gulf oil, and looking forward for supply of oil from Central Asia.

Russia, India and China can also combine to discuss and if necessary deal with terrorism. Islamic extremism in Kashmir, Xinjiang and in Chechnya has grown over the years. Although US war on terrorism will help in reducing the problem, Washington clearly cannot do everything.

There has been a consensus between the three countries on the growing menace of terrorism. In April 1996, the 'Shanghai Five', a multilateral forum composed of China, Russia, Kazakhstan, Tajikistan and Kyrgyzstan, was created with the aim of fighting ethnic separatism as well as Islamic fundamentalism. In March 2000, a meeting was held in Astana, Kazakhstan, to determine a common position on these two issues. This was later confirmed in a joint declaration in July 2000 in Dushanbe followed by a decision to create an anti-terrorist centre in Bishkek, Kyrgzstan. (Djalili, 2001: 64-65). Likewise, in October 2000, during President Putin's visit to Delhi, India and Russia reaffirmed their convergence of view on fighting terrorism, expressing their deep concern over the situation in Central Asia and Afghanistan for which they agreed to set up a working group. (Basu, 1998, 1285-1290).[25]

Since the time of proposal of the triangle in December 1998 to 2001, by and large no concrete steps seem 10 have been taken was by the three concerned steps to realize it. But the more US unilateralism became blatant the more attractive the option seemed. As a result for the first time the three foreign ministers of Russia, China and India net on the sidelines of UN General Assembly meet at New York in 2002 to explore the 'triangle' possibility.

The approach continued to be an extremely cautious one. The three foreign ministers gave no media briefing for the press except that informally they let the press know that they had me' and that these meetings will continue. By comparison at the second 2003 New York meeting the difference in both their body language and press briefing could be clearly noticed. At the conclusion of their second meeting, three foreign ministers were ready to convey to the press that three states had adopted a common approach on Iraq favoring return to political process to ensure quick return of sovereignty to Iraqi people. (Singh, 2005: 14-16).[26]

This clearly had strong connotations for the USA, especially as all three of them had also refused to send troops to Iraq. The 2004 meeting on the eve of the UN General Assembly session in New York could not occur due to change of government in New Delhi leading to some scheduling problems with the Indian establishment. Nevertheless, this was soon rectified and the three foreign ministers had their third 'dialogue' on strategic triangle on the sidelines of the Almaty meet of the 16 nation Conference on Interaction and Confidence Building Measures in Asia

(CICA) in October 2004. In the press briefing all three countries agreed to strengthen a "collective approach" in world affairs. (Singh, 2005: 14-16).[27]

On June 2, 2005 the three foreign ministers of Russia, China and India namely Sergei Lavrov, Li Zhaoxing and Natwar Singh had their first ever stand alone meeting at the port city of Vladivotosk in Russia's Far East. The presence of large number of Western journalists at this meeting indicated that the meet generated curiosity beyond these states. Most experts believe that a meeting solely for this purpose reflects the beginning of the new era in the evolution of the Russia-India-China triangle.

For various reasons, all three countries feel that they are under Western pressure. Russia because of NATO's eastward expansion, Chechnya issue, and more generally, because of perceived CS design on former Soviet republics, including Central Asia and Caspian Sea region. China is experiencing Western pressure on human rights issue and feels threatened by US arms sales to Taiwan and more generally, an East Asian security policy which moves towards greater use of Japan in balancing China. India is experiencing in concealed Western propensity to try to get involved on Kashmir issue and helping Pakistan to internationalizing Kashmir issue; as well as the Western – mainly US attempt to limit country's nuclear and missile programme. (Sakwa, 2003: 5-19).

The international balance of power is changing in favour of world peace. Russia, India and China (RIC) have been interacting trilaterally since 1996. The 11th round of the Russia-India-China (RIC) Foreign Minister's meeting was held on April 13, 2012 in Moscow. The impetus of the RIC Foreign Ministers' recent meeting was strengthened as it was held within a fortnight after the March 29 BRICS summit in New Delhi. RIC's main agenda have been to oppose unilateralism and to promote a pluralistic democratic international order. The three countries believes that the diverse threats and risks cannot be addressed by military power alone but need to be appraised through political, social and economic prisms.

India also accused US for pursuing 'double standard' on fighting with terrorism. India blames that terrorist outfits functioning in Pakistan with covert support of Pakistani establishment are posting grave threat to India's security, but US in eliminating only those terrorists who pose threat for her own interests and not that of India.

IMPACT ON INDIA

India on its side is also willing to engage in great power politics and is looking for international recognition it has been deprived since independence. Nehru wrote movingly of India's desire and its destiny to play a major role in the world politics. He hoped that it would not be military role, but one based on sound moral values. Today although there exists no "white paper" enunciating the objectives of the country's foreign policy, India still strives towards this goal. The most spectacular example of this new assertiveness, largely founded on the self-confidence generated by the relative success of the nuclear tests, is the claim for a permanent seat at the UNSC.

On the issue of triangle, it is only India that seems to be least under pressure to pursue this triangle. India has to carefully weigh its policy options and maintain a delicate balance between promoting strategic triangle and strengthening its engagement with the USA. Individually both Russia and China have maintained good relationship with the US and their trade volume are increasing rapidly with the US.

Fear persists at the bilateral level as well. To some Chinese analysts Russia still represents a potential threat and vice-versa is also true. Both Russia and India presume that in the short and medium term, China may pursue the policy of peace, but in the long term equations may change. China's overt and covert support to Pakistani nuclear and missile development programme pose a great security danger for India.

India-Russia-China can do some sensible things together in the military and geopolitical realm. There is very little prospect that they are going to be allies or even thoroughgoing strategic performers. Moreover there are number of areas where protocol, discussions and agreements might be reached which would enhance their security and contribute to the security of Asia. If the idea of triangle between them mean anything, it is probably means a relatively modest set of understanding on which their view coverage.

Russia, China and India have great historical experience of dealing with such Western influences and preserving their Asian identity despite all challenges. The fundamentals of strategic triangle seem robust and clear and effort must be made to make it effective As of today Russia-India-China stand together in their support for evolving 'just and rational' new international order with democratization of international politics and multipolarization. Also all three have been suffering from transnational and cross-border terrorism and have not been comfortable with uni-polar world led by the US. The trilateral cooperation among themselves holds the key of 'triangle' and how these three Asian giants resolve their internal disputes would be the deciding factor in the emergence of 'Eurasian triangle'.

To conclude, Russian and Chinese interests in Central Asia seem smooth but with growing Chinese influence in the region is the cause of concern for Russia. China has already surpassed Germany to become second largest economy in the world. China's fast growing economy needs continuous energy supply for which Central Asia is its natural choice. Russia treats Central

Asia as its backyard and interests of both countries seems to be at odds here. The proposed with drawl of US from Afghanistan in 2014 and resurgence of Taliban is another issue of concern for three countries and only through joint collaboration they will be able to secure peace in the region. If India and China settle their border dispute amicably which is the biggest hurdle in the formation of RIC, the proposed Asian triangle will become a force to reckon with in the times to come. The induction of Russian aircraft carrier Admiral Gorshkov (renamed as INS Vikramaditya) in November 2013, in Indian navy has increased its strike capability many fold. India has made it categorically clear that induction of state of art weapons like Arihant and Vikramaditya is not aimed to any other country but for the self defence. If these three Eurasian giants, two of them being the permanent members of UNSC can amicably resolve their minor disputes amicably, the dream of 21st century to be an Asian century can be easily realized.

NOTES

1. Chenoy, A.M. (2005), "Russia-India-China: Re-visioning the International Political System", *World Focus* (April, 2005), pp. 11-16.
2. Gorbachev, Mikhail (1987), "*Perestroika: New Thinking for our Country and the World*", London: Collins.
3. Ibid.
4. Imam, Zafar(2001), "*Foreign Policy of Russia, 1991-2000*" New Delhi: New Horizon Publishers.
5. Summary of World Broadcast (*SWB*)/SU/3416 B/5, December 22, 1998).
6. Patnaik, Ajay, (2005) "From Primakov to Putin: 'Stategic Triagle", *World Focus*, pp. 3-10.
7. Shams-ud-din,(2001), *India and Russia: Towards strategic Partnership,* New Delhi: Lancer's Book.

8. Chenoy, A.M. (2005), "Russia-India-China: Revisioning the International Political System", *World Focus* (April, 2005), p. 11-26.
9. Chenoy, A.M. (2001), "The Phases in Indo-Russian Relations" in Shams-ud-din (eds.), *India and Russia: Towards strategic Partnership,* New Delhi: Lancer's Book.
10. Boquerat, G. and Grare, Frederic (2004), "*India-China, Russia Intricacies of an Asian Triangle*", New Delhi; India Research Press.
11. Dutt, V.P. (2003), "Puttin's Russia and India: Overview" in V.D. Chopra (eds.), *New Trends in Indo-Russian Relations,* New Delhi: Kalpaz.
12. Wishnick, Elisabeth (2001), "*Mending Fences, The Evolution of Moscow's China Policy from Brezhnev to Yeltsin*", Seattle, Wash.: University of Washington Press, pp.121-127.
13. Ibid.
14. Bakshi, Jyotsna (2002), "Post Cold War Sino-Russian Relations: An Indian Perspective" *Strategic Analysis,* 26 (1): 80-117.
15. Banerji, A., and Bhattacharya P. (2001), *"Peoples Republic of China at Fifty: Politics Economy and Foreign Relations"*, New Delhi: Lancer.
16. Shambaugh, David (2000), "China's Military Views the World: Ambivalent Security", *International Security,* 24 (3): 72-89.
17. Keith , Crane and William Overholt (2005), "*Modernizing China's Military: Opportunities and Constraints*", Santa Monica, Calif.: RAND Corporation.
18. Li, Jingjie (2000), "Pillars of Sino-Russian Partnership", *Orbis,* 44 (4): 428-439.
19. Jiali, Ma (2003), "Strengthening the Role of UNO Cooperation of India-China and Russia in UN", *China Report,* 39 (3): 385-92.
20. Subramanyam, K. "China-Pakistan Nuclear and missile technology nexus" The Hindu, March 20, 2000.

21. Boquerat, G. and Grare, Frederic (2004), "*India-China, Russia Intricacies of an Asian Triangle*", New Delhi; India Research Press. pp.121-124.

22. SWB/SU/3417 B/4, December 23, 1998.

23. Jingjie, L. (2000), "Pillars of the Sino-Russian Partnership", *Orbis,* 44 (4): 527-539.

24. Yi, Tung (2000), "Russian Experts said helping PRC make high-tech weaponry" *People's Daily*, Sept. 6, 2000.

25. Basu, Baidya Bikas (1998), "Russian National Security Thinking", *Strategic Analysis,* 24 (7): 1285-1305.

26. Singh, Swaran (2003), "India-China-Russia: A Strategic Triangle?" *World Focus,* 24 (1): 9-17.

27. ibid.

28. Sakwa, Richard (2003), "Putin's Foreign Policy: Transforming the East" in Garbriel Gorodetsky (eds.), *Russia Between East and West: Russian Foreign Policy on the Threshold of 21st Century*, London: Frankcass.

8

INDO-RUSSIA RELATIONS: ROLE OF RUSSIA IN ASIA

The Asia-Pacific region has been identified as the world's new center of gravity. The emerging new architecture revolving around Asian powers has given rise to questions about Russia's role in the region, given that the Eurasian giant has an Asian presence in the Far East. The mutual threat perceptions between Russia and other Asian nations have altered over the course of Twenty years since the collapse of communism. Russia is now recognized as a non-threatening great power with global significance. The Asia-Pacific has always been a region of great importance for super powers throughout Cold War and after due to its unique geo-political and geo-economic importance. Both USA and USSR was engaged in a great ideological battle to get hold on this region and this is still continuing even after end of Cold War. Russia has a long and varied history as a serious strategic player in Asia. It is only recently that it has been completely written off by the end of the Cold War and its attendant beliefs in the end of geopolitics. The mutual threat perceptions between Russia and other Asian nations have certainly altered over the course of 20 years since the collapse of communism, and Russia is now widely recognized as a nonthreatening great power with global significance. However, regional analysts are still skeptical over the degree to which Russia's vested interests lie in Asia, and whether these interests are compatible with those of other regional players.

Russia is distinctly interested in Asia-Pacific affairs because more than two-thirds of its territory is situated in this region. Development of the rich natural resources of Siberia and the Far East will be of exceptional importance for the future progress of Russia and the many states of the Asia-Pacific. The population of these areas is small compared to the total population of Russia. This makes it even more important to ensure transparency, predictability, stability, and security along the vast perimeter of Russia's eastern boundaries. On the whole, inter-state relations in the Asia-Pacific region and the trajectories of their evolution are favorable and meet the fundamental interests of Russia. The developments in the Asia-Pacific deeply affect the political and economic climate worldwide. During recent decades, the economic center of the world has been moving gradually toward the Asia-Pacific, and the international relations in the region are becoming more and more important in global affairs.

Russia consistently supports the establishment of a just and democratic world order based on strict observance of the international legal norms, goals, and principles of the UN Charter and on comprehensive security, sovereign equality, and mutual respect for the legitimate interests of all states. The fact that the vast majority of the Asia-Pacific states share this approach seems to explain why peace and stability prevail in the region. Since the Cold War ended, the political situation in the Asia-Pacific has been relatively stable and predictable. Many Asia-Pacific states have mutual territorial claims, and sometimes these contradictory claims can lead to drastic and even dangerous conflicts. However, these states have practical experience in solving such problems, which helps to avoid military action, material damage, and loss of human life. The agreements on the mutually acceptable demarcation of a huge part of the border between China, on the one hand, and Russia, Kazakhstan, Kyrgyzstan, and Tajikistan, on the other hand, are a good example of this problem-solving skill. India and China also have good prospects for settling their border claims.

Although the Southeast Asian countries and China have not agreed on the ownership of the Spratly and Paracel Islands, they have elaborated a Code of Conduct in the South China Sea and are looking forward to arrangements for joint exploitation of the areas in dispute. Russia welcomes the commitment of the countries participating in developing the Code of Conduct because it is an important step in resolving the territorial dispute. Rather than resuming their confrontation over two islands near the east coast of Kalimantan, Malaysia and Indonesia opted to settle their dispute through the International Court of Justice.[1] From time to time, the dispute over the Senkaku Islands ignites, but in words rather than military actions. Today, when inter-state relations in Asia have a five relatively low conflict potential, it is unlikely that territorial disputes could generate a serious challenge to regional security and stability.

The growing interest of Russian military-industrial and energy companies in Southeast Asia will give Russia cause to become increasingly interested in the security and stability of vital water corridors in the waters of East Asia. Despite protests from Beijing, Russia is intensifying its connections with Vietnam, arranging for joint oil and gas exploration and signing military contracts, including the sale of six submarines in 2009. Thailand, Indonesia, Laos and Malaysia are among other potential targets for Russia's armament deals. Most of those countries are America's partners in the "hub and spokes" cooperative security system and their close relations with Russia will only prove beneficial for the US, as Moscow would be more inclined to engage in conflict resolution that might erupt between China and them. Another area of joint interest is North Korea and nuclear non-proliferation. As stated in the Russian Foreign Policy

Concept, political stability in Asia is crucial to Russia foreign policy priorities, especially on the question of non-proliferation. The readiness to participate in Korean talks and enforce a peaceful resolution is even more evident when placed in the context of Moscow's ambition to build a Trans-Korean railroad and a direct pipeline from the Russian Far East to the Korean market.[2]

The USSR was feared until the late 1980s for its bold force projection into the South Pacific and Indian Ocean. Some, such as Richard Herr, openly worried that the US and Australian policy of "strategic denial" vis-à-vis the USSR in the South Pacific had failed, and that regional governments had better acquaint themselves with this new reality. Canberra and Washington even worried that, in a nuclear war with the Soviet Union, the Naval Communications "North West Cape" facility would be a tempting first target – either by a nuclear strike or Special Forces raid – to prevent an American retaliation from the nuclear submarines which the base commanded. In fact, the Soviets, according to one among their ranks, carried out some of their training in the deserts of Kazakhstan to mimic the arid conditions of the Australian desert in the event of a future raid. Since the 1990s, many have perceived Russia as a feeble giant with clay feet. This soundly demonstrates the current dismissive consensus around Russia's role in Asia. This default position made sense when Russia was indeed riddled by chronic internal ills, violent conflicts, economic misery, separatism, a public health collapse, and the largest peace-time depopulation in recorded history. But it no longer makes sense today.

RUSSIA–CHINA STRATEGIC CO-OPERATION AND THE GEOPOLITICS OF ASIA-PACIFIC

Russia being the largest country and China being the most populous country on the planet, both collectively are undoubtedly the two major powers of the international system.

Russia being the successor of erstwhile Soviet Union wishes to regain the role once Soviet Union enjoyed whereas China being a communist country is also showing signs of new ambitions based on her history, population and military power and also her emergence as an important international economic actor. Relations between Moscow and Beijing have gone full circle in the past half century, from alliance to containment and now to strategic partnership.

To understand the ebbs and flows in Moscow's China policy it is necessary to look into the Soviet history. History which is characterized as chronicle of the past provides the solid base for building up future relationships. In International Relations, there is no permanent 'friend or foe', today's bitter enemy can become tomorrow's staunchest ally. It is interest which runs supreme, and Russia and China are not exceptions to it. Despite being communist countries both Soviet Union and China counted each other as enemy number one and targeted each other with their nuclear weapons. But today Russia and China no longer consider each other as enemy and both countries have developed "very deep" relations in the strategic field.

China has the largest population in the world, while Russia is the largest nation in terms of territory. Both are permanent members of the United Nations Security Council. Obviously, the significance of Sino-Russian relations extends far beyond the interests of the two nations. It also affects the stability of Asia and the world at large.

Soviet-China relations before disintegration of USSR were characterized by a number of ups and downs. In February 1950 just four months after establishment of the PRC the two countries signed the Treaty of Friendship, Alliance and Mutual Cooperation. The first half of the 1950s was the honeymoon period. However, by the late 1950s differences in national interest and ideology emerged leading to serious disputes in early 1960s which developed in to acute conflict and border clashes in 1969. Hence in the late 1960s and 1970s the USSR regarded China as one of its main rivals and stationed approximately one million troops and one third of its SS-20 intermediate-range ballistic missile along the Sino-Soviet border, threatening to make a 'surgical' first strike on China', nuclear bases. Under serious threat, China had to prepare for a military intrusion from north. However, in 1980s two countries came to realization that these were not in the interests of either side and they made effort to alleviate the situation. These efforts resulted in the normalization of the relations during a state visit to Beijing by the then Soviet President Mikhail Gorbachev in May 1989. (Qimao, 1999, pp. 206-207).[3] In the words of Gorbachev, 'New Thinking' stood for–

> "We need normal international conditions for our internal progress. But we want a world free of war, without arms races, nuclear weapons and violence, not only because this is an optimal condition for our internal development." (Gorbachev, 1987: 10-12).[4]

On 15 September 1992, President Yeltsin signed the "Order of Russian Federation's Relations with China" and reaffirmed that -

a) there is only one China;
b) the PRC government is the sole legal representative of China;
c) Taiwan is the part of China; and
d) Russia will never establish official relation with Taiwan.[5]

Both Russia and China are opposed to US hegemonic policies and favour a multi-polar world order with different power centres. In April 1997 Chinese president Zemin paid another visit to Moscow on April 23 and the two countries issued a joint statement on the multipolarisation of the world and establishment of new international order. The statement rejected hegemony and power politics, and stated that 'Cold War' mentality must also be abandoned and bloc politics opposed. They called for preservation of the Anti Ballistic Missile (ABM) Treaty of 1972 between Soviet Union and USA and they supported lifting the UN Security Council sanctions against Saddam Hussain regime in Iraq.

On 24 November 1998, when Jiang Zemin paid another crucial visit to Russia, the Russian side reaffirmed its "four nos" position. The basic thrust of which was - no support for any conception of 'Taiwan's independence; no acceptance of the position of 'two Chinas' or 'one China and one Taiwan'; no support for Taiwan's participation in the UNO or other international organizations in which only sovereign states participated; and no sales of weapon to Taiwan. [6]

NATO bombing on Yugoslavia from March end to mid June 1999 without getting any authorization from the UN Security Council sent shock waves in both Russia and China and tended to bring together the two in joint opposition of NATO action. NATO's intervention on 'humanitarian ground' was an ominous development. Being multi-ethnic and multi-religious states, both Russia and China have their own separatist movements, Russia in Chechnya and China in Taiwan, Tibet and Xinjiang province. Being a Slav country, Yugoslavia was traditionally friend of Russia and attack on it, aroused Russian sentiments in the form of massive protests in Moscow.[7]

Both Russia and China have greater common ground to chalk out their strategy to deal with outside world compare to the issues on which they are at odds. Russo-Chinese link is built on a number of shared concerns which includes:

- The struggle against US led unipolar hegemonism;
- Unilateral humanitarian interventionism by passing UN;

- Islamic extremism and secessionism;
- Opposition to NATO enlargement and inter-reference in the internal matters;
- Opposition to NMD(National Missile Defence) and TMD (Theatre Missile Defence);
- Opposition to US withdrawal from ABM Treaty of 1972
- Restructuring of UN
- Opposition to US led NATO forces to stay longer in the Central Asian region;
- Near mutual acceptance of Russia's hegemony as a guarantor of order in Eurasia
- Strengthening the SCO
- Working together in the multilateral forums like WTO etc.

The declaration of 'New World Order in 21st Century' confirms that relations between two 'headed eagle' and 'dragon' have reached on its height. Both countries have gone very far and deep in their defence translations and no longer count each other as enemies. Their defence personnel, scientists, students are getting training in each other's establishments. Russia is building up nuclear reactors in China and has offered parternership in the state in the state owned space agency GLONASS which itself indicates the comfort level in their ever flourishing bilateral relations.

One of the prime reasons for developing close ties between Moscow and Beijing in the US factor, the common cause of concern for the both countries. US's continuous military and economic support to Taiwan and its huge military presence poses grave threat to the Chinese sovereignty. USA has also agreed to deploy TMD technology to Taiwan, which may virtually neutralize Chinese missile capabilities and would disturb the strategic balance in the region.

Russia is consistently under immense pressure from western human rights groups and media on the issue of human rights violations in the Chechnya war. These groups had virtually shut their eyes on Moscow Theatre tragedy and Beslan School crisis in which hundreds of Russian people lost their lives. It shows as if these human rights groups and media people are acting at the behest of their respective governments to settle their political goals with Moscow. When the issue of human rights violations by US forces comes from Iraq or Afghanistan, these groups keep their mouth shut.

To neutralize these double standards on terrorism, both Russia and China call for implementation of UN charter and International Laws globally without any fear or favour. The most frequent violator of international laws, Israel always go unpunished due to overt and covert support from the USA but a single incidence of Tianmen Square in China made her virtually untouchable in the international politics.

Initially there was some opposition within the Russian establishment to the entry of the US troops in Central Asia, an area of traditional Russian influence. However, subsequently, Moscow decided to allow air corridors, the use of its bases for the search and secure operations as well as sharing of intelligence regarding the terrorist networks operating in Afghanistan. Uzbekistan offered its airspace and bases to the US troops ahead of other CARs, whereas Moscow preferred to maintain the façade of coordinated stand of all the CIS states. Kyrgyzstan claimed that the granting of Manas air base was coordinated in advance with its partners in the CIS Collective Security Treaty.

Manas airbase of Kyrgyzstan is just 200 miles away from Chinese territory from where US troops can keep their eye on Chinese troop movements. Presence of US troops in such a close to Chinese border made security expert in Beijing uncomfortable. Beside military bases in Pakistan and Kyrgyzstan, US acquired military bases in Baghram and Kandahar in Afghanistan and bases of Khanabad in Uzbekistan.

Development of closer ties between Russia and US, especially after coming of Obama regime is causing concerns in Beijing. Before Obama regime, Bush administration worked closely with Russia especially after September 2001 terrorist attack.

After the September 11, 2001 attacks on New York and Washington and subsequent military action taken by US and NATO against Al-Queda and Talibans have radically altered the geopolitical situation in Central Asian Region. Russia and Central Asian republics acquired a prominence place in the US military strategy in Afghanistan military bases in Baghram and Kandahar in Afghanistan and the bases of Khanabad in Uzbekistan. It is believed that these facilities helped US military to quickly establish air superiority thought Central Asia and even to the Middle East. It is believed that in offering bases to the USA, the Central Asian States sought security against the threat of terrorist attacks as well as gain maneuvering space vis-à-vis Russia and China. CARs hoped to gain financially from the US presence.

The impact of post-September 11 developments on China has been the mixed one. China gained in so far as combating international terrorism became the number one task of the US policy. Prior to it economically and militarily growing China was increasingly being projected as emerging strategic rival of sole super power. China reluctantly, joined the international community in supporting the US war against terror but with certain conditions. China wanted UNSC to play central role in the war against terrorism as a guarantee against the US unilaterism. In fact China insisted that struggle against terrorism also includes the 'East Turkistan' terrorist forces or the Uighur separatist movement in Xinjiang province.[8]

There is no doubt that the prospects of a prolonged US military presence in Central Asian region are not welcome to either Russia or China. Post September 11 developments in the region are seem as a set back to SCO, because SCO was created to forge Russia-China partnership in the Central Asia for jointly maintaining peace, stability and economic cooperation in the region and keep a check on the Western influence in the region.

Russian and Chinese interests also converge on the issue of eastward expansion of NATO. First time ever NATO crossed the border of a non-NATO remember country i.e. Afghanistan in the name of fight against terrorism. Both Russia and China opposed the bombing on Belgrade, the capital of Yugoslavia in 1999. Also the US B-2 bombers dropped bomb on Chinese embassy in Belgrade causing many casualties. These incidences proved beyond doubt that US led NATO forces are crossing their granted mandate in the name of fight against terrorism and in the name of humanitarian intervention. Russia and China have their own set of problems in Chechnya and Xinjiang respectively.

At the time when NATO bombing was on, the 50th anniversary celebrations of the founding of NATO took place in Washington in which all the former Soviet republics with exception of Russia participated. What aroused the further Russian and Chinese concern and even the concern in countries like India was the enunciation of new strategies doctrine of NATO that permitted use of force by it in regions beyond the areas of its traditional responsibility comprising the territories of its member states. So, now NATO forces could be used anywhere.

Against such unilateral hegemonism of the US and NATO. Russia-China wants a multipolar world with many power centres. The declaration between Yeltsin and Jiang Zemin in 1997 openly talked about establishment of multipolar world based on principles of Panchsheel. Both call for respect of State sovereignty, equality of states eschewing of pursuit of hegemony, non-interference in internal affairs of other states, an equitable and just economic order and the strengthening of UN. Both Russia and China also seeks to work closely with NAM and champion the cause of third world.

The major bone of contention in the smooth relation was border dispute which is now solved. China has not only settled in border dispute with Russia but also with the Central Asian Republics in a peaceful manner. With the border dispute gone there is no any serious issues left between Russia and China to doubt each other's intention.

Peaceful solution of Korean Peninsula problem is also in the priority list of Russia and China. The proposed NMD system of the USA is expressly aimed at providing defence against the 'rogue' states like Iran, Iraq and North Korea etc. The launch of Pyongyong's rocket over Japan in 1998 provided justification to US for such apprehensions. Russia and China therefore, have sought to minimize the perception of North-Korean threat. They favour a rapprochement between North and South Korea and one between US and North Korea.

To counter the eastward expansion of NATO and with drawl of US from ABM Treaty of 1972, President Putin made an overture to European Union and NATO to reach some compromise solution. He called upon to EU and NATO to join forces with Moscow and set up a joint anti-missile shield during his visit to Rome on 5th June, 2000. He said that such a system will avoid creating problems linked to an imbalance in the equilibrium of forces and ensures 100 percent security to European countries.[9]

As far as economic ties between Russia and China are concerned, it lag behind political, diplomatic, strategic and military ties. It is apparent that the two countries are also to create economic interdependence. The economies of the two countries are mutually complementary. Russia is the major producer and supplier of energy while China is energy hungry and its needs are growing. Russia's main exports apart from defence equipments include fertilizer, steel, timber and machinery, while its main imports are consumer goods and food items.

There are some major pre-requisites for further growth in the scale and diversifications of Russo-Chinese economic collaboration. These are implementing joint programmes in the fuel and energy sector; stepping up cooperation in the field of investment; involving Russian companies in the strategy of accelerated development of China's western region; expanding cooperation between the two countries' border region and cooperation in the manufacturing sector and joint mastering of high technologies.

By strengthening trade with China, Russia will try to reduce its shortage of light industrial goods and electronics, create an economic infrastructure using cheap Chinese labour in the less developed areas of Russian Far East. Russia will also be able to reduce the financial crunch of its arms manufacturing units by selling weapons to China which includes more than $2 billion every year. Russia can also benefit by sending part of its well educated labour force to China to help create high technology industries and reduce the chronic unemployment among highly educated youths.[10]

On the other hand China will get benefitted by sending a certain amount of its unskilled labour force to Russia to work in the unstaffed industries. The excess of labour force available in China is about 200 million. This arrangement will reduce some burden of unemployment among Chinese people. In addition, China will have a chance to participate in the economic opening of oil fields resources in Russian Far East and Siberia.[11]

CONCLUSION

Given the contours of the Sino-Russian strategic partnership and its likely durability, what should be the US response? Perceiving this partnership as a full-fledged alliance, directed across the board against US interests, is a mistake. The common rhetoric is easy to sustain, but what will happen if the United States negotiates with Russia in earnest on an antiballistic missile compromise? Would Chinese opposition to changes in the regime really block a bilateral deal? Are China's interests really engaged in NATO enlargement?

Sino-Russian cooperation will not markedly change questions on issues such as Taiwan or NATO enlargement. These issues remain bilateral or regional; the outside partner has little standing. Moreover, issues such as these remain subject to a dynamic outside the control of the distant partner. Russia will act in its own interests in Europe, and China in Asia. For example, China remains comfortable with a framework in Korea that excludes Russia and Japan. Russia's European interests could well lead it much closer to Europe and the European Union in the years ahead. Chinese analysts can not confidently exclude the European turn they feared in the early 1990s. Chinese economic interests place the United States, Japan, and a wide variety of Asian countries far ahead of Russia.

Although Sino-Russian economic ties have expanded, they have not reached the levels outside the arms trade that many in Moscow expected or hoped. Sino-Russian cooperation at the UN could make future peacekeeping operations more difficult to negotiate (e.g., Macedonia) or make vetoes more likely as both countries now hold leverage over this body. Although current US-Russian differences are serious, US-Russian strategic talks on missile defense could yield a satisfactory outcome for Moscow that would complicate the situation in Beijing. Moreover, serious challenges have not yet arisen in Central Asia, though the next decade will bring changes of leadership, regional instability, and other problems there. If sustained Chinese migration pressure appears in the Russian Far East, the current strategic partnership will be difficult to maintain. Washington still controls many levers of influence, and the most ambitious bilateral expressions of solidarity and cooperation have yet to be tested.

The most important near-term consequence of Sino-Russian partnership is a negative one: the Russian contribution to Chinese military modernization. For the foreseeable future, China will have an enduring need for Russian military technology and systems, while Russia will have a variety of reasons to sell. Official statements from senior Russian defense officials indicate that they believe Russia has a long lead on China in key military capabilities and thus that current sales do not create a military threat to Russia itself. Russia's own economic problems and the ideological motivations of some in the Russian foreign policy community create incentives for sales, not restraint. These sales– and the broader defense and technology cooperationthat is linked to them–could in time alter regional military balances in areas of vital US interest in East and Southeast Asia or the Taiwan Strait. China does not need to match the military of the United States and its allies to affect this alteration. It need only develop capabilities that substantially raise the cost of US intervention in the region. At the very least, the upgrading of key Chinese military capabilities places an added burden on the United States and its regional allies in future crises.

NOTES

1. Rouben Azizian and Boris Reznik "*Russia, America, and Security in the Asia-Pacific*"(2006), Asia-Pacific Center for Securities Studies, Honolulu, pp.23-33.

2. Anton Barbashin, "A Pacific Vision for Russia and USA" *The Diplomat*, December 6, 2013.
3. Qimao, Chen (1999), "Sino-Russian Relationship after the Break Up of the Soviet Union" in Chaufrin Gennady (eds.), *Russia and Asia: Emerging Security Agenda,* New York: Sipri, OUP.
4. Gorbachev, Mikhail (1987), "*Perestroika: New Thinking for our Country and the World*", London: Collins. pp.123-128.
5. Chufrin, G. (1999), "*Russia and Asia: The emerging Security Agenda*", New York: Sipri Oxford University Press. pp.292-296.
6. Jingjie, L. (2000), "Pillars of the Sino-Russian Partnership", *Orbis,* 44(4): 527-539.
7. Saiget, Robert J. (2000), "*China, Russia beef up cooperation on Ethnic Separatism, Taiwan, Terrorism*", Hong Kong: Afp, pp.102-110.
8. Moltz, Clay (1995), "Regional Tensions in Russo-China Rapprochement", *Asian Survey,* 35(36): pp. 23-54.
9. Menon, Rajan and Charles E. Ziegler (2002), "The Balance of Power and US Foreign Policy Interest in the Russian Far East" in Thorton J and Ziegler E.C. (eds.), *Russia's Far East a region at risk,* London; University of a Washington Press, pp.17-23.
10. Shaumian, T.L. (2003), "Geopolitical Changes in Central Asia and Positions of Russia, China and India" *China Report,* 38(3): 361-363.
11. Mikhail Alexseev, "The Chinese Are Coming': Public Opinion and Threat Perception in the Russian Far East," *Program on New Approaches to Russian Security: Policy Memo 184,* Washington, D.C.: Council on Foreign Relations, January 2001.

9

RUSSIA-CHINA STRATEGIC CO-OPERATION: IMPLICATIONS FOR INDIA

Russia being the largest country and China being the most populous country on the planet, both collectively are undoubtedly the two major powers of the international system. Russia being the successor of erstwhile Soviet Union wishes to regain the role once Soviet Union enjoyed whereas China being a communist country is also showing signs of new ambitions based on her history, population and military power and also her emergence as an important international economic actor. Relations between Moscow and Beijing have gone full circle in the past half century, from alliance to containment and now to strategic partnership.

To understand the ebbs and flows in Moscow's China policy it is necessary to look into the Soviet history. History which is characterized as chronicle of the past provides the solid base for building up future relationships. In International Relations, there is no permanent 'friend or foe', today's bitter enemy can become tomorrow's staunchest ally. It is interest which runs supreme, and Russia and China are not exceptions to it. Despite being communist countries both Soviet Union and China counted each other as enemy number one and targeted each other with their nuclear weapons. But today Russia and China no longer consider each other as enemy and both countries have developed "very deep" relations in the strategic field.

China has the largest population in the world, while Russia is the largest nation in terms of territory. Both are permanent members of the United Nations Security Council. Obviously, the significance of Sino-Russian relations extends far beyond the interests of the two nations. It also affects the stability of Asia and the world at large.

Soviet-China relations before disintegration of USSR were characterized by a number of ups and downs. In February 1950 just four months after establishment of the PRC the two countries signed the treaty of Friendship, Alliance and Mutual Cooperation. The first half of the 1950s was the honeymoon period. However, by the late 1950s differences in national interest and ideology emerged leading to serious disputes in early 1960s which developed in to acute conflict and border clashes in 1969. Hence in the late 1960s and 1970s the USSR regarded China as one of its main rivals and stationed approximately one million troops and one third of its SS-20 intermediate-range ballistic missile along the Sino-Soviet border, threatening to make a 'surgical' first strike on China', nuclear bases. Under serious threat, China had to prepare for a military intrusion from north. However, in 1980s two countries came to realization that these were not in the interests of either side and they made effort to alleviate the situation. These efforts resulted in the normalization of the relations during a state visit to Beijing by the then Soviet President Mikhail Gorbachev in May 1989. (Qimao, 1999, pp. 206-207).

However, the tense relationship of two communist giants eased with the rise of Gorbachev as the Secretary General of CPSU in 1985. He made epoch making changes in the Soviet history by introducing 'Perestroika' and 'Glasnost'. Some have described him in Soviet history as 'reformer in hurry'. In the realm of international relations he introduced 'New Thinking' which stressed on a deidoelogised foreign policy.

In the words of Gorbachev, 'New Thinking' stood for–

> "We need normal international conditions for our internal progress. But we want a world free of war, without arms races, nuclear weapons and violence, not only because this is an optimal condition for our internal development." (Gorbachev, 1987: 10-12).[2]

Under the slogan of 'New Thinking' Gorbachev's foreign policy was based on shared moral and ethical principles to solve global problems rather than on Marxist-Leninist concept of irreconcilable conflict between capitalism and communism. The historic meeting between Deng and Gorbachev lead to resolution of many outstanding problems between the two. The border dispute was resolved by demarcating the Usuri River; trade was opened up and threat perceptions to a large extent eliminated.

While relations were improving between the two countries, the Soviet Union itself collapsed in December 1991. It was a historical event of global significance. Relations between the two neighbours, Russia and China could not therefore, escape the global effects of this historical event. (Imam, 2001:97-100).[3]

In the initial years after the disintegration of Soviet Union, Russian leaders did everything to become part of the prosperous capitalist world but they got disappointed with their cold response. The bubble of "Common European Home" and "One World from Vancouver to Vladivostok" busted very soon. Disillusioned Russia turned her face towards the Third World, and Asia which had been a natural ally of the erstwhile Soviet Union again got prominence among the policy makers. So in the changed circumstances and policies countries like China, India, Iran got the top priority in Russian foreign policy list.

Soon, Andrei Kozyrev (pro-West Foreign Minister) was replaced by an academician Yevgeny Primakov (pro-Third World) as Russia's new foreign minister who tried to balance between the East and the West. In December 1998, he made an official visit to India. Primakov visited India at the time when India was internationally isolated after conducting five nuclear tests a few months back. He proposed to formulate a triangle between three major Eurasian countries Russia-China-India to counter US hegemony and unilateralism in the world politics. According to him 'Russia favours the creation of a Moscow-Beijing-Delhi triangle and also it would be a good idea'.[4] On 15 September 1992 President Yeltsin signed the "Order of Russian Federation's Relations with China" and reaffirmed that -

a) there is only one China;
b) the PRC government is the sole legal representative of China;
c) Taiwan is the part of China; and
d) Russia will never establish official relation with Taiwan.[5]

On the question of separatism, religious extremism and terrorism both countries share common view today. In March 1995, Chinese president Jiang Zemin visited Moscow to participate in the celebration of 50th anniversary of victory over Fascism. In an agreement between the two, Russia reiterated its support to China on Taiwan issue and on its part; China extended its full support to Russia in dealing with the Chechnya problem.[6]

Both Russia and China are opposed to US hegemonic policies and favour a multi-polar world order with different power centers. In April 1997 Chinese president Jiang Zemin paid another visit to Moscow on April 23 and the two countries issued a joint statement on the multipolarisation of the world and establishment of new international order. The statement rejected hegemony and power politics, and stated that 'Cold War' mentality must also be abandoned and bloc politics opposed. They called for preservation of the Anti Ballistic Missile (ABM) Treaty of 1972 between Soviet Union and USA and they supported lifting the UN Security Council sanctions against Saddam Husain regime in Iraq.

Russia and China shared views on increasing numbers of international issues in the light of the challenge from the USA and its allies. In the first year after the collapse of Soviet Union, Russia adopted a pro-western foreign policy, hoping for economic aid from the west and for recognition as a strong power and an equal partner of the USA. Soon, however, Russia was deeply disappointed by the level of western aid. Moreover, it faced fierce competition from the west over the sphere of influence in the newly independent states. These realities forced Russia to switch to an 'Omni-directional' or 'two headed eagle' (Russia's national emblem) policy, pursuing relations with countries of both the East and the West. Especially after 1995, under heavy pressure from NATO's eastward expansion led by the USA, Russia attached greater importance to its relations with China, India and other Asian countries. Russia termed Asian countries as 'natural allies', among which China got the top priority. Despite odd relationship in the past both countries evolved consensus on various national and international issues.

I) AREAS OF COMMON CONCERN BETWEEN RUSSIA AND CHINA

On the question of separatism, religious extremism and terrorism both countries share common view today. In March 1995, Chinese president Jiang Zemin visited Moscow to participate in the celebration of 50th anniversary of victory over Fascism. In an agreement between the two, Russia reiterated its support to China on Taiwan issue and on its part, China extended its full support to Russia in dealing with the Chechnya problem.

Both Russia and China are opposed to US hegemonic policies and favour a multi-polar world order with different power centres. In April 1997 Chinese president Zemin paid another visit to Moscow on April 23 and the two countries issued a joint statement on the multipolarisation of the world and establishment of new international order. The statement rejected hegemony and power politics, and stated that 'Cold War' mentality must also be abandoned and bloc politics opposed. They called for preservation of the Anti Ballistic Missile (ABM) Treaty of 1972 between Soviet Union and USA and they supported lifting the UN Security Council sanctions against Saddam Husain regime in Iraq.

On 24 November 1998, when Jiang Zemin paid another crucial visit to Russia, the Russian side reaffirmed its "four nos" position. The basic thrust of which was - no support for any conception of 'Taiwan's independence; no acceptance of the position of 'two Chinas' or 'one China and one Taiwan'; no support for Taiwan's participation in the UNO or other international organizations in which only sovereign states participated; and no sales of weapon to Taiwan.[7]

NATO bombing on Yugoslavia from March end to mid June 1999 without getting any authorization from the UN Security Council sent shock waves in both Russia and China and tended to bring together the two in joint opposition of NATO action. NATO's intervention on 'humanitarian ground' was an ominous development. Being multi-ethnic and multi-religious states, both Russia and China have their own separatist movements, Russia in Chechnya and China in Taiwan, Tibet and Xinjiang province. Being a Slav country, Yugoslavia was traditionally friend of Russia and attack on it, aroused Russian sentiments in the form of massive protests in Moscow.[8]

Both Russia and China have greater common ground to chalk out their strategy to deal with outside world compare to the issues on which they are at odds. Russo-Chinese link is built on a number of shared concerns which includes:

- The struggle against US led unipolar hegemonism;
- Unilateral humanitarian interventionism by passing UN;
- Islamic extremism and secessionism;
- Opposition to NATO enlargement and inter-reference in the internal matters;
- Opposition to NMD(National Missile Defence) and TMD (Theatre Missile Defence);
- Opposition to US withdrawal from ABM Treaty of 1972
- Restructuring of UN
- Opposition to US led NATO forces to stay longer in the Central Asian region;
- Near mutual acceptance of Russia's hegemony as a guarantor of order in Eurasia
- Strengthening the SCO
- Working together in the multilateral forums like WTO etc.

The Russian and Chinese economies are among the ten fastest growing economies in the world. Both have vast potentials to become the economic super power. Russian oil and gas pipelines are the life lines for the Western Europe. Russia is the second largest producer of crude oil after Saudi Arabia and it has the largest gas reserves. Whereas China is the energy hungry country with abundant cheap labour and have cutting edge in manufacturing industry. Both countries have ample scope to get benefitted from each other's expertise.

Russian arms sale consists major portion in Russo-Chinese trade. Russian defence industries are facing financial crunch in order to remain competitive in highly volatile defence equipment market to find its buyers. Here China can play vital role to meet much needed financial crunch by using its huge foreign exchange reserves with other countries like India and Iran. China is the largest arms buyer from Russia. China has acquired many advanced weaponry from Russia like SU-30 MKK fighter planes, Akula Class nuclear submarines etc. which have provided advantage to the Chinese armed forces.

The Putin-Hu declaration on the 'New World Order' in 21st century on July 1, 2005 provided a sound base for further converting the relations between the two countries. Both agreed that 'All countries of the world must strictly abide by the principles of mutual respect for sovereignty and territorial integrity, mutual non-aggression, non-interference in internal affairs of each other, equality and mutual benefit and peaceful coexistence. Both attacked US 'double standards' in the war against terrorism (though without mentioning).

The declaration of 'New World Order in 21st Century' confirms that relations between two 'headed eagle' and 'dragon' have reached on its height. Both countries have gone very far and deep in their defence translations and no longer count each other as enemies. Their defence personnel, scientists, students are getting training in each other's establishments. Russia is building up nuclear reactors in China and has offered partnership in the state in the state owned space agency GLONASS which itself indicates the comfort level in their ever flourishing bilateral relations.

One of the prime reasons for developing close ties between Moscow and Beijing in the US factor, the common cause of concern for the both countries. US's continuous military and economic support to Taiwan and its huge military presence poses grave threat to the Chinese sovereignty. USA has also agreed to deploy TMD technology to Taiwan, which may virtually neutralize Chinese missile capabilities and would disturb the strategic balance in the region.

Russia is consistently under immense pressure from western human rights groups and media on the issue of human rights violations in the Chechnya war. These groups had virtually shut their eyes on Moscow Theatre tragedy and Beslan School crisis in which hundreds of Russian people lost their lives. It shows as if these human rights groups and media people are acting at the behest of their respective governments to settle their political goals with Moscow. When the issue of human rights violations by US forces comes from Iraq or Afghanistan, these groups keep their mouth shut.

To neutralize these double standards on terrorism, both Russia and China call for implementation of UN charter and International Laws globally without any fear or favour. The most frequent violator of international laws, Israel always go unpunished due to overt and covert support from the USA but a single incidence of Tianmen Square in China made her virtually untouchable in the international politics.

Initially there was some opposition within the Russian establishment to the entry of the US troops in Central Asia, an area of traditional Russian influence. However, subsequently, Moscow decided to allow air corridors, the use of its bases for the search and secure operations as well as sharing of intelligence regarding the terrorist networks operating in Afghanistan. Uzbekistan offered its airspace and bases to the US troops ahead of other CARs, whereas Moscow preferred to maintain the façade of coordinated stand of all the CIS states. Kyrgyzstan claimed that the granting of Manas air base was coordinated in advance with its partners in the CIS Collective Security Treaty.

Manas airbase of Kyrgyzstan is just 200 miles away from Chinese territory from where US troops can keep their eye on Chinese troop movements. Presence of US troops in such a close to Chinese border made security expert in Beijing uncomfortable. Beside military bases in Pakistan and Kyrgyzstan, US acquired military bases in Baghram and Kandahar in Afghanistan and bases of Khanabad in Uzbekistan.

Development of closer ties between Russia and US, especially after coming of Obama regime is causing concerns in Beijing. Before Obama regime, Bush administration worked closely with Russia especially after September 2001 terrorist attack.

After the September 11, 2001 attacks on New York and Washington and subsequent military action taken by US and NATO against Al-Queda and Talibans have radically altered the geopolitical situation in Central Asian Region. Russia and Central Asian republics acquired a prominence place in the US military strategy in Afghanistan military bases in Baghram and Kandahar in Afghanistan and the bases of Khanabad in Uzbekistan. It is believed that these facilities helped US military to quickly establish air superiority thought Central Asia and even to the Middle East. It is believed that in offering bases to the USA, the Central Asian States sought security against the threat of terrorist attacks as well as gain maneuvering space vis-à-vis Russia and China. CARs hoped to gain financially from the US presence.

The impact of post-September 11 developments on China has been the mixed one. China gained in so far as combating international terrorism became the number one task of the US policy. Prior to it economically and militarily growing China was increasingly being projected as emerging strategic rival of sole super power. China reluctantly, joined the international community in supporting the US war against terror but with certain conditions. China wanted UNSC to play central role in the war against terrorism as a guarantee against the US unilaterism. In fact China insisted that struggle against terrorism also includes the 'East Turkistan' terrorist forces or the Uighur separatist movement in Xinjiang province.

There is no doubt that the prospects of a prolonged US military presence in Central Asian region are not welcome to either Russia or China. Post September 11 developments in the region are seem as a set back to SCO, because SCO was created to forge Russia-China partnership in the Central Asia for jointly maintaining peace, stability and economic cooperation in the region and keep a check on the Western influence in the region.

Russian and Chinese interests also converge on the issue of eastward expansion of NATO. First time ever NATO crossed the border of a non-NATO remember country i.e. Afghanistan in the name of fight against terrorism. Both Russia and China opposed the bombing on Belgrade, the capital of Yugoslavia in 1999. Also the US B-2 bombers dropped bomb on Chinese embassy in Belgrade causing many casualties. These incidences proved beyond doubt that US led NATO forces are crossing their granted mandate in the name of fight against terrorism and in the name of humanitarian intervention. Russia and China have their own set of problems in Chechnya and Xinjiang respectively.

At the time when NATO bombing was on, the 50th anniversary celebrations of the founding of NATO took place in Washington in which all the former Soviet republics with exception of Russia participated. What aroused the further Russian and Chinese concern and even the concern in countries like India was the enunciation of new strategies doctrine of NATO that permitted use of force by it in regions beyond the areas of its traditional responsibility comprising the territories of its member states. So, now NATO forces could be used anywhere.

Against such unilateral hegemonism of the US and NATO. Russia-China wants a multipolar world with many power centres. The declaration between Yeltsin and Jiang Zemin in 1997 openly talked about establishment of multipolar world based on principles of Panchsheel. Both call for respect of State sovereignty, equality of states eschewing of pursuit of hegemony, non-interference in internal affairs of other states, an equitable and just economic order and the strengthening of UN. Both Russia and China also seeks to work closely with NAM and champion the cause of third world.

The major bone of contention in the smooth relation was border dispute which is now solved. China has not only settled in border dispute with Russia but also with the Central Asian Republics in a peaceful manner. With the border dispute gone there is no any serious issues left between Russia and China to doubt each other's intention.

Peaceful solution of Korean Peninsula problem is also in the priority list of Russia and China. The proposed NMD system of the USA is expressly aimed at providing defence against the 'rogue' states like Iran, Iraq and North Korea etc. The launch of Pyongyong's rocket over Japan in 1998 provided justification to US for such apprehensions. Russia and China therefore, have sought to minimize the perception of North-Korean threat. They favour a rapprochement between North and South Korea and one between US and North Korea.

To counter the eastward expansion of NATO and with drawl of US from ABM Treaty of 1972, President Putin made an overture to European Union and NATO to reach some compromise solution. He called upon to EU and NATO to join forces with Moscow and set up a joint anti-missile shield during his visit to Rome on 5th June, 2000. He said that such a system will avoid creating problems linked to an imbalance in the equilibrium of forces and ensures 100 percent security to European countries.

As far as economic ties between Russia and China are concerned, it lag behind political, diplomatic, strategic and military ties. It is apparent that the two countries are also to create economic interdependence. The economies of the two countries are mutually complementary. Russia is the major producer and supplier of energy while China is energy hungry and its needs are growing. Russia's main exports apart from defence equipments include fertilizer, steel, timber and machinery, while its main imports are consumer goods and food items.

There are some major pre-requisites for further growth in the scale and diversifications of Russo-Chinese economic collaboration. These are implementing joint programmes in the fuel and energy sector; stepping up cooperation in the field of investment; involving Russian companies in the strategy of accelerated development of China's western region; expanding cooperation between the two countries' border region and cooperation in the manufacturing sector and joint mastering of high technologies.

By strengthening trade with China, Russia will try to reduce its shortage of light industrial goods and electronics, create an economic infrastructure using cheap Chinese labour in the less developed areas of Russian Far East. Russia will also be able to reduce the financial crunch of its arms manufacturing units by selling weapons to China which includes more than $2 billion every year. Russia can also benefit by sending part of its well educated labour force to China to help create high technology industries and reduce the chronic unemployment among highly educated youths.

On the other hand China will get benefitted by sending a certain amount of its unskilled labour force to Russia to work in the unstaffed industries. The excess of labour force available in China is about 200 million. This arrangement will reduce some burden of unemployment among Chinese people. In addition, China will have a chance to participate in the economic opening of oil fields resources in Russian Far East and Siberia.

II) DIVERGENT VIEWS BETWEEN RUSSIA AND CHINA

A Russo-China border issues of considerable sensitivity concerns the extensive Chinese migration much of it illegal in to Russian territory. The demographic imbalance along the border with 150 million Chinese crowded in the North Eastern part of China and only 7 million Russians in the vast bordering territories of Siberia and the Far East has been a source of concern for Soviet and Russian citizens, officials and journalists for many years.

Moscow is unhappy with China's massive production of copycat versions of Russian weapons. Russian arms manufacturers have been taken by surprise with the sheer speed and scale of China's copycat capabilities. Often, Chinese dealers say they want to buy Russian arms, begin negotiations, and ask as many technical questions as possible. They then take photos and videos of the weapons, request all available documents, and repeatedly come back to the table to discuss technical issues.

Another trouble spot in China's Xinjiang province, whose population is ethnically kin to that of the neighbouring post-Soviet states, is troubled by sporadic anti-Beijing rebellious that could potentially spark a cross-border "liberation war". From that perspective even with respect to the near future by closely associating with China and by selling it arms, Russia risks upsetting the delicate military balance in Asia and even being drawn in to China's territorial disputes with Taiwan, Vietnam, Japan, and ultimately the US.[9]

At a more generalized level, there exists a cultural divide that frequently obscures and undermines commonalities of interests. Many Russians who even advocate strategic partnerships, subscribe to the image of Russia as a "civilizational barrier" against the barbarian, 'East'. Although these days the principle danger is seen as Islamic radicalism emanating from the South, the very concept of Russian as a guardian of 'western' values inhibits rapprochement with China. It foster a superiority complex that many Chinese find unwarranted in a state they view as economically backward, militantly crippled and of diminishing international influence.[10]

The burden of historical and civilizational prejudices, an increasingly dominant West-centrism in Moscow and Beijing and the Russian anxieties regarding China's rise as the next superpower continue. Within this overall dynamic, three issue areas will bear particular a1tention i.e. (i) development over the Angarsk-Nakhodka oil pipeline; (ii) security management on the Korean peninsula; and (iii) strategic projections of former Soviet Central Asia.[11]

In Central Asia, Moscow is engaged in much more activist project i.e., re-establishing itself in the traditional sphere of influence. Here Russia sees itself as a regional hagemon, a position it is reluctant to cede. However, China's geographical proximity to Central Asia and considerable security and economic interests there mean that it will not simply 'go away'. As Russia seeks to reassert its presence and influence in the region, and China attempts to maximize its economic stake Central Asia looms as perhaps the most likely theatre for renewed bilateral tensions.[12]

IMPLICATIONS FOR INDIA

India on its side is also willing to engage in great power politics and is looking for international recognition it has been deprived since independence. Nehru wrote movingly of India's desire and its destiny to play a major role in the world politics. He hoped that it would not be military role, but one based on sound moral values. Today although there exists no "white paper" enunciating the objectives of the country's foreign policy, India still strives towards this goal. The most spectacular example of this new assertiveness, largely founded on the self-confidence generated by the relative success of the nuclear tests, is the claim for a permanent seat at the UNSC.

On the issue of triangle, it is only India that seems to be least under pressure to pursue this triangle. India has to carefully weigh its policy options and maintain a delicate balance between promoting strategic triangle and strengthening its engagement with the USA. Individually both Russia and China have maintained good relationship with the US and their trade volume are increasing rapidly with the US.

Fear persists at the bilateral level as well. To some Chinese analysts Russia still represents a potential threat and vice-versa is also true. Both Russia and India presume that in the short and medium term, China may pursue the policy of peace, but in the long term equations may change. China's overt and covert support to Pakistani nuclear and missile development programme pose a great security danger for India.

India-Russia-China can do some sensible things together in the military and geopolitical realm. There is very little prospect that they are going to be allies or even thoroughgoing strategic performers. Moreover there are number of areas where protocol, discussions and agreements might be reached which would enhance their security and contribute to the security of Asia. If the idea of triangle between them mean anything, it is probably means a relatively modest set of understanding on which their view coverage.

The Eurasian security in future will depend a lot on how these three largest countries harmonise their relationships. They represent world's most populous segment, rich with natural resources and are on a fast track to emerge as leading global economic power. The June 2, 2005 concluded meeting at Vladivostok recently solely for this purpose indicate that future of triangle is very promising and the picture will be clearer in the time to come. At the same time the future of triangle rests with how India and China solve their own long standing problem of border disputes.

To conclude, therefore, if Asia has to make any positive contribution towards the evolution of new global order and if world has to evolve an adequately representative framework for international security then, increasingly mutual cooperation of these three Asian powers amongst themselves and also their cooperation with other major players remains the most critical pre-requisite to all initiative:; in building the future world order.

Russia, China and India have great historical experience of dealing with such Western influences and preserving their Asian identity despite all challenges. The fundamentals of strategic triangle seem robust and clear and effort must be made to make it effective As of today Russia-India-China stand together in their support for evolving 'just and rational' new international order with democratization of international politics and multipolarization. Also all three have been suffering from transnational and cross-border terrorism and have not been comfortable with unipolar world led by the US. The trilateral cooperation among themselves holds the key of 'triangle' and how these three Asian giants resolve their internal disputes would be the deciding factor in the emergence of 'Eurasian triangle'.

Russian and Chinese interests in Central Asia seems smooth but with growing Chinese influence in the region is the cause of concern for Russia. China has already surpassed Germany to become third largest economy in the world. China's fast growing economy needs continuous energy supply for which Central Asia is its natural choice. Russia treats Central Asia as its backyard and interests of both countries seems to be at odds here.

NOTES

1. Qimao, Chen (1999), "Sino-Russian Relationship after the Break Up of the Soviet Union" in Chaufrin Gennady (eds.), *Russia and Asia: Emerging Security Agenda*, New York: SIPRA, OUP.
2. Gorbachev, Mikhail (1987), "*Perestroika: New Thinking for our Country and the World*", London: Collins. pp. 123-128.
3. Imam, Zafar (2001), "*Foreign Policy of Russia, 1991-2000*" New Delhi, New Horizon Publishers, pp.23-27.
4. *Summary of World Broadcasting*/SU/3416 B/5, December 22, 1998.
5. Chufrin, G. (1999), "*Russia and Asia: The emerging Security Agenda*", New York: Sipri Oxford University Press, pp.292-296.
6. Ibid.
7. Jingjie, L. (2000), "Pillars of the Sino-Russian Partnership", *Orbis,* 44(4): 527-539.
8. Saiget, Robert J. (2000), "*China, Russia beef up cooperation on Ethnic Separatism, Taiwan, Terrorism*", Hong Kong: AFP.
9. Moltz, Clay (1995), "Regional Tensions in Russo-China Rapprochement", *Asian Survey,* 35(36): pp.23-54.
10. Menon, Rajan and Charles E. Ziegler (2002), "The Balance of Power and US Foreign Policy Interest in the Russian Far East" in Thorton J and Ziegler E.C. (eds.), *Russia's Far East a region at risk,* London; University of a Washington Press, pp.17-23.

11. Lo, Bobo (2004), "Long Sunset of Strategic Partnership: Russia's Evolving China Policy", *International Affairs*, 50(2): 295-309.

12. Shaumian, T.L. (2003), "Geopolitical Changes in Central Asia and Positions of Russia, China and India" *China Report*, 38(3): 361-363.

10

INDO-VIETNAM RELATIONS: A GATEWAY TO SOUTH EAST ASIA

India-Vietnam relations have been exceptionally friendly and cordial since their foundations were laid by Prime Minister Nehru and President Ho Chi Minh more than 50 years ago. The traditionally close and cordial relations have their historical roots in the common struggle for liberation from foreign rule and the national struggle for independence. Jawaharlal Nehru was one of the first visitors to Vietnam after its victory against the French at Dien Bien Phu in 1954. President Ho Chi Minh went to India in February, 1958. President Rajendra Prasad visited Vietnam in 1959.

In recent times, political contacts have strengthened as reflected in several high-level visits by leaders from both sides. Trade and economic linkages continue to grow. India's thrust under the 'Look East' policy combined with Vietnam's growing engagement within the region and with India has paid rich dividends. Vietnam is an important regional partner in South East Asia. India and Vietnam closely cooperate in various regional forums such as ASEAN, East Asia Summit, Mekong Ganga Cooperation, Asia Europe Meeting (ASEM) besides UN and WTO.

India supported Vietnam's independence from France, opposed American involvement in the Vietnam War, and supported unification of Vietnam. During the Vietnam War, India supported the North, albeit not by conducting military hostilities against the South. This can be contrasted with the policies of the US, who strongly supported the South and engaged in military conflict with the North, albeit without issuing an official declaration of war. India and North Vietnam established official diplomatic relations in 1972 and have since maintained friendly relations, especially in wake of Vietnam's hostile relations with the People's Republic of China, with which India had some diplomatic disputes.

Vietnam is an important regional partner in South East Asia. India and Vietnam closely cooperate in various regional forums such as ASEAN, East Asia Summit, Mekong Ganga Cooperation, Asia Europe Meeting (ASEM). Converging long-term political, economic and strategic interests, aspirations and concerns have driven the partnership. This partnership will enable both countries to harness the vast potential of bilateral relations, drawing upon complementarities and each other's intrinsic strengths, and work together to address regional and global challenges. The evolving strategic partnership is meant for mutual benefit that would work together to meeting the common concerns for the long-term partnership and does not lead to alliance against any third country.

India and Vietnam experience commonalities in their relationship with China, which saw further convergence of interests and strengthening of mutual defence ties. Harsh Pant, Professor at King's College argues that India's foremost interest in Vietnam lies in the realm of defence. New Delhi looks at Vietnam as counterweight to China. Both countries are concerned with China's rise, for India it is China's increasing presence in the Indian Ocean and South Asia while Vietnam is alarmed by China's sovereignty claims in the South China Sea. Besides, China's growing military might is also a common concern.

The relationships between the two countries make a lot of sense when they share common interest- maritime security, fighting terrorism, security of the sea lanes of communications, piracy and natural disasters. Ever since India and Vietnam signed the New Strategic Partnership in 2007, there witnessed significant improvement in a multifaceted ties ranging from political and economic engagements, security and defence cooperation, science and technology and close cultural contacts. Despite Chinese objections, India and Vietnam went a step ahead to signing six agreements encompassing promote oil exploration in South China Sea, extradition treaty, deepen trade, security and strategic ties, etc. The visit of Vietnam President Truong Tan Sang's to India aims to affirm Vietnam's consistent policy of giving high priority to the strategic partnership with India and to promote the two countries' cooperation in all fields and at regional and international forums. What makes this relationship special is because of the close understanding that both countries share over the growing rise of China and its subsequent implication on the security of both countries.[1]

POLITICAL INTERACTIONS

In terms of political and diplomatic cooperation between India and Vietnam, the convergence of interests, once again tend to get focused on China. To pre-empt China apologists from disputing the above, attention needs to be drawn to the following worthwhile analysis of China:

> "Clearly it is both foolish and dangerous to depreciate China or to doubt its long term potential. Yet that very potential could well be threatening for other nations including US Pacific allies like Japan, Korea and Indonesia, not to mention countries like India and Vietnam, even should China not so intend. The Middle Kingdom's expansive territorial claims and pronounced

> self-absorption virtually guarantee that foreign anxieties will persist".[2]

The same author further amplifies the reasons for apprehensions about China, thus:

> "A major element in foreign apprehension about China is the pervasive uncertainty about its long term geostrategic intentions. Some of this is rooted in the unpredictability of Chinese politics, which have been extraordinarily volatile across the past half century and may well continue to be so. But such uncertainty is greatly intensified by the chronic lack of transparency in Chinese defence planning, weapons acquisitions and even defense budgeting".[3]

General Secretaries of CPV Le Duan (1984), Nguyen Van Linh (1989), Do Muoi (1992) and NongDucManh (2003) have visited India. During NongDucManh's visit to India, the two sides signed a Joint Declaration on the framework of comprehensive cooperation between India and Vietnam as they enter the 21st century. President Tran DucLuong visited India in 1999. Prime Ministers Pham Van Dong (1978, 1980), Vo Van Kiet (1997) and Nguyen Tan Dung (July 2007) have also visited India. During Nguyen Tan Dung's visit to India, the two sides signed a Joint Declaration to officially establish strategic partnership between the two countries. Chairman of the National Assembly of Vietnam visited India in 1994. Other important high-level visits during recent years include; visits by Foreign Minister of Vietnam Nguyen DyNien, Defence Minister General Pham Van Tra, and Fisheries Minister Ta Quang Ngoc in 2005; a Vietnamese delegation led by Former Vice President Nguyen ThiBinh attended Vietnam-India Friendship Festival in September 2007. President Rajendra Prasad visited Vietnam in 1959. Subsequently, President R. Venkatraman (1991) Vice-President K.R. Narayanan (1993), Prime Minister Rajiv Gandhi (1985, 1988), Prime Minister

Narsimha Rao (1994) and Prime Minister Atal Behari Vajpayee (2001) visited Vietnam. Speaker of Lok Sabha Somnath Chatterjee visited Vietnam in March, 2007. Indian Minister of Home Affairs Shiva Patel visited Vietnam in October, 2007.[4]

India granted the "Most Favoured Nation" status to Vietnam in 1975 and both nations signed a bilateral trade agreement in 1978 and the Bilateral Investment Promotion and Protection Agreement (BIPPA) on March 8, 1997. The Indo-Vietnam Joint Business Council has worked to promote trade and investment since 1993. In 2003, both nations promulgated a Joint Declaration on Comprehensive Cooperation when the General Secretary of the Communist Party of Vietnam NongDucManh visited India and both nations are negotiating a free trade agreement. In 2007, a fresh joint declaration was issued during the state visit of the Prime Minister of Vietnam Nguyen Tan Dung.

Bilateral trade has increased rapidly since the liberalisation of the economies of both Vietnam and India. India is the 13th largest exporter to Vietnam, with exports have grown steadily from $ 11.5 million in 1985-86 to $ 395.68 million by 2003. Vietnam's exports to India rose to $ 180 million, including agricultural products, handicrafts, textiles, electronics and other goods. Between 2001 and 2006, the volume of bilateral trade expanded at 20-30 per cent per annum to reach $ one billion by 2006. Continuing the rapid pace of growth, bilateral trade rose to $ 2.48 billion in the year 2008, 2 years ahead of the official target of reaching $ 2 Billion by 2008. India and Vietnam have also expanded cooperation in information technology, education and collaboration of the respective national space programmes.[5]

India attaches great importance to the development of its relations with Vietnam and move forward on the strategic partnership by adding more content in all areas. The year 2012 marked the 40th anniversary of the establishment of full diplomatic relations between India and Vietnam, the 5th anniversary of the India-Vietnam Strategic Partnership, and the 20th anniversary of partnership between India and ASEAN. The two sides celebrated it as the 'Year of Friendship between India and Vietnam'.

During the visit of Binh Minh, and after the 15th meeting of India-Vietnam Joint Commission, it transpired that the strategic partnership which included exchange of a cooperative agenda on bilateral relations and regional and global issues has been strengthened further. Salman Khurshid also testified to this commitment to the media. Both the leaders agreed to consolidate their activities and add greater content to the partnership and bilateral relations in the fields of defence and security, trade and investment, science and technology, information technology, capacity building and human resource development, agriculture, education and culture and other areas of common interest. The potentials are huge and both need to work together to tap into those opportunities.[6]

Seeking a more dynamic relationship with strategically-important Vietnam, external affairs minister Sushma Swaraj arrived here on Sunday for talks with the country's top leadership during which cooperation in defence, agriculture, pharmaceuticals and textiles would be in focus. The crucial three-day visit comes just days after Vietnam renewed India's lease of two oil blocks in South China Sea for another year, a move that could rile China. It also comes ahead of next month's visit by President Pranab Mukherjee.

ECONOMIC AND DEFENCE COOPERATION

Economic ties between the two countries have also expanded. Vietnam has received substantial Indian private sector investments. Bilateral trade has grown to $6.1 billion in 2012-13.

Both expect to cross the target of $7 billion by 2015. Investments by Indian companies totals about $936 million in 86 projects in sectors such as oil and gas exploration, mineral exploration and processing, sugar manufacturing, agro-chemicals, IT, and agricultural processing.

Vietnam has a lot to offer in terms of trade and investment. Vietnam supports Indian businesses to explore more opportunities in oil exploration, electricity, science and technology and agriculture. A vivid example is that Tata Power has won a $1.8 billion contract to build the 2X660 MW Long Phu Thermal 2 Power Project in SocTrang Province in southern Vietnam, despite strong competition from Korean and Russian companies, thus taking India from 40th to 12th biggest foreign investor to Vietnam.

Principle commodities: the major items of India's export to Vietnam were feed ingredients (37.38 %), Machinery and equipment (7.29%), Steel of all kinds (6.43%), pharmaceuticals (5.05%), cottons of all kinds (3.82%), leather and textile materials (2.72%), plastic materials (2.56%). India's imports (2008): Coal (14.08%), computer hardware and electronics goods (7.47%), Coffee (2.73%), Cinnamon (2.43%), Garment and textile (2.42%), pepper (2.32%), rubber (1.68%)

Investments into India: Vietnam's investment into India is still modest with one project of FPT in India at the capital of US$ 0.15 million only.

Investment from India: (Volume/area) According to the Vietnamese official statistics, as of December 2008, India has 30 investment projects in Vietnam with total registered capital of US$185.47 million. Indian companies are investing in oil and gas exploitation, mineral exploitation and processing, sugar manufacturing, agro-chemicals, IT, and agricultural processing. Due to the economic crisis, Essar Steel withdrew their project for setting up a cold rolled steel plant in Ba RiaVung Tau. Tata Steel has planned to invest more than US$4.5 billion to set up a steel complex in Ha Tinh, Vietnam. Once it obtains the licenses for setting up their steel complex in Ha Tinh Province, India will rank among the top four foreign investors in Vietnam.[7]

A major turning point was reached in November 2007 when India and Vietnam raised their bilateral relations to a strategic partnership during the official visit to India by Vietnam's Prime Minister Nguyen Tan Dung. The Joint Declaration on Strategic Partnership included thirty-three points and mapped out cooperation in five major areas: political, defense and security; closer economic cooperation and commercial engagement; science and technology; cultural and technical; and multilateral and regional cooperation.

The Joint Declaration set out six areas of cooperation under the political, defense and security heading: First, India and Vietnam agreed to hold a Strategic Dialogue at deputy minister level. These have been held annually since 2007. Second, India and Vietnam agreed to place future emphasis on defense supplies, joint projects, training cooperation and intelligence exchanges. Third, India and Vietnam agreed to enhance contacts and exchange visits between their defense and security establishments. Fourth, in light of shared maritime interests, India and Vietnam agreed to enhance cooperation in capacity building, technical assistance and information sharing between relevant agencies with a particular attention to security of sea-lanes, anti-piracy, prevention of pollution and search and rescue. Fifth, India and Vietnam resolved to strengthen bilateral cooperation to combat terrorism and to promote cooperation in cyber security. Sixth, India and Vietnam agreed to cooperate to address non-traditional security issues including drug trafficking, natural disasters, climate change, energy security, HIV/AIDS, avian influenza and other epidemics.

CONCLUSION

India and Vietnam are both geostrategically important countries, vital to all major nations with a stake in the freedom of high seas. Both countries share disputed borders with China and both have been subjected to military aggression by China. A highly proud and nationalistic country with rugged determination and plucky courage, Vietnam enjoys the unique distinction in the second half of the twentieth century of having inflicted military defeats on three major powers i.e. France, USA and China.

Current indicators in the Asia Pacific security environment point towards China's emergence as a major strategic destabilising entity, bent on challenging United States predominance in the region. It also claims South and South East Asia as its natural and historical area of influence. China in its pursuance of its power aspirations stands guilty of strategically destabilising India's and Vietnam's neighbourhood i.e. Pakistan and Cambodia earlier. The changing international security environment also presents an ironic picture where Russia which earlier stood by India and Vietnam in terms of strategic needs, today is engaged in building up the military might and force projection capabilities of China- a threat perception common to both India and Vietnam.

NOTES

1. Mohammad Samir Hussain & Vinayak Subhash Lashkar, *India-Vietnam Strategic Partnership Getting Stronger*, 3 December 2011.
2. Kent E. Calder, '*Asia's Deadly Triangle: How Arms, Energy and Growth Threatens to Destabilise Asia Pacific*'. London, Nicholas Brealy Publishing, 1996, p. 216.
3. Ibid.
4. India-Vietnam Relations at http://www.vietnamconsulate-mumbai.org/cn/nr070521165956/news_object_view?

newsPath=/vnemb.vn/cn_vakv/ca_tbd/nr040819102240/ns071207145643

5. Vietnam-India Relations at http://inchamhanoi.org/cms/index.php?option=com_content&view=article&id=116&Itemid=111.
6. Rajaram Panda, India & Vietnam: Defence Cooperation, Economic Ties and a Strategic Partnership at http://www.ipcs.org/article/india/ipcs-special-commentary-india-vietnam-defence-cooperation-economic-ties-and-4080.html
7. ibid.

11

INDIA-RUSSIA-CHINA AND THE RECENT UKRAINE CRISIS

Russia being the largest country and China being the most populous country on the planet, both collectively are undoubtedly the two major powers of the international system. Russia being the successor of erstwhile Soviet Union wishes to regain the role once Soviet Union enjoyed whereas China being a communist country is also showing signs of new ambitions based on her history, population and military power and also her emergence as an important international economic actor. Relations between Moscow and Beijing have gone full circle in the past half century, from alliance to containment and now to strategic partnership.

To understand the ebbs and flows in Moscow's China policy it is necessary to look into the Soviet history. History which is characterized as chronicle of the past provides the solid base for building up future relationships. In International Relations, there is no permanent 'friend or foe', today's bitter enemy can become tomorrow's staunchest ally. It is interest which runs supreme, and Russia and China are not exceptions to it. Despite being communist countries both Soviet Union and China counted each other as enemy number one and targeted each other with their nuclear weapons. But today Russia and China no longer consider each other as enemy and both countries have developed "very deep" relations in the strategic field.

China has the largest population in the world, while Russia is the largest nation in terms of territory. Both are permanent members of the United Nations Security Council. Obviously, the significance of Sino-Russian relations extends far beyond the interests of the two nations. It also affects the stability of Asia and the world at large.

Soviet-China relations before disintegration of USSR were characterized by a number of ups and downs. In February 1950 just four months after establishment of the PRC the two countries signed the Treaty of Friendship, Alliance and Mutual Cooperation. The first half of the 1950s was the honeymoon period. However, by the late 1950s differences in national interest and ideology emerged leading to serious disputes in early 1960s which developed in to acute conflict and border clashes in 1969. Hence in the late 1960s and 1970s the USSR regarded China as one of its main rivals and stationed approximately one million troops and one third of its SS-20 intermediate-range ballistic missile along the Sino-Soviet border, threatening to make a 'surgical' first strike on China', nuclear bases. Under serious threat, China had to prepare for a military intrusion from north. However, in 1980s two countries came to realization that these were not in the interests of either side and they made effort to alleviate the situation. These efforts resulted in the normalization of the relations during a state visit to Beijing by the then Soviet President Mikhail Gorbachev in May 1989. (Qimao, 1999, pp. 206-207).[1]

However, the tense relationship of two communist giants eased with the rise of Gorbachev as the Secretary General of CPSU in 1985. He made epoch making changes in the Soviet history by introducing 'Perestroika' and 'Glasnost'. Some have described him in Soviet history as 'reformer in hurry'. In the realm of international relations he introduced 'New Thinking' which stressed on a deidoelogised foreign policy.

In the words of Gorbachev, 'New Thinking' stood for–

> "We need normal international conditions for our internal progress. But we want a world free of war, without arms races, nuclear weapons and violence, not only because this is an optimal condition for our internal development". (Gorbachev, 1987: 10-12).[2]

Under the slogan of 'New Thinking' Gorbachev's foreign policy was based on shared moral and ethical principles to solve global problems rather than on Marxist-Leninist concept of irreconcilable conflict between capitalism and communism. The historic meeting between Deng and Gorbachev lead to resolution of many outstanding problems between the two. The border dispute was resolved by demarcating the Usuri River; trade was opened up and threat perceptions to a large extent eliminated.

While relations were improving between the two countries, the Soviet Union itself collapsed in December 1991. It was a historical event of global significance. Relations between the two neighbors, Russia and China could not therefore, escape the global effects of this historical event. (Imam, 2001:97-100).[3]

In December 1998, he made an official visit to India. Primakov visited India at the time when India was internationally isolated after conducting five nuclear tests a few months back. He proposed to formulate a triangle between three major Eurasian countries Russia-China-India to counter US hegemony and unilateralism in the world politics. According to him 'Russia favours the creation of a Moscow-Beijing-Delhi triangle and also it would be a good idea.'[4] On 15 September 1992 President Yeltsin signed the "Order of Russian Federation's Relations with China" and reaffirmed that -

a) there is only one China;

b) the PRC government is the sole legal representative of China;

c) Taiwan is the part of China; and

d) Russia will never establish official relation with Taiwan.[5]

On the question of separatism, religious extremism and terrorism both countries share common view today. In March 1995, Chinese president Jiang Zemin visited Moscow to participate in the celebration of 50th anniversary of victory over Fascism. In an agreement between the two, Russia reiterated its support to China on Taiwan issue and on its part; China extended its full support to Russia in dealing with the Chechnya problem.[6]

Both Russia and China are opposed to US hegemonic policies and favour a multi-polar world order with different power centers. In April 1997 Chinese president Jiang Zemin paid another visit to Moscow on April 23 and the two countries issued a joint statement on the multipolarisation of the world and establishment of new international order. The statement rejected hegemony and power politics, and stated that 'Cold War' mentality must also be abandoned and bloc politics opposed. They called for preservation of the Anti Ballistic Missile (ABM) Treaty of 1972 between Soviet Union and USA and they supported lifting the UN Security Council sanctions against Saddam Hussain regime in Iraq.

Russia and China shared views on increasing numbers of international issues in the light of the challenge from the USA and its allies. In the first year after the collapse of Soviet Union, Russia adopted a pro-western foreign policy, hoping for economic aid from the west and for recognition as a strong power and an equal partner of the USA. Soon, however, Russia was deeply disappointed by the level of western aid. Moreover, it faced fierce competition from the west over the sphere of influence in the newly independent states. These realities forced Russia to switch to an 'Omni-directional' or 'two headed eagle' (Russia's national emblem) policy, pursuing relations with countries of both the East and the West. Especially after 1995, under heavy pressure from NATO's eastward expansion led by the USA, Russia attached greater importance to its relations with China, India and other Asian countries. Russia termed Asian countries as 'natural allies', among which China got the top priority. Despite odd relationship in the past both countries evolved consensus on various national and international issues.

AREAS OF COMMON CONCERN BETWEEN RUSSIA AND CHINA

On the question of separatism, religious extremism and terrorism both countries share common view today. In March 1995, Chinese president Jiang Zemin visited Moscow to participate in the celebration of 50th anniversary of victory over Fascism. In an agreement between the two, Russia reiterated its support to China on Taiwan issue and on its part, China extended its full support to Russia in dealing with the Chechnya problem.

Both Russia and China are opposed to US hegemonic policies and favour a multi-polar world order with different power centres. In April 1997 Chinese president Zemin paid another visit to Moscow on April 23 and the two countries issued a joint statement on the multipolarisation of the world and establishment of new international order. The statement rejected hegemony and power politics, and stated that 'Cold War' mentality must also be abandoned and bloc politics opposed. They called for preservation of the Anti Ballistic Missile (ABM) Treaty of 1972 between Soviet Union and USA and they supported lifting the UN Security Council sanctions against Saddam Hussain regime in Iraq.

On 24 November 1998, when Jiang Zemin paid another crucial visit to Russia, the Russian side reaffirmed its "four nos" position. The basic thrust of which was - no support for any conception of 'Taiwan's independence; no acceptance of the position of 'two Chinas' or 'one China and one Taiwan'; no support for Taiwan's participation in the UNO or other international organizations in which only sovereign states participated; and no sales of weapon to Taiwan.[7]

NATO bombing on Yugoslavia from March end to mid June 1999 without getting any authorization from the UN Security Council sent shock waves in both Russia and China and tended to bring together the two in joint opposition of NATO action. NATO's intervention on 'humanitarian ground' was an ominous development. Being multi-ethnic and multi-religious states, both Russia and China have their own separatist movements, Russia in Chechnya and China in Taiwan, Tibet and Xinjiang province. Being a Slav country, Yugoslavia was traditionally friend of Russia and attack on it, aroused Russian sentiments in the form of massive protests in Moscow.[8]

Both Russia and China have greater common ground to chalk out their strategy to deal with outside world compare to the issues on which they are at odds. Russo-Chinese link is built on a number of shared concerns which includes:

- The struggle against US led unipolar hegemonism;
- Unilateral humanitarian interventionism by passing UN;
- Islamic extremism and secessionism;
- Opposition to NATO enlargement and inter-reference in the internal matters;
- Opposition to NMD(National Missile Defence) and TMD (Theatre Missile Defence);
- Opposition to US withdrawal from ABM Treaty of 1972;
- Restructuring of UN;
- Opposition to US led NATO forces to stay longer in the Central Asian region;
- Near mutual acceptance of Russia's hegemony as a guarantor of order in Eurasia;

- Strengthening the SCO;
- Working together in the multilateral forums like WTO etc.

UKRAINE CRISIS 2014

The Ukraine crisis is an ongoing international crisis involving Russia and Ukraine, and centered on the peninsula of Crimea–a region of Ukraine that comprises a majority of ethnic Russians but that has undergone dramatic changes in its population for the past 200 years. The region is also bases. The crisis unfolded in late February 2014 in the aftermath of the 2014 Ukrainian revolution: after months of protests by Euromaidan and days of armed violence by government forces in the Ukrainian capital of Kiev, the president of Ukraine was impeached in a procedure that Russia contends was done improperly and was, therefore, according to Russia, "unconstitutional" and "illegal".[9]

Beginning on 27 February 2014, unidentified pro-Russian troops seized control of the majority of the Crimean peninsula in the southeastern area of Ukraine. The region has fallen into crisis as a result of the uncertain outcome of the 2014 Ukrainian revolution, and Russia's apparent seizure of this strategic peninsula.

The Crimean Peninsula is Russia's strategic link to the Mediterranean Sea, Black Sea, and the Balkans. The Russian government maintains that its involvement in Crimea seeks to protect ethnic Russians in the region against Ukrainian authorities.[10] Russia does not recognize the newly installed interim government in Ukraine, instead considering now-ousted-President Viktor Yanukovych Ukraine's legitimate leader. Russia states that Yanukovych asked Russia to intervene in Ukraine militarily to maintain peace and order.[11] Russia claims that its regular forcesare not involved in the present stand-off, and also asserts that use of force for the purposes of humanitarian intervention in Ukraine, has not yet occurred.[12]

The Ukrainian response so far has been muted as its leaders seek diplomatic solutions, with military reaction on their part limited to a mobilization of Ukraine's armed forces and reserves. Russia, however, has vowed that its troops will stay until the political situation has been "normalised".Internally, Crimea is scheduled to hold a referendum on 16 March 2014 on whether Crimea shall join the Russian Federation or remain part of Ukraine. The events have caused alarm among the Crimean Tatar ethnic group, whose members were deported *en masse* to Central Asia in 1944 under orders from Joseph Stalin, claiming a huge death toll.

At the international level, the United States, the United Kingdom, France, Germany, Italy, Poland, Canada, Turkey and the European Union condemned Russia, accusing it of breaking international law and violating Ukrainian sovereignty. China neither publicly supported nor criticized Russia while showing support for Ukraine's territorial integrity. India considers that Russia has legitimate interests in Crimea.[13]

At the same time, the Port of Sevastopol and the town of Kacha are located in Sevastopol, a city in the southwestern area of the peninsula that does not belong to Crimea administratively. Both locations hold key strategic value for Russia, economically and militarily. The Port of Sevastopol, which Russia currently leases from Ukraine, is considered a key hold for maritime routes between the Black Sea and the Sea of Marmara, and by extension the Mediterranean Sea and Atlantic Ocean. It is also one of the few warm deepwater ports in the Black Sea available to Russia. As the Ukrainian revolution unfolded–and as the newly installed Ukrainian government began to distance itself from Russia–Russia felt that its access to the port and its military bases in the Crimean peninsula were in jeopardy.[14] Ensuring access to the port and Russia's military bases in the Crimean peninsula are considered one of the main factors that sparked Russia's military intervention. On the other hand, the town of Kacha serves as military headquarters for Russia's 25th Independent Anti-submarine Helicopter Regiment (25th AHR) and the 917th Independent Composite Air Regiment (917th ICAR) of the Black Sea Fleet Naval Air Force.

Responding to the recent Ukraine crisis Chinese president Xi Jinping has urged a *political solution* to the crisis in Ukraine and for all parties to exercise calm and restraint, during separate telephone calls with US president Barack Obama and German chancellor Angela Merkel. "The situation in Ukraine is extremely complex, and what is most urgent is for all sides to remain calm and exercise restraint to avoid an escalation in tensions," China's foreign ministry on Monday cited Xi as telling Obama. "Political and diplomatic routes must be used to resolve the crisis," Xi added. [15]

The People's Daily, one of China's top-selling newspapers, condemned what it viewed as attempts by Washington and Europe to shape the Ukraine's future following the ouster of its Kremlin-backed President Viktor Yanukovych last week. "The theories related to politics, economics and security during the Cold War period is still influencing many people on their concept of the world, and some Western people are still imbued with resentment towards Russia." It called on Western countries to "abandon their outdated thinking" and focus more on cooperation. "Ridding the shackles of the Cold War mentality will reduce unnecessary confrontation, thereby allowing for a smoother transition in international relations," it said.[16]

China also has a growing trade relationship with Ukraine and imports arms from the former Soviet state, the world's fourth-leading arms exporter. Beijing purchased its first aircraft carrier from Ukraine. But Russia remains a far more important partner for China both in terms of trade and geopolitics. Beijing and Moscow often share positions at the United Nations Security Council, where they are both permanent members with veto powers, and Russia is an important supplier of oil and natural gas to China. On Wednesday, Global Times, a nationalistic newspaper, ran an editorial urging Beijing to stand by its neighbor Russia. "We prefer to agree with voices supporting Russia," Global Times said. "Russia has been resisting the eastward trend of Western forces in Ukraine, which is important not only to its own fate but also to China's strategic interests."[17]

To conclude, the crisis in Ukraine has strengthened Russia's strategic partnership with China, says Vassily Kashin from the Moscow-based Center for Analysis of Strategies and Technologies, according to Vedomosti, a Russian-language business daily. China is currently the only nation on the UN Security Council to retain cordial relations with Russia after the latter moved its troops into Crimea, said Kashin. Even if the United States and other NATO countries do not impose sanctions against Russia, it will be very difficult for Moscow to continue normal economic relations with Western countries.

As Japan may become the only nation of the Group of Eight which will still seek cooperation with Russia, China's position as one of Russia's only trusted allies can be strengthened. Russia will seek to speed up its negotiations with China regarding both military and economic cooperation pacts, Kashin said, specifically suggesting that Moscow should sign contracts on the provision of natural gas and the sale of the Sukhoi Su-35 fighter to China before President Vladimir Putin embarks on a visit to Beijing in May. To demonstrate Russia's sincerity towards China, it is believed that the advanced Su-35 fighters may be turned over to China earlier than expected. Russia may also launch more joint military exercises and even expand its military relationship with China, according to Kashin, who told Vedomosti that China may become the only beneficiary of the Ukraine crisis.

NOTES

1. Qimao, Chen (1999), "Sino-Russian Relationship after the Break Up of the Soviet Union" in Chaufrin Gennady (eds.), *Russia and Asia: Emerging Security Agenda,* New York: SIPRA, OUP.
2. Gorbachev, Mikhail (1987), "*Perestroika: New Thinking for our Country and the World* ", London: Collins. pp.123-128.
3. Imam, Zafar (2001), "*Foreign Policy of Russia, 1991-2000*" New Delhi, New Horizon Publishers, pp.23-27.
4. *Summary of World Broadcasting* /SU/3416 B/5, December 22, 1998.
5. Chufrin, G. (1999), "*Russia and Asia: The emerging Security Agenda*", New York: Sipri Oxford University Press, pp.292-296.
6. Ibid.
7. Jingjie, L. (2000), "Pillars of the Sino-Russian Partnership", *Orbis,* 44(4): 527-539.
8. Saiget, Robert J. (2000), "*China, Russia beef up cooperation on Ethnic Separatism, Taiwan, Terrorism*", Hong Kong: AFP, pp.23-28.
9. Lally, Kathy; Englund, Will (4 March 2014). "Putin defends Ukraine stance, cites lawlessness". *The Washington Post.*
10. Radyuhin, Vladimir (1 March 2014). "Russian Parliament approves use of army in Ukraine". *The Hindu.*
11. Borger, Julian (4 March 2014). "Putin offers Ukraine olive branches delivered by Russian tanks". *The Guardian.*
12. "Ukraine crisis: Crimea MPs vote to join Russia". BBC News. 6 March 2014.

13. FlorCruz, Jaime (6 March 2014). "Russia may find ally in China – albeit a passive one for now". CNN.
14. Hille, Kathrin (27 February 2014). "Ukrainian port is key to Russia's naval power". *Financial Times.*
15. China Slams West Over 'Cold War Mentality' Amid Ukraine Crisis *By Alexander Smith http://www.nbcnews. com/storyline/ukraine-crisis/china-slams-west-over-cold-war-mentality-amid-ukraine-crisis-n39871*
16. Russia may find ally in China – albeit a passive one for now" By Jaime A. FlorCruz and Paul Armstrong, CNN March 6, 2014 http://edition.cnn.com/2014/03/05/world/asia/china-russia-ukraine-analysis/
17. http://www.nbcnews.com/storyline/ukraine-crisis/china-slams-west-over-cold-war-mentality-amid-ukraine-crisis-n39871
18. "Ukraine crisis strengthens China's partnership with Russia" http://www.wantchinatimes.com/news-subclass-cnt.aspx?id=20140307000099&cid=1101.

12

INDO-IRAN RELATIONS: WITH REFERENCE TO ITS NUCLEAR PROGRAMME

On December 8, 1953, President Eisenhower delivered his "*Atoms for Peace*" speech before the United Nations General Assembly. In his speech, Eisenhower remarked that "...if a danger exists in the world, it is a danger shared by all; and equally, that if hope exists in the mind of one nation, that hope should be shared by all." Eisenhower recognized the paradoxical danger and promise offered by the atomic age: on one hand, the militarization of the atom for nuclear weapons and, on the other hand, the peaceful utilization of the atom to produce energy. Atoms for Peace provided technology and educational resources for states wanting civilian nuclear programs.[1] As a participant in the program, Atoms for Peace laid the foundation for Iran's nuclear program beginning in 1957. Today, given the concerns about Iran's nuclear program, it is worthwhile to examine how much Atoms for Peace contributed to Iran's nuclear program, specifically the elements that have concerned the international community most.

The nuclear program of Iran was launched in the 1950s with the help of the United States as part of the Atoms for Peace program. The participation of the United States and Western European governments in Iran's nuclear program continued until the 1979 Iranian Revolution that toppled the Shah of Iran. After the 1979 revolution, a clandestine nuclear weapons research program was disbanded by Ayatollah Khomeini (1902-1989), who considered such weapons as haram (sinful) and forbidden as unethical and immoral in Muslim jurisprudence. Iran has signed treaties repudiating the possession of weapons of mass destruction including the Biological Weapons Convention, the Chemical Weapons Convention, and the Nuclear Non-Proliferation Treaty (NPT).[2]

Iran's nuclear program has included several research sites, two uranium mines, a research reactor, and uranium processing facilities that include three known plants. Iran's first nuclear power plant, Bushehr I reactor was complete with major assistance of Russian government agency Rosatom and officially opened on 12 September 2011.[3] Iran has announced that it is working on a new 360 MW nuclear power plant to be located in Darkhovin. The Russian engineering contractor Atomenergoprom said the Bushehr Nuclear Power Plant would reach full capacity by the end of 2012. Iran has also indicated that it will seek more medium-sized nuclear power plants and uranium mines in the future.

In a 2007 National Intelligence Estimate, the United States Intelligence Community assessed that Iran had ended all "nuclear weapon design and weaponization work" in 2003. In 2012, U.S. intelligence agencies reported that Iran was pursuing research that could enable it to produce nuclear weapons, but was not attempting to do so.

In November 2011, the International Atomic Energy Agency (IAEA) Board of Governors criticized Iran after an IAEA report concluded that before 2003 Iran likely had undertaken research and experiments geared to developing a nuclear weapons capability. The IAEA report details allegations that Iran conducted studies related to nuclear weapons design, including detonator development, the multiple-point initiation of high explosives, and experiments involving nuclear payload integration into a missile delivery vehicle. A number of Western nuclear experts have stated there was very little new in the report, that it primarily concerned Iranian activities prior to 2003 and that media reports exaggerated its significance. Iran threatened to reduce its cooperation with the IAEA.[4]

One of the central ironies about Iran is that its controversial nuclear program has become a defining political issue, even though many of the program's details remain shrouded in secrecy. Tehran is public about its quest to acquire peaceful nuclear energy to serve a population that has doubled since the 1979 revolution. But the theocracy vehemently denies any interest in developing a nuclear weapon–even as it boasts about its growing ability to enrich uranium, a capability that can be used to generate power or for a weapons program.

Technically, Iran does not yet need to enrich, since Russia is providing the fuel for the new reactor it built in Bushehr. Tehran counters that it has the right to enrich uranium as a signatory to the Nuclear Non-Proliferation Treaty (NPT). It also intends to build additional reactors and says it does not want to be dependent on foreign powers for fuel. But since 2002, international suspicions about Iran's long-term intentions have deepened because of revelations–by other governments or Iranian exile groups–that it has built secret facilities that could be used for a weapons program. The Islamic Republic has only acknowledged them after the fact. And as of mid-2010, Tehran had still not provided full details about its programs to the International Atomic Energy Agency, as it is also required to do under the NPT.[6]

Iran appears to have wanted to start a secret program for several reasons, from its experience during Iran-Iraq War to the fact that five of the world's nine nuclear powers are nearby or on its borders. At the same time, it also appears to have adopted a strategy of nuclear hedging–or maintaining the option of a weapons program, while trying to remain within the nuclear treaty. But the disclosures between 2002 and 2009 about its secret facilities and the subsequent international pressure have turned the program into a major political issue at home. In the already tense environment after disputed 2009 presidential elections, Iran's nuclear program became a political issue that pittedthe hardliner regime against both conservatives and the Green Movement opposition.

IRANIAN JUSTIFICATION FOR PEACEFUL USE OF NUCLEAR TECHNOLOGY

The Iranians believe that concerns about nuclear weapons proliferation are pretextual, and any suspension of enrichment is simply intended to ultimately deprive Iran of the right to have an independent nuclear technology:

> "We had a suspension for two years and on and off negotiations for three ... Accusing Iran of having "the intention" of acquiring nuclear weapons has, since the early 1980s, been a tool used to deprive Iran of any nuclear technology, even a light water reactor or fuel for the American-built research reactor ... the United States and EU+3 never even took the trouble of studying various Iranian proposals: they were – from the very beginning – bent on abusing this Council and the threat of referral and sanctions as an instrument of pressure to compel Iran to abandon the exercise of its NPT guaranteed right to peaceful nuclear technology".[6]

Iran says that its inalienable right to peaceful nuclear technology has been the subject of "the most extensive and intensive campaign of denial, obstruction, intervention and misinformation" and that the international community has been subject to "bias, politicized and exaggerated information" on the Iranian nuclear program and activities.[7]

After the 1979 Iranian Revolution, Iran informed the International Atomic Energy Agency (IAEA) of its plans to restart its nuclear program using indigenously made nuclear fuel, and in 1983 the IAEA planned to provide assistance in uranium conversion (not enrichment) to Iran under its Technical Assistance Program, until the program was terminated under US pressure. An IAEA report at the time stated clearly that its aim was to "contribute to the formation of local expertise and manpower needed to sustain an ambitious program in the field of nuclear power reactor technology and fuel cycle technology". Iran's enrichment program was openly discussed on national radio in the early 1980s, and IAEA inspectors were even invited to visit Iran's uranium mines in 1992.

Iran argues that it disclosed information about its programs in which "in nearly all cases, it was not any way obliged to disclose in accordance with its obligations under its safeguards agreement with the IAEA." Iran says its voluntary confidence building measures were only "reciprocated by broken promises and expanded requests" and that the EU3 "simply wanted prolonged and fruitless negotiations" to inhibit Iran from exercising its inalienable right to peaceful nuclear technology.

Iran says it has suggested to the EU3 to ask the IAEA to develop monitoring modalities for Iran's enrichment program as objective guarantees to ensure that Iran's nuclear program will remain exclusively for peaceful purposes and has also provided its own set of Western suggested modalities to the Agency. However, Iran says it will not suspend its enrichment because "it would further be deprived from its inalienable right to work on nuclear fuel cycle, with the aim of producing required fuels for its research reactors and nuclear power plants."

Iran also believes it has a legal right to enrich uranium for peaceful purposes under the Nuclear Non-Proliferation Treaty (NPT), a right which in 2005 the US and the EU-3 began to assert had been forfeited by a clandestine nuclear program that came to light in 2002. Iranian politicians compare its treatment as a signatory to the NPT with three nuclear-armed nations that have not signed the NPT: Israel, India, and Pakistan. India and Pakistan developed an indigenous nuclear weapons capability, and it is widely suspected that Israel has as well: Israel by 1966, India by 1974, and Pakistan by 1990.[9]

The Iranian authorities assert that they cannot simply trust the United States or Europe to provide Iran with nuclear energy fuel, and point to a long series of agreements, contracts and treaty obligations which were not fulfilled. Developing nations say they do not want to give up their rights to uranium enrichment and do not trust the United States or other nuclear countries to be consistent suppliers of the nuclear material they would need to run their power plants.

Some have argued that there is a double standard between the treatment of Iran, which was reported to the Security Council for undeclared enrichment and reprocessing activities, and South Korea, which had failed to report enrichment and reprocessing experiments but was not found in non-compliance.[8] In South Korea's case, issues were reported by the IAEA Secretariat but the IAEA Board of Governors did not make a formal finding of non-compliance. In making its decision, the Board said "there is no indication that the undeclared experiments have continued" and observed that the "Republic of Korea has an Additional Protocol in force and that developments in the Republic of Korea demonstrate the utility of the Additional Protocol. Pierre Goldschmidt, former head of the department of safeguards at the IAEA, has called on the Board of Governors to adopt generic resolutions which would apply to all states in such circumstances and has argued "political considerations played a dominant role in the board's decision" to not make a formal finding of non-compliance.

OPPOSITION TO IRAN'S NUCLEAR PROGRAMME BY US LED WEST

President Bush said that Iran's pursuit of nuclear weapons could trigger "World War III", while in 2007 Undersecretary of State Nicholas Burns warned that Iran may be seeking a nuclear weapons capability.[10]

In June, IAEA director Mohammad El Baradei suggested that Iran should be allowed limited uranium enrichment under strict supervision of the IAEA. His remarks were formally criticised by Nicholas Burns, the US Under-Secretary of State, who said: "We are not going to agree to accept limited enrichment." El Baradei later criticized the US position and said, "I have seen the Iranians ready to accept putting a cap on their enrichment program in terms of tens of centrifuges, and then in terms of hundreds of centrifuges. But nobody even tried to engage them on these offers. Now Iran has 5,000 centrifuges. The line was, 'Iran will buckle under pressure.' But this issue has become so ingrained in the Iranian soul as a matter of national pride."[11]

In September, Undersecretary of State Nicholas Burns called for the UN Security Council members and US allies to help push for a third round of sanctions against Iran over the nuclear program. Meanwhile, French Foreign Minister Bernard Kouchner said that although the international community is focused on diplomacy, the international community should prepare for the possibility of war if Iran obtains nuclear weapons.

In the same month, French Foreign Minister Bernard Kouchner, while discussing penalties that Europe might impose on Iran, said that they could be "economic sanctions regarding financial movements... Our German friends proposed this. We discussed it a few days ago. The international community's demand is simple: They must stop enriching uranium. Our Iranian friends want to create, they say, civilian nuclear energy. They have the right to that, but all that they are doing proves the contrary. That is why we are worried. In November, President Bush said that Iran has a sovereign right to civilian nuclear technology, but expressed concern that the enrichment process could lead to a nuclear weapon. Bush also expressed concerns over Iranian leaders' threats against Israel, and said that all options, including a military option, were "on the table" in regards to preventing Iran from obtaining nuclear weapons.[12]

Tensions were raised by media reports of an Israeli air incursion over north-eastern Syria on 6 September 2007. One U.S. official said the attack hit weapons heading for the Lebanese militant group Hezbollah, an ally of Syria and Iran, but there also has been speculation the Israelis hit a nascent nuclear facility or were studying routes for a possible future strike on Iran. Others suspect Israel was performing an intelligence operation for the U.S.[13]

On 15 June 2013, Hassan Rohani won the Iranian presidential election and assumed office on 3 August 2013. Rouhani is considered "the most moderate and outward-looking of the presidential candidates deemed fit to contest the election by the supreme leader, Ayatollah Ali Khamenei" and subsequently "has raised hopes for a nuclear deal between Iran and the international community."[14] The Economist, however, argues that neither a moderate Iranian president, nor sanctions, or military threats will divert Iran from attaining the capability to rapidly "produce enough weapons-grade uranium for one or more bombs before the IAEA or Western intelligence agencies would even know it had done so.

Rohani's election means the next round of negotiations will be conducted in a better atmosphere. But to what end? ... For Iran, the continuation of talks is a means of getting some easing of sanctions in exchange for concession that will have little impact on its nuclear program." The newspaper thinks that a more accommodating Iranian president can be a trap for the international community as well as an opportunity for it. Rohani can improve relations with the West through constructive engagement and ultimately ease the burden of sanctions on Iran. But Iran could take advantage of its rosier international standing by continuing to enrich uranium and achieve a breakout capability. Abulof argues that "the 2013 election of Hassan Rouhani as president demonstrated the regime's legitimacy crisis, while upping the ante for both mitigating the crisis and exacerbating it. If the latter transpires, the regime may opt to further escalate its diversionary nuclear strategies.[15]

COMPREHENSIVE AGREEMENT ON THE IRANIAN NUCLEAR PROGRAMME

The comprehensive agreement on the Iranian nuclear programme is a topic of the final phase of the negotiations among Iran and the P5+1 – United States, Russia, China, France, United Kingdom and Germany – plus the European Union regarding Iran's nuclear program. The term "P5+1" refers to the five permanent members of the United Nations Security Council, China, France, Russia, the United Kingdom, and the United States, plus Germany.

The prospective agreement is to be achieved based on the 24 November 2013 Geneva agreement, officially titled the Joint Plan of Action (JPA). The Geneva agreement was an interim deal, in which Iran agreed to roll back parts of its nuclear program in exchange for relief from some sanctions and which went into effect on 20 January 2014. The parties agreed to extend their talks with a first extension deadline on 24 November 2014 and a second extension deadline set to 1 July 2015.[16]

Based on the March/April 2015 negotiations on Iran nuclear deal framework, completed on 2 April 2015, Iran agreed tentatively to accept significant restrictions on its nuclear program, all of which would last for at least a decade and some longer, and to submit to an increased intensity of international inspections under a framework deal. These details are to be negotiated by the end of June 2015. Based on the March/April 2015 negotiations on Iran nuclear deal framework, completed on 2 April 2015, Iran agreed tentatively to accept significant restrictions on its nuclear program, all of which would last for at least a decade and some longer, and to submit to an increased intensity of international inspections under a framework deal. These details are to be negotiated by the end of June 2015.

According to the joint statement,

> "As Iran pursues a peaceful nuclear program, Iran's enrichment capacity, enrichment level and stockpile will be limited for specific durations and there will be no other enrichment facility than Natanz. Fordow will be converted into a nuclear physics and technology center and Iran's research and development on centrifuges will be carried out based on a mutually agreed framework. A modernized heavy water research reactor in Arak will be redesigned and rebuilt with the assistance of an international joint venture that will not produce weapons-grade plutonium. There will be no nuclear reprocessing, and spent fuel will be exported. Monitor the provisions of the JCPOA including implementation of the modified code 3.1 and provision of the additional protocol, will be done based on a set of measures. To clarify past and present issues regarding Iran's nuclear program, the International Atomic Energy Agency will be permitted the use of modern technologies and will have announced

access through agreed procedures. Iran will take part in international cooperation in the field of civilian nuclear energy including supply of power and research reactors as well as nuclear safety and security. The European Union will terminate the implementation of all nuclear-related economic and financial sanctions and the United States will cease the application of all nuclear-related secondary economic and financial sanctions simultaneously with the IAEA-verified implementation by Iran of its key nuclear commitments. To endorse the Joint Comprehensive Plan of Action (JCPOA), a new UN Security Council resolution will be approved which terminates all previous nuclear-related resolutions, and incorporate certain restrictive measures for a mutually agreed period of time."[17]

CONCLUSION

Overall, if the deal does what it is meant to, it should make the region a bit safer, heading off, at least for now, the prospect of a dangerous nuclear arms race involving Saudi Arabia and perhaps Egypt and Turkey as well. Israel will surely be more secure if Iran's breakout capability is extended to over a year from just a month or so and its whole nuclear programme becomes vastly more transparent. What a deal is most unlikely to do, at least in the short-term, is to make Iran a more cooperative, less aggrandising player in the region's geopolitics. If Iran feels richer, there is a risk it may actually interfere more. This is an arms-control deal between adversaries, not a friendship hug. Interests will continue to diverge between Iran and the West. Just possibly, however, if Iran's economy becomes re-integrated with the world, and a degree of trust is established on all sides by Iran's meeting the obligations they have signed up to, something more fruitful could eventually emerge.

NOTES

1. Ariana Rowberry, "*Sixty Years of "Atoms for Peace"and Iran's Nuclear Programme*" Brookings Institute, I December 18, 2013.
2. Yossi Melman, Meir Javedanfar, *The Nuclear Sphinx of Tehran*, Basic Books, 2008 pp.89-90.
3. "U.S. does not believe Iran is trying to build nuclear bomb", *Los Angeles Times*, 23 February 2012.
4. "Iran parliament to review ties with U.N. nuclear body". *Washington Post.* 20 November 2011.
5. ShahramChubin, "*The Politics of Iran's Nuclear Program*"United States Institute of Peace,The Iran Primer.
6. Statement by Dr. M. Javad Zarif, Permanent Representative of the Islamic Republic of Iran before the Security Council, 23 December 2006.
7. "U.S. in 1983 stopped IAEA from helping Iran make UF6" by Mark Hibbs, *Nuclear Fuel*, 4 August 2003, Vol. 28, No. 16; p. 12.
8. "Perceptions and Courses of Actions toward Iran" *Military Review*, September-October 2005".
9. Pierre Goldschmidt, "Concrete Steps to Improve the Nonproliferation Regime". *Survival: Global Politics and Strategy*, vol. 51, no. 1, February–March 2009, pp. 143-164.
10. Jonathan S. Landay (November 4, 2007). "Experts: No firm evidence of Iranian nuclear weapons". *McClatchy Washington Bureau.*
11. Christopher Dickey (2009-05-22). "Mohamed El Baradei: 'They are not Fanatics'". *Newsweek.*
12. Ali Akbar Dareini (19 September 2007). "Iran: Retaliation for any Israeli attack". *USA Today.* Associated Press.
13. "European leaders considering Iran sanctions, French foreign minister says". *International Herald Tribune.* Associated Press.

14. Iran's nuclear programme: Breakout beckons". *The Economist.* 22 June 2013.
15. Abulof, Uriel. 2013. "Nuclear Diversion Theory and Legitimacy Crisis: The Case of Iran." *Politics & Policy,* 41 (5):693.
16. "Iran, world powers reach historic nuclear deal", *Washington Post.*
17. "Joint Statement by EU High Representative Federica Mogherini and Iranian Foreign Minister Javad Zarif Switzerland". *eeas.europa.eu.* 2 April 2015.

13

INDO-MYANMAR RELATIONS IN TWENTY-FIRST CENTURY

India had long historical relationship with Myanmar since ancient time. The cultural exchanges included Buddhism and the Burmese script, which was based on the Indian Grantha script. In particular, *Theravada Buddhism* has tremendously influenced Burmese society and culture for millennia, with 90% continuing to follow the religion to this day. Myanmar (formerly Burma) was made a province of British India by British rulers and again separated in 1937. India established diplomatic relations after Myanmar's independence from Great Britain in 1948.[1] For many years, Indo-Burmese relations were strong due to Myanmar previously having been a province of India, due to cultural links, flourishing commerce, common interests in regional affairs and the presence of a significant Indian community in Myanmar. India provided considerable support when Myanmar struggled with regional insurgencies. However, the overthrow of the democratic government by the Military of Myanmar led to strains in ties. Along with much of the world, India condemned the suppression of democracy and Myanmar ordered the expulsion of the Burmese Indian community, increasing its own isolation from the world.[2] Only China maintained close links with Myanmar while India supported the pro-democracy movement.

Myanmar shares a long, sensitive and porous land border of over 1600 Km with India as well as a maritime boundary in the Bay of Bengal. Four north-eastern States viz. Arunachal Pradesh, Nagaland, Manipur and Mizoram share an international boundary with Myanmar. These geo-strategic realities affect India's north-eastern region, security of the Andaman & Nicobar Islands and our broader interests in the Indian Ocean region. Both countries share a heritage of religious, linguistic and ethnic ties. Myanmar has a substantial population of Indian origin (around 1.5 million to 2.0 million). People-to-people contacts need to be fostered to keep alive our common Buddhist heritage. Further, Myanmar is the only ASEAN country adjoining India and, therefore, our gateway to South East Asia with which we are seeking greater economic integration through India's 'Look East' and now 'Act East' Policy. Myanmar also offers us an alternative access route to the Northeast.

India's move to forge close relations with Burma are motivated by a desire to counter China's growing influence as a regional leader and enhance its own influence and standing. Concerns and tensions increased in India over China's extensive military involvement in developing ports, naval and intelligence facilities and industries, specifically the upgrading of a naval base in Sittwe, a major seaport located close to the eastern Indian city of Kolkata. India's engagement of the Burmese military junta has helped ease the regime's international isolation and lessen Burma's reliance on China. Both nations sought to cooperate to counteract drug trafficking and insurgent groups operating in the border areas.[3] India and Myanmar are leading members of BIMSTEC and the Mekong-Ganga Cooperation, along with Vietnam, Laos, Cambodia and Thailand, helping India develop its influence and ties amongst Southeast Asian nations.

India was hesitant in reacting to the 2007 Burmese anti-government protests that had drawn overwhelming international condemnation. India also declared that it had no intention of interfering in Burma's internal affairs and that the Burmese people would have to achieve democracy by themselves as it respects the sovereignty of Myanmar. This low-key response has been widely criticized both within India and abroad as weakening India's credentials as a leading democratic nation. Indo-Burma relations went into pleasant phase over Burmese steps towards democracy.

Since the 1990s, India has adopted a policy of working on improved Government-to-Government relations, keeping our geo-political and strategic interests in view as well as extending support to democratic forces. Myanmar's transition to a Constitution-based quasi-civilian Government in 2011, dialogue that the Myanmar Government commenced a dialogue with Aung San Suu Kyi and appeal to overseas dissidents to return home and participate in the reform process opened up new possibilities for India's engagement. The landslide victory by the National League for Democracy (NLD) in the November 8, 2015 elections in which the NLD won 255/323 seats (lower house) and 135/168 (upper house) and 475/630 (in regional/state Parliament) and formation of NLD government has further provided opportunities to strengthen the engagement.

India's policy is shaped primarily by our desire to safeguard our national security interests, especially in the North East. The activities of Indian insurgent groups in particular NSCN (I/M), PLA, UNLF and ULFA and arms smuggling into India through Myanmar remain an important security concern for India. These groups find shelter and operate from camps in Myanmar and have been able to procure arms consignments from and via Myanmar from China's Yunnan province. Enabling access to North-East is another key objective, while creating road and trade links between India and ASEAN is central to our Look

East policy. With the emergence of Myanmar as India's largest supplier of pulses it is integral to our food security, while possibilities of energy supply from offshore blocks in Myanmar and business opportunities that emerging from an opening economy underpin relations.

Myanmar's vast oil and natural gas reserves and other resources make it a natural partner for many countries in the world. India, being its next door neighbour, cannot be indifferent to this reality. Besides, geo-political considerations, historical and civilizational links, and the ethnic overlap across their borders, have all come together to make India's North-East the land bridge between the South and South-East Asia through Myanmar. India expects to reap various economic benefits by bolstering bilateral trade and investment, which critically depends upon better connectivity in the region.[4]

ECONOMIC COOPERATION

India is the largest market for Burmese exports, buying about US$ 220 million worth of goods in 2000; India's exports to Burma stood at US$75.36 million. India is Burma's 4th largest trading partner after Thailand, China and Singapore, and second largest export market after Thailand, absorbing 25 percent of its total exports. India is also the seventh most important source of Burma's imports. The governments of India and Burma had set a target of achieving $1 billion and bilateral trade reached USD 650 million US dollars by 2006. The Indian government has worked to extend air, land and sea routes to strengthen trade links with Myanmar and establish a gas pipeline. While the involvement of India's private sector has been low and growing at a slow pace, both governments are proceeding to enhance cooperation in agriculture, telecommunications, information technology, steel, oil, natural gas, hydrocarbons and food processing. The bilateral border trade agreement of 1994 provides for border trade to be carried out from three designated border points, one each in Manipur, Mizoram and Nagaland.[5]

Commercial cooperation is another area of focus. India and Myanmar signed a trade agreement in 1970. Bilateral trade has been growing steadily to reach $ 2052.47 million in 2015-16 and India is the fifth largest trade partner of Myanmar but trade remains below potential. Agriculture sector dominates bilateral trade, particularly supply of beans and pulses to India (813.85 million in 2014-15) and Timber and wood products (US$ 382.12 million). India's exports to Myanmar include pharmaceuticals products, steel & iron products, electrical machinery, Mineral oil, Rubber and articles, plastics etc. US$ 169.17 million worth of pharmaceutical products were exported to Myanmar in 2014-15.[6] Border trade via Moreh and Zawkhatar has reached to US$ 51.68 million in 2013-14.

India is presently the ninth largest investor with an approved investment of US$ 730.649 million by 22 Indian companies, out of the total estimated investments of US$ 58.03 billion from 41 countries by 1001 enterprises (as of 29 Feb 2016). Most of India's investments have been in the oil and gas sector. Following the New Foreign Investment Law (02 Nov 2012) and the by-laws and rules framed by the respective departments/ministries (31 January 2013) investments into the country is increasing. Now FDI is allowed 100 per cent in select sectors. Indian companies have evinced interest in investing in Myanmar and major contracts have been won by Indian companies include Jubilant Energy India-PSC-1 onshore bloc; Punj Lloyd; Jindal Saw; Welspun India; Vihaan Networks; Nipha Exports and Troika Exports; L&T. More facilitative environment that includes greater air, sea and road connectivity options would give a fillip to the cooperation. Cooperation in banking sector is crucial for investment and trade. United Bank of India signed number of banking agreements with banks of Myanmar

(MFTB, MICB, MEB, and 9 private banks) in order to facilitate trade transactions between the two countries. United Bank of India (UBI) opened its representative office in November 2012. In addition to UBI, Indian Overseas Bank, EXIM bank and State Bank of India have opened representative office in Yangon. Mechanisms such as Joint Trade Committee, Double Taxation Avoidance Agreement and Bilateral Investment Protection Agreement and technical level committee on trade have contributed to strengthening trade and investment relations. The first Joint Trade and Investment Forum (JTIF) was held in Yangon on 7 June 2013 co-chaired by Sunil Mittal and U Aung Win (President UMFCCI, Myanmar).[7]

Connectivity is increasingly being seen as the key to promoting bilateral commercial, cultural, touristic and other exchanges. India is undertaking some important development projects that will enhance connectivity: these include the Kaladan project, construction/upgradation of Rhi-Tiddim Road, MOU for which was signed during the visit of EAM to Myanmar in December 2012. Both countries have agreed to Myanmar's request to build 69 bridges along the Tamu-Kalamyo-Kalewa (TKK) Friendship Road and construct the 126 km Kalewa-Yargyi road segment forming part of the Trilateral Highway from Moreh in India to Mae Sot in Thailand via Myanmar. Both are also working on boosting air, rail and sea links. During the visit of Prime Minister in May 2012, Air Services Agreement was signed and agreed to set up JWGs to determine the technical and commercial feasibility of cross-border rail links and direct shipping links between the two countries. The bilateral Air Services Agreement enables third, fourth and fifth freedom rights to both Indian and Myanmar carriers. An MOU to establish a direct Imphal-Mandalay bus service and the broad framework for the operation of this service has been negotiated and initialized and awaiting formal signing. The Air India has launched a direct flight between Delhi-Gaya-Yangon once in a week and Gaya-Kolkata-Yangon flights twice a week. The Shipping Corporation of India launched a direct sea link in October 2014.

DEFENCE COOPERATION

The past few years have witnessed a growing defence bilateral ties. Myanmar welcomes India's cooperation as it enables it counter-balance its dependency on a few countries. The cooperation has been boosted by regular exchange of visits at the Service Chief level, the Indian Chiefs Army and Navy visited Myanmar in January 2012 and August 2011 respectively. In November 2012, Chairman COSC and CAS Air Chief Marshal Browne led tri-services delegation visited Myanmar from 26 to 30 November 2012 and Gen. Bikram Singh, COAS visited Myanmar from Oct 29-Nov 02, 2013. During the visit, the delegation held formal discussion with C-in-C Senior General Min Aug Hlaing and Service Chiefs of Armed Forces. The delegation also made courtesy call on with President U Thein Sein and Myanmar Army was presented a set of five Handgliders and INFCOTT and CDR wargame software, jointly developed by the Indian Army and DRDO.[8]

As Myanmar seeks to enhance its defence ties with India, nearly 200 officials from Myanmar Defence Services were trained in India during 2015, 2 PG slots in AFMC, training in fixed and rotary wing aircraft and in VIP security duties at NSG centre. India is now supplying defensive military hardware for the use of the Myanmar Navy. This marks restoration of supply of hardware which was halted following demonstrations in September 2007. There has also been close interaction between the two Navies including participation of Myanmar Navy Ship during International Fleet Review held at Visakhapatnam in February 2016 and presence of Myanmar Navy Chief during the event.

From Myanmar side, Commander-in-Chief and Sr Gen Min Aung Hlaing led a 21 member delegation to India from 01-08 August 2012. Myanmar CNS Vice Admiral Thura Thet Swe visited India from 29 July- 1 August 2013. Vice Senior Gen. U Soe Win paid an official visit to India from 11-15 December 2013 and called on *Raksha Mantri* and had discussions with COAS Gen. Bikram Singh and reviewed passing out parade at OTA Gaya. The Second Naval Staff Talks were held in Nay Pyi Taw, Myanmar from November 6-8, 2013. CNS Admiral Thura Thet Swe, Commander-in-Chief of Myanmar visited India from July 29 to August 1, 2013. Lt Gen Khin Aung Myint, Chief of Staff (Air) attended the 9th edition of Aero India show at Bangalore. INS Darshak undertook a joint hydrological survey along with Myanmar Navy off the coast of Sittwe including the Kaladan Multimodal Transport-Transit Port in Sittwe.

Commencement of Army and Air Force Staff Talks in 2015 in addition to the ongoing Naval talks have further enhanced our relations. Cooperation along the border areas has also improved post the signing of MoU on Border Cooperation in May 2014. This was evident by successful handling of the fallouts from the alleged cross border raid by Indian Army after an ambush by IIG's based in Myanmar on a Indian Army column in Jun 2015. In accordance with this MoU, border meetings are regularly held in a four-tiered structure and communication lines have been established between three locations across the border. However, Myanmar Army has not shown any worthwhile cooperation in controlling the Indian insurgent groups based in Myanmar territory and their links with other foreign countries.

India responded promptly and effectively to assist Myanmar in humanitarian relief operations following natural calamities like Cyclone Nargis in 2008, the earthquake in Shan State in 2010 and cyclone Komen in 2015. India provided immediate relief material, medical assistance, supplies for rehabilitation work, biomass gasifiers, solar torches & lanterns. We have also replaced 16 damaged transformers and given a grant of $ 200,000 to repair the Shwedagon Pagoda complex in Yangon. India also gave assistance of $ 1 million for relief and reconstruction work in the quake affected zone in Shan State of which 250,000 was given as a cash grant and the remainder used to finance reconstruction of 1 high school and 6 primary schools. India has also donated US$200,000 in cash for Rakhine State rehabilitation. India again provided a sum of US$ 1 million to Government of Myanmar for promoting inter-communal harmony in Rakhine State which the Myanmar Government has chosen to use to construct 10 schools to serve both communities and promoting communal harmony. The construction of 10 schools has hence been completed and classes commenced from the new building. Our emergency supply of food, medicines and relief supplies through four airforce flights to Kalay and Mandalay, soon after the Cyclone Komen has been widely appreciated.

PM Dr. Manmohan Singh paid a State Visit to Myanmar from May 27-29, 2012, after a gap of 25 years. PM and then President U Thein Sein signed 12 Agreements and MOUs including on $ 500 million Line of Credit, on Air Services, Border Areas Development, Establishment of the Advanced Centre for Agriculture Research & Education (ACARE), Rice Bio Park Myanmar and Institute of Information Technology with Indian assistance, Establishment of Border Haats, Joint Trade and Investment Forum, CEP for 2012-2015, MoUs for Cooperation amongst Think Tanks/ Institutes of the two countries and support for HRD through 500 training slots. With new road projects like the Trilateral Highway and Rhi-Tiddim road, India's commitment to Myanmar's development stands at about US$ 2 billion, which is more than the assistance offered by other countries.

PM Narendra Modi visited Nay Pyi Taw from Nov 11-13, 2014 to attend the 12th ASEAN-India Summit and 9th East Asia Summit. PM called on President U Thein Sein and met Daw Aung San Suu Kyi. PM also interacted with around 300 members of the PIO community of Myanmar. NSA attended the Nation wide Ceasefire Agreement ceremony on 15 October 2015 as India's witness signatory; other signatories included China, Thailand, EU, UN and Japan. NSA met President, Commander-in-Chief Min Aung Hlaing and Minister U Aung Min on the sidelines.[10] The NCA was a landmark event in over 67 years of internal strife and was signed between Myanmar Government and with eight ethnic armed organisations.[9] India's presence was a demonstration of support to the peace process.

CONCLUSION

Indo-Myanmar relations have suffered through willful negligence in the past. But we should not forget the present that goes back to at least a generation. It indicated that the relationship has been moving towards an upward trend and has experienced apositivepeak in the last 4 years. It gained peak during the Manmohan Singh Government and has again gathered momentum during the time of Prime Minister Narendra Modi. There is a national consensus now in India on Indo-Myanmar policy but the future relations will depend on the domestic developments within Myanmar. What happens to Myanmar is important to India and the neighbors of Myanmar.

Beyond economic and infrastructure issues, India's political leadership needs to be more aware of Myanmar's concerns and use the insights learned to its own advantage.India, too, has to show more sensitivity when dealing with Myanmar. For instance, when Indian commandos crossed into Myanmar in June 2015 to launch retaliatory strikes on insurgent groups operating at the border to Sagaing Region, some Indian ministers made rather indiscreet statements, claiming that the operations were carried out with the Myanmar government's support.No doubt that security cooperation between both countries has increased, but statements made by the minister put the Myanmarese in an awkward situation. New Delhi had to indulge in damage control.

NOTES

1. Subir Bhaumik "Explaining India's silence over Burma "*BBC News*, Calcutta
2. Tony Allison "Myanmar shows India the road to Southeast Asia"*Asia Times*, February 1, 2001.
3. Simon Robinson, "India's Burma Silence Says Volumes". *TIME*, 29 September 2007.
4. Shristi Pukhrem, "The Significance of Connectivity in India-Myanmar Relations" *IDSA Comment*, July 06, 2012.
5. Syed Ali Mujtaba, "India-Myanmar Trade Relations" bilaterals.org, http://www.bilaterals.org/?india-myanmar-trade-relations.
6. Tridivesh Singh Maini, "What are the options for India's policy toward Myanmar?" *The Globalist*, 2015.
7. "India Myanmar Relations", Embassy of India to Myanmar, Yangon.http://www.indiaembassyyangon.net/index.php?option=com_content&view=category&layout.blog&id.20&Itemid.121&lang.en
8. ibid.
9. ibid.
10. Elizabeth Roche, "The connectivity projects will open up Northeast India to Asean economies" *The Mint*,18 July 2016.

14

INDIAN FOREIGN POLICY AND THE RELEVANCE OF NON-ALIGNMENT MOVEMENT (NAM)

The principles of nonalignment, as articulated by Nehru and his successors, were preservation of India's freedom of action internationally through refusal to align India with any bloc or alliance, particularly those led by the United States or the Soviet Union; nonviolence and international cooperation as a means of settling international disputes. Nonalignment was a consistent feature of Indian foreign policy by the late 1940s and enjoyed strong, almost unquestioning support among the Indian elite. The Non-Aligned Movement (NAM) was created and founded during the collapse of the colonial system and the independence struggles of the peoples of Africa, Asia, Latin America and other regions of the world and at the height of the Cold War. During the early days of the Movement, its actions were a key factor in the decolonization process, which led later to the attainment of freedom and independence by many countries and peoples and to the founding of tens of new sovereign States. Throughout its history, the Movement of Non-Aligned Countries has played a fundamental role in the preservation of world peace and security.

While some meetings with a third-world perspective were held before 1955, historians consider that the Bandung Asian-

African Conference is the most immediate antecedent to the creation of the Non-Aligned Movement. This Conference was held in Bandung on April 18-24, 1955 and gathered 29 Heads of States belonging to the first post-colonial generation of leaders from the two continents with the aim of identifying and assessing world issues at the time and pursuing out joint policies in international relations.

The term "Non-Alignment" was coined by V K Menon in his speech at UN in 1953 which was later used by Indian Prime Minister Jawaharlal Nehru during his speech in 1954 in Colombo, Sri Lanka.[1] In this speech, Nehru described the five pillars to be used as a guide for Sino-Indian relations, which were first put forth by Chinese Premier Zhou Enlai. Called Panchsheel (five restraints), these principles would later serve as the basis of the Non-Aligned Movement. Jawaharlal Nehru was the architect of the Non-Alignment Movement. The five principles were:

1. Mutual respect for each other's territorial integrity and sovereignty
2. Mutual non-aggression
3. Mutual non-interference in domestic affairs
4. Equality and mutual benefit
5. Peaceful co-existence

Jawaharlal Nehru's concept of nonalignment brought India considerable international prestige among newly independent states that shared India's concerns about the military confrontation between the superpowers and the influence of the former colonial powers. New Delhi used nonalignment to establish a significant role for itself as a leader of the newly independent world in such multilateral organisations as the United Nations (UN) and the Non-aligned Movement. The principles that would govern relations among large and small nations, known as the "Ten Principles of Bandung", were proclaimed at that Conference. Such principles were adopted later as the main goals and objectives of the policy of non-alignment. The fulfilment of those principles became the essential criterion for Non-Aligned Movement membership it is what was known as the "quintessence of the Movement" until the early 1990s.

In 1960, in the light of the results achieved in Bandung, the creation of the Movement of Non-Aligned Countries was given a decisive boost during the Fifteenth Ordinary Session of the United Nations General Assembly, during which 17 new African and Asian countries were admitted. A key role was played in this process by the then Heads of State and Government Gamal Abdel Nasser of Egypt, Kwame Nkrumah of Ghana, Jawaharlal Nehru of India, Ahmed Sukarno of Indonesia and Josip Broz Tito of Yugoslavia, who later became the founding fathers of the movement and its emblematic leaders.[2]

Thus, the primary of objectives of the non-aligned countries focused on the support of self-determination, national independence and the sovereignty and territorial integrity of States; opposition to apartheid; non-adherence to multilateral military pacts and the independence of non-aligned countries from great power or block influences and rivalries;[3] the struggle against imperialism in all its forms and manifestations; the struggle against colonialism, neo-colonialism, racism, foreign occupation and domination; disarmament; non-interference into the internal affairs of States and peaceful coexistence among all nations; rejection of the use or threat of use of force in international relations; the strengthening of the United Nations; the democratization of international relations; socioeconomic development and the restructuring of the international economic system; as well as international cooperation on an equal footing.

THE TEN PRINCIPLES OF BANDUNG CONFERENCE

1. Respect of fundamental human rights and of the objectives and principles of the Charter of the United Nations;
2. Respect of the sovereignty and territorial integrity of all nations;
3. Recognition of the equality among all races and of the equality among all nations, both large and small;
4. Non-intervention or non-interference into the internal affairs of another country;
5. Respect of the right of every nation to defend itself, either individually or collectively, in conformity with the Charter of the United Nations;
6. (A) Non-use of collective defence pacts to benefit the specific interests of any of the great powers;

   (B) Non-use of pressures by any country against other countries;
7. Refraining from carrying out or threatening to carry out aggression, or from using force against the territorial integrity or political independence of any country;
8. Peaceful solution of all international conflicts in conformity with the Charter of the United Nations;
9. Promotion of mutual interests and of cooperation;
10. Respect of justice and of international obligations.[4]

Consisting of many governments with vastly different ideologies, the Non-Aligned Movement is unified by its declared commitment to world peace and security. At the seventh summit held in New Delhi in March 1983, the movement described itself as "history's biggest peace movement".[5] The movement places equal emphasis ondisarmament. NAM's commitment to peace pre-dates its formal institutionalisation in 1961. The Brioni meeting between heads of governments of India, Egypt and Yugoslavia in 1956 recognized that there exists a vital link between struggle for peace and endeavours for disarmament.

During the 1970s and early 1980s, the NAM also sponsored campaigns for restructuring commercial relations between developed and developing nations, namely the New International Economic Order (NIEO), and its cultural offspring, the New World Information and Communication Order (NWICO). The latter, on its own, sparked a Non-Aligned initiative on cooperation for communications, the Non-Aligned News Agencies Pool, created in 1975 and later converted into the NAM News Network (NNN) in 2005.

The Non-Aligned Movement espouses policies and practices of cooperation, especially those that are multilateral and provide mutual benefit to all those involved. Many of the members of the Non-Aligned Movement are also members of the United Nations. Both organisations have a stated policy of peaceful cooperation, yet the successes the NAM has had with multilateral agreements tend to be ignored by the larger, western and developed nation dominated UN.[6] African concerns about apartheid were linked with Arab-Asian concerns about Palestine and multilateral cooperation in these areas has enjoyed moderate success. The Non-Aligned Movement has played a major role in various ideological conflicts throughout its existence, including extreme opposition to apartheid governments and support of guerrilla movements in various locations, including Rhodesia and South Africa.

The Movement played an important role in the support of nations which were struggling then for their independence in the Third World and showed great solidarity with the most just aspirations of humanity. It contributed indisputably to the triumph in the struggle for national independence and decolonization, thus gaining considerable diplomatic prestige. As one Summit after another was held in the 1960s and 1970s, "non-alignment", turned already into the "Movement of Non-Aligned Countries" that included nearly all Asian and African countries, was becoming a forum of coordination to struggle for the respect of the economic and political rights of the developing world. After the attainment of independence, the Conferences expressed a growing concern over economic and social issues as well as over strictly political matters. Something that attested to that was the launching at the Algiers Conference in 1973 of the concept of a "new international economic order."

RELEVANCE OF NAM AFTER THE END THE COLD WAR

Since the end of the Cold War and the formal end of colonialism, the Non-Aligned Movement has been forced to redefine itself and reinvent its purpose in the current world system. A major question has been whether many of its foundational ideologies, principally national independence, territorial integrity, and the struggle against colonialism and imperialism, can be applied to contemporary issues. The movement has emphasised its principles of multilateralism, equality, and mutual non-aggression in attempting to become a stronger voice for the global South, and an instrument that can be utilised to promote the needs of member nations at the international level and strengthen their political leverage when negotiating with developed nations. In its efforts to advance Southern interests, the movement has stressed the importance of cooperation and unity amongst member states,[7] but as in the past, cohesion remains a problem since the size of the organisation and the divergence of agendas and allegiances present the on-going potential for fragmentation. While agreement on basic principles has been smooth, taking definitive action vis-à-vis particular international issues has been rare, with the movement preferring to assert its criticism or support rather than pass hard-line resolutions.

The movement continues to see a role for itself, as in its view, the world's poorest nations remain exploited and marginalised, no longer by opposing superpowers, but rather in a uni-polar world, and it is Western hegemony and neo-colonialism that the movement has really re-aligned itself against. It opposes foreign occupation, interference in internal affairs and aggressive unilateral measures, but it has also shifted to focus on the socio-economic challenges facing member states, especially the inequalities manifested by globalization and the implications of neo-liberal policies. The Non-Aligned Movement has identified economic underdevelopment, poverty, and social injustices as growing threats to peace and security.[8]

By the end of the 1980s, the Movement was facing the great challenge brought about by the collapse of the socialist block. The end of the clash between the two antagonistic blocks that was the reason for its existence, name and essence was seen by some as the beginning of the end for the Movement of Non-Aligned Countries. The Movement of Non-Aligned Countries could not spare itself difficulties to act effectively in an adverse international political situation marked by hegemonic positions and unipolarity as well as by internal difficulties and conflicts given the heterogeneity of its membership and, thus, its diverse interests.

The early 1990s demise of the bipolar world system, which had existed since the end of World War II, shook the underpinnings of India's foreign policy. The Cold War system of alliances had been rendered meaningless by the collapse of the East European communist states, the dissolution of the Warsaw Pact, and the demise of the Soviet Union. In the early 1990s, most colonies had become independent, and apartheid in South Africa was being dismantled, diminishing the value of anti-colonialism and making it impossible for antiracism to serve as a rallying point for international political action (India and South Africa restored full diplomatic relations in 1993 after a thirty nine year lapse). The Panchsheel (PanchShila), peaceful resolution of international disputes, and international cooperation to spur economic development which was being enhanced by domestic economic reforms were broad objectives in a changing world. Thus, the 1990s saw India redefining nonalignment and the view of India's place in the world.

India also is a founding member of the Group of fifteen, a group of developing nations established at the ninth Non-aligned Movement summit in Belgrade in 1989 to facilitate dialogue with the industrialised countries. India played host to the fourth Group of Fifteen summit in March 1994. At the summit, Prime Minister Narsimha Rao and other leaders expressed concern over new trade barriers being raised by the industrialised countries despite the conclusion of a new world trade agreement.

Nevertheless, and in spite of such setbacks,the principles and objectives of non-alignment retain their full validity and force at the present international juncture. The primary condition that led to the emergence of the Movement of Non-Aligned Countries, that is, non-alignment from antagonistic blocks, has not lost its validity with the end of the Cold War. The demise of one of the blocks has not done away with the pressing problems of the world. On the contrary, renewed strategic interests bent on domination grow stronger and, even, acquire new and more dangerous dimensions for underdeveloped countries.

India has been victim of colonialism and racism and was as such opposed to these evils in any form. India considers colonialism and imperialism as the threat to international peace and security India was the first to bring the issue of Apartheid in the UN in 1946. India raised her voice for the independence of Indonesia and organized Asian Relations Conference for this purpose. Due to India's consistent efforts through NAM and other international forums, 14 African countries were liberated from the yoke of colonialism in 1964. India made sincere efforts to end the scourge of apartheid in South Africa. At India's initiative, NAM set up the Africa Fund (Action for Resisting Imperialism, Colonialism and Apartheid) in 1986 to help the frontline states, which were victims of aggression of South Africa for supporting the cause of fight against apartheid. India made generous contribution to this fund. The end of racialism in South Africa in 1990 was a great success for Indian policy.

As the world faces greater threat from a unipolar world led by US after the disintegration of Soviet Union, the NAM can act as a check against undue dominance and hegemony of any country or block. The developed (North) and developing (South) world have divergent views over several global and economic issues. The NAM may provide a forum for third world countries to engage the developed nations in a productive dialogue. The NAM can prove to be a powerful mechanism to forge South-South cooperation, which is essential for their collective self-reliance in the present market driven global order. The NAM can provide an important forum for developing countries to discuss and deliberate upon various global problems, issues and reforms including the reform of UN and other international financial institutions like World Bank and IMF in order to make them more democratic and effective.

The global thrust on economic integration has certainly accrued greater space to India that the non-alignment actually stands for. It allows India to reach out to both the US and China without fear of taking sides and draw in the benefits from both of manufacturing, investments, trade and commerce. It has also enabled India to rope in Japan in developing its backward northeast region much to the irritation of the Chinese. In fact, both Japan and China are competing to strengthen economic ties with India. This gives India leverage to bargain for the best economic deals conducive to its national interest.[9]

In recent years the NAM has criticized certain aspects of US foreign policy. The 2003 invasion of Iraq and the War on Terrorism, its attempts to stifle Iran and North Korea's nuclear plans, and its other actions have been denounced by some members of the Non-Aligned Movement as attempts to run roughshod over the sovereignty of smaller nations; at the most recent summit, Kim Yong-nam, the head of North Korea's parliament, stated that, "The United States is attempting to deprive other countries of even their legitimate right to peaceful nuclear activities."

The movement is publicly committed to the tenets of sustainable development and the attainment of the Millennium Development Goals, but it believes that the international community has not created conditions conducive to development and has infringed upon the right to sovereign development by each member state. Issues such as globalization, the debt burden, unfair trade practices, the decline in foreign aid, donor conditionality, and the lack of democracy in international financial decision-making are cited as factors inhibiting development.[10]

The movement has collaborated with other organisations of the developing world– primarily the Group of 77– forming a number of joint committees and releasing statements and documents representing the shared interests of both groups. This dialogue and cooperation can be taken as an effort to increase the global awareness about the organisation and bolster its political clout. The movement accepts the universality of human rights and social justice, but fiercely resists cultural homogenisation. In line with its views on sovereignty, the organisation appeals for the protection of cultural diversity, and the tolerance of the religious, socio-cultural, and historical particularities that define human rights in a specific region.

INDIA AND THE 17TH SUMMIT OF NON-ALIGNED MOVEMENT (NAM) IN VENEZUELA *(17-18 SEPTEMBER 2016)*

India was represented by Vice President Hamid Ansari at the 17th Summit of NAM held on 17-18 September 2016, in Venezuela. He said "The world of today, would certainly appear very different to the leaders who took the initiative to meet in Belgarde in 1961. While the global landscape has changed, the values and principles on which they laid the foundations of our Movement, namely "respect for sovereignty", "peaceful settlement of disputes" and "international cooperation" – are as relevant today as they were at the time of our first Summit. Our theme for the next three years – *"Peace, Sovereignty and Solidarity for Development"* – is in congruence with our founding principles and I congratulate you, Mr. Chairman, for shouldering the responsibility to carry it forward in this Summit.We do believe that cooperation, and Development Cooperation, is an essential means of promoting and developing international solidarity, of putting a human face on the impact of economic globalization. This becomes all the more important in the light of the adoption of the Sustainable Development Goals in the Agenda 2030 which, if implemented successfully, will transform the lives of all our citizens. It would be a reaffirmation of our commitment as a Movement to ensure the dignity and development of all humankind.

The Vice President further reiterated that "The United Nations lies at the heart of the multilateral system set up at the end of the Second World War. Today we need to ask whether an organization designed in 1945 with just 51 member States, is really appropriate to serve the needs of an international community that now comprises 193 independent sovereign States facing 21st century challenges to their citizens' well-being and security. World leaders at their Summit at the UN in 2005 had called for urgent reform of the Security Council as part of the effort to make the United Nations fit for the 21st century. The Inter-governmental Negotiations process currently underway in the UN General Assembly seeks to fulfil that mandate. We must use the forthcoming 71st UNGA to ensure that our discussions in the IGN move forward.

In 1983, at New Delhi, the NAM Summit had noted that 'the earth belongs to us all' – and had implored humanity to 'cherish it in peace' based on the 'dignity and equality' of humanity. As the largest peace movement of the world, NAM must be in the vanguard of the principal international debates on political, strategic and even economic and social issues to achieve that ideal. I do hope that one of the priorities during your Chairmanship of this Movement will be to modernize the manner in which we function. We began a discussion on this at the Cartagena Summit in 1995; this discussion must continue and fructify so that NAM may achieve its full potential."[11]

The Heads of State and Government of the Non-Aligned Movement, gathered in the Island of Margarita, Bolivarian Republic of Venezuela, within the framework of the XVII Conference Summit, on 17-18 September 2016, under the theme "Peace, Sovereignty and Solidarity for Development", undertook a review of the state of the international situation. Mindful of the fact that the history and reality of the world in which we live in today demonstrates that it is the developing countries of the world the ones who suffer more intensely from the disregard of international law, from invasions, from the ravages of war and armed conflicts, caused mostly by the geopolitical interests of the great centres of power, as well as from protracted conflicts inherited from colonialism and neo-colonialism. Emphasizing that many of these crises have been triggered by the violation of the purposes and principles enshrined in the Charter of the United Nations and the Principles of Bandung, recognising that solidarity, the highest expression of respect, friendship and peace among States, is a broad concept encompassing the sustainability of international relations, the peaceful coexistence, and the transformative objectives of equity and empowerment of developing countries, whose ultimate goal is to achieve the full economic and social development of their peoples. At the 55th anniversary of the Movement, determined to defend the right to peace, sovereignty and solidarity for the development of their peoples.

21 POINT DECLARATION OF THE 17TH NAM SUMMIT

1. **Strengthening and Revitalization of the Movement:** They reaffirmed their full and decisive support to the consolidation, strengthening and revitalization of the Non-Aligned Movement, as the only guarantee to preserve its legacy and historical validity and to ensure therefore its strength, cohesion and resilience, on the basis of unity in diversity and the solidarity of its Member States.

2. **Strengthening International Peace and Security:** They reiterated that they will continue to promote the peaceful settlement of disputes, in accordance with Article 2 and Chapter VI of the Charter of the United Nations, as well as with the UN Resolution 26/25 of 24 October 1970 and international law, in order to contribute to achieve said objective and to save future generations from the scourge of war and military conflict. They further rejected the illegal policies of regime change aimed at overthrowing constitutional Governments, in contravention of international law. Furthermore, they stressed that overcoming conflicts and the achievement of a firm and lasting peace requires a holistic approach that addresses the structural causes of conflicts, in order to realize the three pillars of the United Nations: peace and security, development and human rights.

3. **Right to Self-Determination:** They stressed the inalienable right of all peoples, including those of non-self-

governing territories, as well as those of territories under foreign occupation or under colonial or foreign domination, to self-determination.

4. **Disarmament and International Security:** They reaffirmed their intention to redouble efforts towards eliminating the threat posed to the human species the existence of weapons of mass destruction, particularly nuclear weapons.

5. **Human Rights:** They reaffirmed their commitment to the promotion and protection of all human rights, which are universal, indivisible, interdependent and interrelated, through a constructive and cooperative international dialogue, capacity building, technical assistance and the recognition of good practices, while ensuring the full enjoyment of all human rights,

6. **Unilateral Sanctions:** They expressed their condemnation at the promulgation and application of unilateral coercive measures against countries of the Movement, in violation of the Charter of the United Nations and international law, particularly the principles of non-intervention, self-determination and independence of States subject of such practices.

7. **Terrorism:** They reiterated that terrorism constitutes one of the most serious threats to international peace and security. Hence, they reaffirmed their firm condemnation of terrorist acts in all their forms and manifestations, whatever their motivations, wherever and by whomsoever they are committed.

8. **Dialogue Among Civilizations:** They stressed the importance of promoting respect for religious, social and cultural diversity, in order to promote a culture of peace, tolerance and respect between societies and nations, through intercultural, interreligious and inter-civilizations dialogue.

9. **Situation in the Middle East, including the Question of Palestine:** They reaffirmed once again that the Israeli occupation of the Occupied Palestinian Territories, including East Jerusalem, constitutes a destabilising factor in the region, and as such they demanded the withdrawal of the Occupying Power from those territories occupied since June 1967, in accordance with resolutions 242, and 338 as well as other relevant resolutions of the Security Council and the General Assembly of the United Nations.

10. **Reform of the United Nations:** They reiterated the need to recover and strengthen the authority of the General Assembly as the most democratic, accountable, universal and representative body of the Organization.

11. **Selection and Appointment of the Secretary General of the United Nations:** They underlined the central role that corresponds to the General Assembly in the process of selection and appointment of the Secretary General of the United Nations, while reaffirming the need for greater transparency and inclusiveness in the current process of selection and appointment with due regard to the principles of geographical rotation and gender equality in the process of selection and appointment of the Secretary General of the United Nations.

12. **Peacekeeping Operations:** They reaffirmed that peacekeeping operations must be carried out with strict adherence to the principles and purposes enshrined in the Charter, and emphasized that respect of the principles of sovereignty, territorial integrity and independence of States,as well as non-intervention in internal affairs, are key elements of the joint efforts in the promotion of international peace and security.

13. **Sustainable Development Goals:** They reiterated that their will to work towards the full implementation of the 2030 Agenda for Sustainable Development, leaving no one behind,

remembering that the Agenda is based on people and is universal and transformative.

14. **Promotion of Education, Science and Technology for Development:** They reaffirmed their commitment to combat illiteracy as a way to contribute to overcoming poverty and social exclusion, while noting that education is an inalienable human right that must include all sectors of society.

15. **Climate Change:** They reaffirmed that climate change is one of the greatest challenges of their times and expressed profound alarm that emissions of greenhouse gases continue to raise globally. They expressed concern about the increased adverse impacts of climate change, particularly on developing countries, which are severely undermining their efforts to eradicate poverty and achieve sustainable development.

16. **Economic Governance:** They reaffirmed that the reform of the international financial architecture requires the democratization of the decision-making institutions of Bretton Woods (IMF and World Bank). Therefore, it is necessary to widen and strengthen the level of participation of developing countries in the international decision and economic law making processes and in the governance of a new world economic order.

17. **South-South Cooperation:** They reiterated that South-South Cooperation is an important element of international cooperation for the sustainable development of their peoples, as a complement and not as a substitute to the North-South Cooperation, which allows for the transfer of appropriate technologies, in favourable conditions and preferential terms.

18. **International Solidarity:** They recognized that the response of the international community to pandemics that constitute a threat to public health and to various natural disasters is an example to follow in terms of solidarity and international cooperation. In this sense, they highlighted the

efforts of the international community to counter and eradicate the spread of various pandemics, among them the Ebola, as well as for confronting the aftermath of natural disasters around the world.

19. **Refugees and Migrants:** They welcomed the convening of the High Level Meeting to address large movements of refugees and migrants, to be held on 19 September 2016, in New York, and which represents an opportunity for international community to discuss responses to this growing global phenomenon that mainly affects women and children

20. **Youth, Women, Peace and Security:** They recognized the important role that youth and women play in the prevention and resolution of conflicts, as well as in peacekeeping and peace building efforts. In this regard, they underscored the need to achieve full gender equality and the empowerment of women, including their participation in these processes.

21. **New World Information and Communication Order:** They emphasized the need for information and communication strategies to be deeply rooted in historical and cultural processes and called on the media of developed countries to respect developing countries in the formulation of their opinions, models and perspectives with a view to enhancing the dialogue among civilizations. They also reiterated their deep concern on the use of media as a tool for hostile propaganda against developing countries aimed at undermining their governments and stressed the need to promote alternative, free, pluralistic and responsible media and communication sources that reflect the realities and interests of the peoples of the developing world.

CONCLUSION

The NAM has succeeded to create a strong front on the International level, representing countries of the third world in the International organizations on top of which the United

Nations. Current Challenges facing the NAM include the necessity of protecting the principles of International law, eliminating weapons of mass destruction, combating terrorism, defending human rights, working toward making the United Nations more effective in meeting the needs of all its member states in order to preserve International Peace, Security and Stability, as well as realizing justice in the international economic system. On the other hand, the long-standing goals of the Movement remain to be realized. Peace, development, economic cooperation and the democratization of international relations, to mention just a few, are old goals of the non-aligned countries. In conclusion, The Non-Aligned Movement, faced with the goals yet to be reached and the many new challenges that are arising, is called upon to maintain a prominent and leading role in the current International relations in defence of the interests and priorities of its member states and for achievement of peace and security for mankind. In 1983, at New Delhi, the NAM Summit had noted that 'the earth belongs to us all' – and had implored humanity to 'cherish it in peace′ based on the `dignity and equality' of humanity. As the largest peace movement of the world, NAM must be in the vanguard of the principal international debates on political, strategic and even economic and social issues to achieve that ideal.

NOTES

1. Ma'Aroof, Mohammad Khalid (1 January 1987). "Afghanistan in World Politics: a Study of Afghan-US Relations".
2. Grant, Cedric. "Equity in Third World Relations: a third world perspective". *International Affairs* 71, 3 (1995), pp.567-587.
3. Suvedi, Sûryaprasâda (1996). *Land and Maritime Zones of Peace in International Law.*Oxford: Clarendon Press; New York: Oxford University Press. pp.169-170.

4. "Meeting of the Ministerial Committee on Methodology of the Movement of the Non-Aligned Countries, Caratagena de Indias, May 14–16, 1996". *Head of State and Government of the Non-Aligned Countries.* Government of Zaire. 14-16 May 1996.

5. Ohlson, Thomas; Stockholm International Peace Research Institute (1988). *Arms Transfer Limitations and Third World Security.* Oxford: Oxford University Press. p.198.

6. Morphet, Sally. "Multilateralism and the Non-Aligned Movement: What Is the Global South Doing and Where Is It Going?" *Global Governance: A Review of Multilateralism and International Organizations.* 10 (2004), pp. 517-537.

7. Staff (7 August 2009). "Profile: Non-Aligned Movement". BBC News.

8. XII Summit, Durban, South Africa, 2-3 September 1998: NAM XII Summit: Basic Documents – Final Document: 1 Global Issues. Nam.gov.za.

9. http://www.idsa.in/idsacomments/NonAlignmentinModisIndia_abhattacharya_290614.

10. XII Summit, Durban, South Africa, 2-3 September 1998: *Final Document,* no. 55.

11. https://www.mea.gov.in/Speeches-Statements.htm?dtl/27412/address+by+vice+president+at+the+17th+nam+plenary+ meeting+september+18+2016.

15

US WITHDRAWAL FROM AFGHANISTAN AND THE ROLE FOR INDIA AND RUSSIA

Afghanistan has always played a very crucial role in the Asian and world politics and acted as playground for the 'Great Game'. Due to its unique geographical location and presence of abundant natural resources, controlling of Afghanistan has been a long cherished dream for the colonial powers in the past. In the nineteenth century, Afghanistan served as a 'strategic buffer' state between Czarist Russian and the British Empire in the subcontinent. Afghanistan's relations with Moscow became more cordial after the Bolshevik Revolution in 1917. The Soviet Union was the first country to establish diplomatic relations with Afghanistan in 1919[1] after the Third Anglo-Afghan war and signed an Afghan-Soviet non-aggression pact in 1921, which also provided for Afghan transit rights through the Soviet Union. Early Soviet assistance included financial aid, aircraft and attendant technical personnel, and telegraph operators.

The Soviets began a major economic assistance program in Afghanistan in the 1950s. Between 1954 and 1978, Afghanistan received more than $1 billion in Soviet aid, including substantial military assistance. In 1973, the two countries announced a $200-million assistance agreement on gas and oil development, trade, transport, irrigation, and factory construction. Following the 1979 invasion, the Soviets augmented their large aid commitments to shore up the Afghan economy and rebuild the Afghan military. They provided the Karmal regime an unprecedented $800 million. The Soviet Union supported the Najibullah regime even after the withdrawal of Soviet troops in February 1989. Today, unresolved questions concerning Soviet MIA/POWs in Afghanistan remain an issue between Russia and Afghanistan.

The Union of Soviet Socialist Republics (USSR) had been a major power broker and influential mentor in Afghan politics, ranging from civil-military infrastructure to Afghan society. In the 1980s, many Afghans were Russian language proficient. Since 1947, Afghanistan had been under the influence of the Russian government and received large amounts of aid, economic assistance, military equipment training and military hardware from the Soviet Union.[2]

The economic assistance and aid had been provided to Afghanistan as early as 1919, shortly after the Russian Revolution and when the regime was facing the Russian Civil War. Provisions were given in the form of small arms, ammunition, a few aircraft, and (according to debated Soviet sources) a million gold rubles to support the resistance during the Third Anglo-Afghan War. In 1942, the USSR again moved to strengthen the Afghan Armed Forces, by providing small arms and aircraft, and establishing training centers in Tashkent (Uzbek Soviet Socialist Republic). Soviet-Afghan military cooperation began on a regular basis in 1956, and further agreements were made in the 1970s, which saw the USSR send advisers and specialists. The Soviet Union built an extensive amount of infrastructure, notably giving assistance building the Kabul University, Polytechnical institutes, hospitals, civilian infrastructure, power plants, and local schools. During the 1980s, Soviets established the universities in Blakhe, Herate, Takhar, Nangarhar and Fariyab provinces. The Russian faculty soon joined the universities, teaching Afghan students in proficient Russian languages.

In 1978, President Daoud Khan began to take initiatives for building the massive military after witnessing India's nuclear test, *Smiling Buddha*, to counter Pakistan's armed forces and Iranian military influence in Afghanistan's politics. A final pre-war treaty, signed in December 1978, allowed the PDPA to call upon the Soviet Union for military support.[3] Following the Herat uprising, President Taraki contacted Alexei Kosygin, chairman of the USSR Council of Ministers, and asked for "practical and technical assistance with men and armament". Kosygin was unfavorable to the proposal on the basis of the negative political repercussions such an action would have for his country, and he rejected all further attempts by Taraki to solicit Soviet military aid in Afghanistan.[4] Following Kosygin's rejection Taraki requested aid from Leonid Brezhnev, the general secretary of the Communist Party of the Soviet Union and Soviet head of state, who warned Taraki that full Soviet intervention "would only play into the hands of our enemies – both yours and ours". Brezhnev also advised Taraki to ease up on the drastic social reforms and to seek broader support for his regime.[5]

In 1979, Taraki attended a conference of the Non-Aligned Movement in Havana, Cuba. On his way back, he stopped in Moscow on March 20 and met with Brezhnev, foreign minister Andrei Gromyko and other Soviet officials. It was rumored that Karmal was present at the meeting in an attempt to reconcile Taraki's Khalq faction and the Parcham against Amin and his followers. At the meeting, Taraki was successful in negotiating some Soviet support, including the redeployment of two Soviet armed divisions at the Soviet-Afghan border, the sending of 500 military and civilian advisers and specialists and the immediate delivery of Soviet armed equipment sold at 25 percent below the original price; however, the Soviets were not pleased about the developments in Afghanistan and Brezhnev impressed upon Taraki the need for party unity. Despite reaching this agreement with Taraki, the Soviets continued to be reluctant to intervene further in Afghanistan and repeatedly refused Soviet military intervention within Afghan borders during Taraki's rule as well as later during Amin's short rule.

The arrival of Mikhail Gorbachev on the scene in 1985 and his 'new thinking' on foreign and domestic policy was probably the most important factor in the Soviets' decision to leave. Gorbachev was attempting to change the stagnant years of Brezhnev and reform the Soviet Union's economy and image across the board with Glasnost and Perestroika. Gorbachev was also trying to ease cold war tensions by signing the Intermediate-Range Nuclear Forces Treaty in 1987 with the U.S. and withdrawing the troops from Afghanistan whose presence had garnered so much international condemnation. Gorbachev regarded confrontation with China and resulting military build ups on that border as one of Brezhnev's biggest mistakes. Beijing had stipulated that a normalization of relations would have to wait until Moscow withdrew its army from Afghanistan (among other things) and in 1989 the first Sino-Soviet summit in 30 years took place. At the same time, Gorbachev pressured his Cuban allies in Angola to scale down activities and withdraw even though Soviet allies were faring somewhat better there. The Soviets also pulled many of their troops out of Mongolia in 1987 where they were also having a far easier time than in Afghanistan and restrained the Vietnamese invasion of Kampuchea to the point of an all out withdrawal in 1988. This mass withdrawal of Soviet forces from contested areas shows that the Soviet government's decision to leave Afghanistan was based on a general change over in Soviet foreign policy.[6]

US INVOLVEMENT IN AFGHANISTAN

US engagement with Afghanistan goes long back in the history books. The first recorded contact between Afghanistan and the United States occurred in 1830s when Josiah Harlan, an American adventurer and political activist from the Philadelphia area of Pennsylvania, traveled to the Indian subcontinent with intentions of becoming the King of Afghanistan. It was when the British Indian army invaded Afghanistan, during the First Anglo-Afghan War (1838–1842) when Afghan kings Shuja Shah Durrani and Dost Mohammad Khan were fighting for the throne of the Durrani Empire. Harlan became involved in Afghan politics and factional military actions, eventually winning the title Prince of Ghor in exchange for military aid. The British-Indian forces were defeated and forced to make a complete withdraw a few years later, with around 16,500 of them being reported to be killed and captured in 1842. There is no clear evidence as to what happened because the claim is made by William Brydon, the lone survivor. Harlan is believed to have left Afghanistan around the same period, eventually returning to the United States.

Afghan-American relations became important during the start of the Cold War, between the United States and Soviet Union. Prince Mohammed Naim, King Zahir Shah's cousin, became the Chargé d'affaires in Washington, D.C. At that time, U.S. President Harry S. Truman commented that the friendship between the two countries would be "preserved and strengthened" by the presence of senior diplomats in each capital. The first official Afghanistan Ambassador to the United States was Habibullah Khan Tarzi, who served until 1953. The U.S. Kabul Legation was elevated to the U.S. Embassy Kabul on May 6, 1948. Louis Goethe Dreyfus, who previously served as Minister Plenipotentiary, became the U.S. Ambassador to Afghanistan from 1949 to 1951.[6] The first American expedition to Afghanistan was led by Louis Dupree, Walter Fairservis, and Henry Hart. In 1953, Richard Nixon who was serving as U.S. Vice President at the time made an official diplomatic visit to Kabul. He also took a short tour around the city and met with local Afghans.

U.S. President Dwight D. Eisenhower's state visit to Afghanistan on December 9, 1959. In 1958, Daoud Khan became the first Afghan to speak before the United States Congress in Washington, DC. He was serving as Prime Minister of Afghanistan at the time. His presentation focused on a number of issues, but most importantly, underscored the importance of US-Afghan relations. While in the US capital of Washington, Daoud met with President Dwight Eisenhower, signed an important cultural exchange agreement, and reaffirmed personal relations with Vice President Nixon that had begun during the latter's trip to Kabul in 1953. The Prime Minister also traveled around the United States visiting the New York Stock Exchange, the Empire State Building, hydroelectric facilities at the Tennessee Valley Authority (TVA), and other sites. King Zahir Shah of Afghanistan and U.S. President John F. Kennedy in Washington, D.C. two months before his assassination.

At that time the United States declined Afghanistan's request for defense cooperation but extended an economic assistance program focused on the development of Afghanistan's physical infrastructure–roads, dams, and power plants. Later, US aid shifted from infrastructure projects to technical assistance programs to help develop the skills needed to build a modern economy. Contacts between the United States and Afghanistan increased during the 1950s, especially during the Cuban Revolution between 1953 and 1959. While the Soviet Union was supporting Cuba's Fidel Castro, the United States was focusing on Afghanistan for its strategic purposes. This was mainly to counter the spread of communism and the strength of the Soviet Union into South Asia, particularly the Persian Gulf.

President Eisenhower made a state visit to Afghanistan in December 1959 to meet with its leaders. He landed at Bagram Airfield and then drove from there to Kabul in a motorcade. He met with King Zahir Shah, Prime Minister Daoud and a number of high-ranking government officials. He also took a tour of Kabul. After this important visit, the United States began to feel that Afghanistan was safe from ever becoming a Soviet satellite state. From the 1950s to 1979, U.S. foreign assistance provided Afghanistan with more than $500 million in loans, grants, and surplus agricultural commodities to develop transportation facilities, increase agricultural production, expand the educational system, stimulate industry, and improve government administration.

In 1963, King Zahir Shah of Afghanistan made a special state visit to the United States where he was met by John F. Kennedy and Eunice Kennedy Shriver. Zahir Shah also took a special tour of the United States, visiting Disney World in California, New York and other places. Habibullah Karzai, uncle of Hamid Karzai who served as representative of Afghanistan at the United Nations, is also believed to have accompanied Zahir Shah in the course of the King's state visit. During this period the Soviets were beginning to feel that the United States was turning Afghanistan into a satellite state. In 1965, Afghanistan and Cuba saw the establishment of communist parties, the Communist Party of Cuba and the People's Democratic Party of Afghanistan (PDPA).

Vice President Spiro Agnew, accompanied by Apollo 10 astronauts Thomas Stafford and Eugene Cernan, visited Kabul during an eleven-nation tour of Asia. At a formal dinner hosted by the Royal Family, the American delegation presented the King with a piece of lunar rock, a small Afghan flag carried on the Apollo 11 flight to the moon, and photographs of Afghanistan taken from space. By the 1970s, numerous American teachers, engineers, doctors, scholars, diplomats, and explorers had traversed Afghanistan's rugged landscape where they lived and worked. The Peace Corps was active in Afghanistan between 1962 and 1979. Many other American programs were running in the country such as CARE, American Scouting overseas (Afghanistan Scout Association), USAID, and others.

After the April 1978 Saur Revolution, relations between the two nations deteriorated. In February 1979, U.S. Ambassador Adolph "Spike" Dubs was murdered in Kabul after Afghan security forces burst in on his kidnappers. The U.S. then reduced bilateral assistance and terminated a small military training program. All remaining assistance agreements were ended after the Soviet invasion of Afghanistan.

Following the Soviet invasion, the United States supported diplomatic efforts to achieve a Soviet withdrawal. In addition, generous U.S. contributions to the refugee program in Pakistan played a major part in efforts to assist Afghan refugees. U.S. efforts also included helping the population living inside Afghanistan. This cross-border humanitarian assistance program aimed at increasing Afghan self-sufficiency and helping resist Soviet attempts to drive civilians out of the rebel-dominated countryside. During the period of Soviet occupation of Afghanistan, the U.S. provided about 3 billion US dollars in military and economic assistance to the Mujahideen groups stationed on the Pakistani side of the Durand Line. The U.S. Embassy in Kabul was closed in January 1989 for security reasons.

TWELVE YEARS AFTER US-NATO JOINT OPERATION "OPERATION ENDURING FREEDOM"

It is beyond doubt that presence of US and NATO forces in Afghanistan has broken the backbone of Taliban. Following the September 11 attacks in the United States, believed to be orchestrated by Osama bin Laden who was residing in Afghanistan under asylum at the time, the US-led "Operation Enduring Freedom" was launched. This major military operation was aimed at removing the Taliban government from power and to capture or kill Al Qaeda members, including Osama bin Laden. Following the overthrow of the Taliban, the U.S. supported the new government of Afghan President Hamid Karzai by maintaining a high level of troops to establish the authority of his government as well as combat Taliban insurgency. Both Afghanistan and the United States resumed diplomatic ties in late 2001.

The U.S. and its allies quickly drove the Taliban from power and captured all major cities and towns in the country. Many Al Qaeda and Taliban leaders escaped to neighboring Pakistan or retreated to rural or remote mountainous regions. In December 2001, the U.N. Security Council established the International Security Assistance Force (ISAF), to oversee security in the country and train the Afghan National Army. At the Bonn Conference in December 2001, Hamid Karzai was selected to head the Afghan Interim Administration, which after a loyajirga in Kabul in June 2002, became the Afghan Transitional Administration. In the popular elections of 2004, Karzai was elected the president of the new permanent Afghan government, the Islamic Republic of Afghanistan.[7]

In 2003, NATO assumed leadership of ISAF, included troops from 43 countries, with NATO members providing the core of the force. Only a portion of U.S. forces in Afghanistan operate under NATO command; the rest remained under direct American command. Mullah Omar reorganized the Taliban movement and launched the insurgency against the Afghan government and ISAF forces in the spring of 2003.Though vastly outgunned and outnumbered by NATO forces and the Afghan National Army, the Taliban and its allies, most notably the Haqqani Network and Hezb-e-Islami Gulbuddin, have waged asymmetric warfare with guerilla raids and ambushes in the countryside, suicide attacks against urban targets, and turncoat killings against coalition forces. The Taliban exploited the weak administration of the Afghan government, among the most corrupt in the world, to reassert influence across rural areas of southern and eastern Afghanistan. NATO countries responded in 2006 by increasing troops for operations to "clear and hold" villages and "nation building" projects to "win hearts and minds".[8] On 2 May 2011, U.S. forces killed Osama bin Laden in Abbotabad, Pakistan. On 2 May 2011, U.S. officials announced that Al-Qaeda leader Osama bin Laden was killed in a Special Operation (code-named *Operation Neptune Spear*) to kill or capture Osama Bin Laden, conducted by the CIA and U.S. Navy SEALs, in Pakistan. Crowds gathered outside the White House in Washington, DC, chanting "USA, USA" after the news emerged, and President Barack Obama addressed the nation and the world from the East Room of the White House to tell the world of the operation.[9] On 21 May 2012 the leaders of the NATO-member countries endorsed an exit strategy for removing NATO soldiers from Afghanistan.

With the death of Osama Bin Laden, US has got an golden opportunity to exit Afghanistan and to stop spending billions of Dollars, although it is a pre-mature withdrawal. Eleven years later, there are many Afghans who barely know anything about the September 11. They don't know that the attacks were the reason for the huge United States and NATO presence in Afghanistan. They don't know that they led to the ousting of the Taliban. What they do know is that Afghanistan has been fundamentally transformed since 2001.

It would be a mistake to interpret these accomplishments as a clear Taliban defeat in the south. Yes, the Taliban there is no longer capable of mounting major military operations. But it has learned that targeted assassinations of key political and tribal figures and government officials and persistent insidious intimidation accomplish many of its objectives. Some supposedly-cleared areas, such as Mallajat, an important sub district of Kandahar City, have seen a substantial deterioration of security already. The quality of the Afghan national security forces, on which preserving stability hinges to a great extent, also still remains questionable. The Afghan National Police in particular continue to suffer from many vices and deficiencies, not the least of which is an absolute lack of capacity to suppress crime – the scourge of the lives of Afghans that eviscerates their security and provides a perfect mobilization platform for the Taliban. The Afghan National Army (ANA) has made large progress: Not only has it grown in size, but also its quality has improved. The coming two years will show how much capacity to tackle the Taliban and other forms of insecurity it has. But even the ANA represents hardly a clear-cut success. Worrisomely, it appears that it is deeply ethnically-factionalized, not to mention the fact that most of its high-level commanders continue to be northerners and that southern Pashtuns exhibit little interest in signing up for even rank-and-file positions. Thus, there is a real danger that the ANA may fracture along ethnic lines and around particular commanders when the foreigners leave.

The militias mushrooming around Afghanistan with or without the encouragement of ISAF often prove unreliable and incapable of standing up to the Taliban, yet they frequently bring other forms of insecurity to an area and undermine good governance and peaceable relations within and among Afghan communities. The Afghan Local Police, one of such militia forces, has the most stringent oversight mechanisms compared to the other militias, but even in its case, the oversight exists mainly during the vetting phase of standing it up. Even in the ALP's case, established mechanisms are lacking for rolling it back should some of its units go rogue. Moreover, precisely because the absolutely necessary vetting takes time, the ALP currently numbers in the low thousands, with a growth of about 1,000 ALP fighters per half a year; thus the ALP can hardly be counted upon as a game-changer. However, sacrificing the vetting procedures and rushing to stand up the ALP faster will likely plunge it into the same abuse and unreliability problems that other militia forces have exhibited, only intensifying conflict dynamics in Afghanistan.[10]

RETURN OF RUSSIA TO AFGHANISTAN

Russia's heavily troubled past in Afghanistan as well as its unique experience there, coupled with a long history of economic and security dominance in the neighbouring region of Central Asia, both define and constrain Russia's interests and policy vis-à-vis Afghanistan, now as much as after 2014. This role should be primarily analysed in the economic and security context. Russia has some role to play in reconstruction and economic cooperation. It also provides limited security assistance to the Afghan government and has a genuine interest in the improved security and functionality of the state in Afghanistan, especially in view of its genuine security and counter-narcotics concerns.

Even after disintegration of USSR, the influence of Russia still dominates in the Central Asian region and Russia treats Central Asia as its backyard and is always concern about growing influence of US and China in the region. Upon Vladimir Putin's return to power in May 2012, Moscow is increasingly adopting a 'Russia first' strategy, and has begun to provide a better definition of its priorities. Moscow will only get involved in those areas that it considers crucial to its security and domestic development. Other sectors will be 'marketized', left to the private sector or to market competition. The fight against drug-trafficking passing through Central Asia from Afghanistan is one of Moscow's security priorities. Another is the control of labour migration from Central Asia. The Kremlin is also concerned about the risks of interaction between its own Islamic networks and those in Central Asia and Afghanistan.

To support its domestic development, Russia is prioritizing the creation of a Eurasian Economic Space and promoting greater regional coordination in key sectors such as hydrocarbons, electricity, and transport and cereals production. This strategy, which is still in the making, is built on the assumption that Russia will partially retract its interest in states that resist its influence, such as Uzbekistan and Turkmenistan. Instead, it will privilege regional structures with fewer members – Kazakhstan, Kyrgyzstan and Tajikistan – but a higher degree of cohesion. Examples of this include the Collective Security Treaty Organization (CSTO), and the yet incomplete Customs Union/Eurasian Economic Space.

On the one hand, Russia's economic cooperation with Afghanistan is likely to modestly expand, depending on security conditions after 2014. While Russian companies may lose in subcontracting in the likely case of reduced Western economic/reconstruction aid to Afghanistan after the NATO security presence ends, they might even gain if they are ready – as they often are in other insecure parts of the world – to more actively subcontract to the West for projects in certain parts of Afghanistan with a potentially more volatile context. On the other hand, the lion's share of Russia's economic attention, projects and investments in the broader region will be absorbed by Central Asia, not Afghanistan.

RUSSIA'S CONCERNS ABOUT THE IMPLICATIONS FOR CENTRAL ASIA

Moscow has voiced serious concerns about the potential effects of the post-2014 situation in Afghanistan on stability in

Central Asia. The potential spill-over of instability and militancy from Afghanistanis seen by Central Asian governments, including Russia's security allies, as a major cross-border threat. While the Taliban-led insurgency poses no direct threat to Afghanistan's northern neighbours, overall in stability in Afghanistan is likely to increase, the already weak central government in Kabul may further weaken, and cross-border trafficking, sporadic violence and further militarization of northern Afghanistan may intensify. The scale of the spill-over threat though, should not be over-estimated. Violent rifts between Tajik government forces and some former commanders of the United Tajik Opposition in Rasht or Gorno-Badakhshan Autonomous Region in 2010-2012 show that the spill-over of militancy and instability goes in both directions across the Tajik-Afghan border (not only from Afghanistan to Tajikistan, but also the other way round).[11]

Despite insufficient or speculative evidence on an Afghanistan-related 'spill-over effect' and a lack of solid international expertise on domestic sources of violence in Central Asia, the threat from 'external militants' has been systematically overrated by all Central Asian governments (but also, to an extent, by Russia, Pakistan and China). It is not clear how much of this overrating is accounted for by:

(a) conspiracy-obsessed thinking widespread among the region's mostly autocratic rulers;

(b) a degree of genuine concern about the cross-border factor as an additional complication in the case of major internal calamity (e.g. during the looming regime succession in Uzbekistan); or

(c) manipulation of the 'cross-border' threat for domestic and foreign policy purposes.

For Central Asian regimes, apart from blaming domestic unrest on external scapegoats, such purposes include attracting foreign security assistance. Russia emphasizes the external threat from Afghanistan-based 'militants and terrorists' as one of the main justifications for its security presence in Central Asia and the need to reinforce the CSTO role. Despite a tendency to routinely link any violence in northern Afghanistan to the Islamic Movement of Uzbekistan (IMU), the picture is actually more complicated. Not all violence in northern Afghanistan is accounted for by remnants of militant exiles from Central Asia such as the IMU.

The IMU – the core of which had been formed in the course of the Tajik civil war by exiled Islamists from Uzbekistan – was pushed out of Tajikistan, following an end to the civil war, and suffered a major blow in northern Afghanistan from the Northern Alliance and the US-led military coalition in 2001. Several hundred remaining fighters relocated to Pakistan's 'tribal areas' where they tried to survive by serving as 'hired guns' and linking up with local militants.[12] Since 2007, the Pakistani government, under increased pressure from the United States on antiterrorism grounds, tried to use 'the Uzbek card' to split the Taliban elements in the FATA and to blame local and cross-border violence primarily on 'foreigners' such as the IMU.[13] While there was some influx of IMU remnants and splinter militants back to Afghanistan in late 2000s – early 2010s, as a result of tribal infighting in the FATA and of pressure by Pakistani government forces, this influx was not massive enough, given the overall limited numbers of IMU fighters, to solely account for the rise in violent incidents in northern Afghanistan after 2009. Nor is there strong evidence that such militant elements in northern Afghanistan still see Central Asia as their final destination.

AFGHAN DRUG TRAFFICKING CHALLENGE TO RUSSIA

The only direct large-scale threat that Russian society faces from Afghanistan emanates from the deeply-embedded Afghan opium economy, with Central Asia as the main transit corridor to the Russian market. The Russian government has become increasingly aware of the gravity of this threat to Russian society and elevated its importance to a first-order security challenge rather than a secondary aspect to other threats such as terrorism. In post-Taliban Afghanistan, opiate cultivation, production and export levels increased exponentially and far exceeded the levels under the Taliban back in the 1990s. In 2007, cultivation reached an all-time historical peak (it was 25 times larger than in 2001when it declined by 91 percent as a result of the Taliban ban on poppy cultivation); in 2012, cultivation was still 19 times larger than it had been under the Taliban in 2001.[14]

To conclude, the drug trafficking, terrorism, return of Taliban, political instability are some major problems that are haunting the world community after US withdraws from Afghanistan in 2014. Countries like India and Central Asian nations will face the daunting task of fighting terrorism alone if the Taliban returns with the overt and covert support of Pakistan. After 2014, both end-consumers of Afghan heroin such as Russia and transit countries will need to rely on whatever governance will be in place in Afghanistan for drug control and counter-narcotics measures at the source. But, as foreign forces leave, the central government in Kabul stands little chance of establishing even basic control either in the main drug-producing areas in the south or in major manufacturing areas in the north.

So Russia has a very pragmatic and genuine interest in supporting any political solution for Afghanistan that could improve governance capacity, i.e. increase the functionality and legitimacy of the Afghan state. In areas where the drug economy is compounded by an ongoing, protracted armed conflict, there is no solution to the drug problem without a solution to the conflict. As long as the armed confrontation continues, it both impedes central state access to the areas affected by drugs and conflict and complicates the functioning of any de facto governance structures (i.e. run by the insurgency). In addition, in the absence of functional governance, both neither tough, nor soft counter-narcotics and drug control measures, neither 'security' nor 'development' solutions, nor even a combination of the two, will work.

Against this background, Russia has a very genuine interest in supporting any kind of political solution for Afghanistan that could bring relative stabilization (in terms of the end of a major armed conflict) and increase the functionality of the Afghan state. And this hinges upon progress towards a political settlement and power-sharing between all major veto players in post-2014 Afghanistan, including the insurgency. Also a joint and genuine effort from other regional powers like Pakistan, China, India, Iran is the need of the hour to stop Taliban to return to power in Kabul. This heightened responsibility does not mean Russia should be directly involved in Afghan events. Russia should never intervene in infighting in Afghanistan, especially militarily. Its goal should be protecting Russian interests by using diplomatic and other nonviolent means in Afghanistan and in the region. Moscow should also pursue an active and comprehensive policy in Central Asia–the territory where the first Russian line of defence against security threats emanating from Afghanistan lies. Having effective working relations with all significant Afghan elites and with all regional powers is an important condition for the success of Russian policy in Afghanistan.

NOTES

1. Amin Saikal, Ravan Farhadi, Kirill Nourzhanov. *Modern Afghanistan: A History of Struggle and Survival.* I.B. Tauris, 2006, p.64.
2. Press Release (February 13, 2009). "*Tips for Soviet in Afghanistan*". *BBC, 1979*, pp.3-5.

3. The Russian General Staff (2002). Lestwer W. Grau, Michael A. Gress, ed. *The Soviet Afghan-War: How a Superpower Fought and Lost.* University Press of Kansas. p.10.
4. Misdaq, Nabi (2006). *Afghanistan: Political Frailty and External Interference.* Taylor & Francis. p.134.
5. Grigory, Paul (2008). *Lenin's Brain and Other Tales from the Secret Soviet Archives.* Hoover Press. p.121.
6. Maley, William and Saikal, Amin (1989).*The Soviet Withdrawal from Afghanistan.* Cambridge University Press. p.127.
7. Felbab-Brown, V. (2012) Slip-Sliding on a Yellow Brick Road: Stabilization Efforts in Afghanistan. Stability: *International Journal of Security and Development* 1(1): 4-19, DOI: http://dx.doi.org/10.5334/sta.af.
8. Rothstein, Hy S (2006). "*Afghanistan: and the troubled future of unconventional warfare" Rothstein.* pp306-308.
9. "Al-Qaeda leader Osama Bin Laden dead – Obama". *BBC News* (BBC). 2 May 2011.
10. Vanda Felbab-Brown, September 6, 2011) "Afghanistan Ten Years after 9/11: Counterterrorism Accomplishments while a Civil War Is Lurking" Brookings Institute, See at.http://www.brookings.edu/research/opinions/2011/09/06-afghanistan-felbabbrown
11. Stepanova E., "Islamist terrorism in the Caucasus and Central Asia", in A. Schmid and G. Hindle (eds), *After the War on Terror: Regional and Multilateral Perspectives on Counter-terrorism Strategy,* (London: RUSI, 2009), pp. 112-121.
12. Van der Schriek D., "*The IMU: fish in search of a sea,*" Eurasianet.org, 14 March 2005.
13. Mirsayitov I., "The Islamic Movement of Uzbekistan: development stages and its present state," *Central Asia and the Caucasus,* vol. 42, no. 6 (2006), pp.110-114.
14. *Afghanistan Opium Survey* 2008 (Vienna: UNODC, 2008), p. 7; Afghanistan Opium Survey 2012: Summary Findings (Vienna: UNODC, 2012), p. 5.

16

INDIA'S FIGHT AGAINST TERRORISM: PATHANKOT AIRBASE ATTACK

On 2nd January 2016, a heavily armed group attacked the Pathankot Air Force Station, part of the Western Air Command of the Indian Air Force. Six attackers and three security forces personnel were killed in the initial battle. The gun battle and the subsequent combing operation lasted about 17 hours on 2 January. The attackers, who were wearing Indian Army fatigues, were suspected to belong to Jaish-e-Mohammed, an Islamist militant group designated a terrorist organization by India, US, UK and the UN. The attack was described as a terrorist incident in the Indian and foreign media. A further three soldiers who were admitted to hospital with injuries died, raising the death toll to seven soldiers. On 3 January, fresh gunshots were heard, and another security officer was killed by an IED explosion. The Pathankot–Jammu highway was sealed off as soon as news of the attack broke.[1] According to Indian intelligence officers, the attackers may have entered India on 31st December 2015 along the banks of the Beas River which cuts across the Pakistani border.[2] The attackers were aiming to destroy the aircraft and helicopters in the base, according to a call interception report.[3]

Gunshots were heard on the morning of 3rd January, 2016, leading to speculation that more attackers were still in the airbase. A fresh IED explosion on3rd January injured three

National Security Guard personnel. A National Security Guard officer who was injured during the blast died in a hospital. Around noon, it was discovered that two attackers were still at large in the airbase. Security forces continued the operation on 4 January with reinforcements being deployed to the location. A fifth attacker was confirmed killed later during the day. The neutralisation of the sixth attacker was reported at 4.15 PM on5th January. The operation launched by the Indian Army to neutralise the attackers was called "Operation Dhangu" or "Dhangu Suraksha", named after the place Dhangu where the base is located.[4] The operation continued on 4 January, and a fifth attacker was confirmed killed. The United Jihad Council claimed responsibility for the attack on 4th January, 2016.[4]

The hijacking of a car of a superintendent of the Punjab Police the previous day was reportedly linked to the attack. People hijacked his car for transport. They did not know that it was a police car since the police lights were off. Media reports suggested that the attack was an attempt to derail a fragile peace process meant to stabilize the deteriorated relations between India and Pakistan, as several pieces of evidence were found linking the attackers to Pakistan. In mid-January, Pakistan made the arrests of several members of the Jaish-e-Mohammed, which India suspects of involvement in attack.

Reports claimed that the people who carried out the attack in Pathankot were in regular touch with their Pakistani handlers. A report revealed that the two phone numbers to which calls were made by the attackers were from Pakistan. According to the report, the first number probably belonged to the mother of one of the militants, while the second one belonged to one of the handlers of the attackers. Intelligence Bureau officials told TOI that the attackers called their handler "ustaad" while describing their positions inside Punjab after crossing over from Pakistan.

The attackers called a number at 21:12 on 31 December from the phone of taxi driver Ikaagar Singh. Perpetrators also received four phone calls on Ikrar Singh's number. "On this number, in fact, the terrorist is heard telling the attacker to kill the taxi driver," the official told TOI. One of the attackers called up his mother in the middle of attack from the mobile phone of jeweller Rajesh Verma. The call was made at around 08:30, five hours after the attack was launched on the airbase. Maulana Masood Azhar, chief of Jaish-e-Mohammad, and his brother Abdul Rauf Asghar, mastermind of IC-814 hijack case, are among four persons identified by Indian intelligence agencies as "handlers" behind the attack. The agencies found evidence that the conspiracy was hatched near Lahore. Indian defense Minister Manohar Parrikar said there are indications that some of the materials used were made in Pakistan.[5]

The Pakistan Ministry of Foreign Affairs issued a press release condemning the attack and offered condolences. Foreign office spokesman Qazi Khalilullah said. "Building on the goodwill created during the recent high-level contacts between the two countries, Pakistan remains committed to partner with India as well as other countries in the region to completely eradicate the menace of terrorism afflicting our region."[6] Pakistan also complained that India accused the Pakistani state of the attack. Special assistant to Prime Minister Nawaz Sharif, Irfan Siddiqui, said, "India should understand that Pakistan itself had been one of the greatest victims of terrorist attacks on its soil." He regretted that only after a few terrorist attacks India begins hurling baseless allegations. He advised India to review its stance by further saying, "India should create an environment of trust, as unfounded allegations only hamper the process of dialogue." Former foreign secretary of Pakistan Riaz Khokhar said, "India was trying to tarnish Pakistan's image and is using such attacks to derail talks. Pakistani news channel ARY News reported today that "some arrests" have been made in this regard but police did not confirm any arrest related to the Pathankot attack, as per PTI.

INDIA'S STRATEGY TO FIGHT AGAINST TERRORISM

Terrorism in India, according to the Home Ministry, poses a significant threat to the people of India. Terrorism found in India includes ethno-nationalist terrorism, religious terrorism, left wing terrorism and narco terrorism.[8] The regions with long term terrorist activities have been Jammu and Kashmir, east-central and south-central India (Naxalism) and the Seven Sister States. In August 2008, National Security Advisor M K Narayanan has said that there are as many as 800 terrorist cells operating in the country.[9] As of 2013, 205 of the country's 608 districts were affected by terrorist activity. Terror attacks caused 231 civilian deaths in 2012 in India, compared to 11,098 terror-caused deaths worldwide, according to the State Department of the United States; or about 2 per cent of global terror fatalities while it accounts for 17.5 per cent of global population.[10]

The Indian government uses the following working definition of terrorism, same as one widely used by Western nations as well as the United Nations, proposed by Schmid and Jongman in 1988.[11]

"Terrorism is an anxiety-inspiring method of repeated violent action, employed by (semi-) clandestine individual, group or state actors, for idiosyncratic, criminal or political reasons, whereby the direct targets of violence are not the main targets. The immediate human victims of violence are generally chosen randomly (targets of opportunity) or selectively (representative or symbolic targets) from a target population, and serve as message generators. Threat and violence-based communication processes between terrorist organization, victims, and main targets are used to manipulate the main target (audience(s)), turning it into a target of terror, a target of demands, or a target of attention, depending on whether intimidation, coercion, or propaganda is primarily sought."–*Alex Schmid and Albert Jongman*[12.]

India subdivides terrorism in four major groups: [13]

1. ***Ethno-nationalist Terrorism*** - This form of terror focuses either (a) on creating a separate State within India or independent of India or in a neighboring country, or (b) on emphasizing the views/response of one ethnic group against another. Violent Tamil Nationalist groups from India to address the condition of Tamils in Sri Lanka, as well as insurgent tribal groups in North East India are examples of ethno-nationalist terrorist activities.[14]
2. ***Religious Terrorism*** - This form of terror focuses on religious imperatives, a presumed duty or in solidarity for a specific religious group, against one or more religious groups. Mumbai 26/11 terror attack in 2008 from an Islamic group in Pakistan is an example of religious terrorism in India.[15]
3. ***Left wing Extremism*** - This form of terror focuses on economic ideology, where all the existing socio-political structures are seen to be economically exploitative in character and a revolutionary change through violent means is essential. The ideology of Marx, Engel, Mao, Lenin and others are considered as the only valid economic path. Maoist violence in Jharkhand and Chhattisgarh are examples of left wing terrorism in India.[16]
4. ***Narco Terrorism*** - This form of terror focuses on creating illegal narcotics traffic zones. Drug violence in northwest India is an example of narco-terrorism in India.[17]

MAJOR TERRORIST GROUPS ACTIVE IN INDIA

There are scores of insurgent and terrorist groups operating in the country. Those recognized by the U.S. State Department as Foreign Terrorist Organizations (FTO) or other "groups of concern" are: [18]

- *Lashkar-e-Taiba* (LeT), whose name means "Army of the Pure," is a militant Islamist group operating in Pakistan as well as in Jammu and Kashmir. The group reportedly received funding from Pakistan's intelligence services until 2001, when the United States designated it an FTO and Pakistan froze its assets. LeT, which has ideological, but unconfirmed operational ties to al-Qaeda, aims to win sovereignty for Jammu and Kashmir and spread Islamic rule across India. The group is blamed for some of the most high-profile terrorist attacks in India, including the July 11, 2006 bombing of the Mumbai commuter rail.
- *Jaish-e-Muhammad*, (JeM), meaning "Army of Mohammed," is another Pakistan-based terrorist group operating in Jammu and Kashmir. Founded in 2000 by the former leader of the now-defunct group Harkat-ul-Ansar, Jaish-e-Muhammed seeks to drive India out of Jammu and Kashmir and transfer control of the region to Pakistan.
- *Harakatul-Mujahadeen* (HuM), or the "Islamic Freedom Fighters' Group," was founded in 1985 as an anti-Soviet group fighting in Afghanistan. When Soviet forces withdrew in 1989, the Pakistan-based HuM shifted its focus to Jammu and Kashmir. HuM seeks to battle "anti-Islamic forces" and its members have helped carry out operations as far away as Myanmar, Tajikistan, and Bosnia.
- *The Communist Party of India (Maoist)* was formed by a merger of Naxalite groups in 2004 after talks between the Indian government and the leftist militants broke down. The group seeks to establish a "revolutionary zone" of control extending from the Nepalese border down to the southern part of Andhra Pradesh that would ultimately become a sovereign state.
- *Harakatul-Jihad-I-Islami* (HUJI) was founded in 1980 to fight Soviets in Afghanistan but has since concentrated

its efforts in Jammu and Kashmir. HUJI, which is based in Pakistan and Kashmir, primarily attacks Indian military targets, but it is believed to be linked to the abduction and slaying of five Western tourists in Jammu and Kashmir in 1995.

- *Jamiatul-Mujahadeen* is a small group of pro-Pakistan Kashmiri separatists operating in or near Pakistan. It is thought to be responsible for a pair of 2004 grenade attacks against political targets in India.
- *The United Liberation Front of Assam* (ULFA) has sought to establish an independent socialist state in Assam since its founding in 1979. In the 1990s, ULFA's attacks on political leaders, security forces, and infrastructure provoked a harsh response from the Indian government, causing it to lose some support among the residents of Assam. The U.S. State Department reports a December 2003 attack on a ULFA base by Indian forces caused the group's numbers to drop from more than 3,000 to several hundred.

STRATEGIES TO COUNTER TERRORISM IN INDIA

India's vulnerability to terrorism to a large measure is attributable to its geography – its borders are not secure. An open border with Nepal, a porous border with Bangladesh as well as the long Line of Control in Jammu and Kashmir which allows for infiltration, contribute to the unhindered movement of terrorists from across the borders.

India's coastal security also needs to be beefed up, as the Mumbai terrorist attack has demonstrated. Home grown terrorist groups, abetted and aided by external help, have also established a foothold. Socio economic and political motivations have also been contributing factors to violent activities.[21]

National Counter Terrorism Centre (NCTC) - The National Counter Terrorism Center (NCTC) is a proposed federal anti-terror agency to be created in India, modelled on the National

Counter terrorism Center of the USA. The proposal arose after the 2008 Mumbai attacks and 26/11 attacks where several intelligence and operational failures revealed the need for a federal agency with real time intelligence inputs of actionable value specifically to counter terrorist acts against India. The proposal has however met with much criticism from the Chief Ministers of various states who see this as a means of weakening India's federalism. The NCTC will derive its powers from the Unlawful Activities Prevention Act, 1967. It is to be a part of the Intelligence Bureau and will be headed by a Director who will report to the Director IB and the Home Secretary. But the modified original draft of NCTC says that this system does not come under purview of Intelligence Beaureu and states are taken into confidence before the Centre carries on any operation in their territories. The NCTC will execute counter-terror operations and collect, collate and disseminate data on terrorism besides maintaining a data base on terrorists and their associates including their families. The NCTC has been empowered to analyses intelligence shared by agencies like the Intelligence Bureau and select what it deems suitable. It has also been granted powers to conduct searches and arrests in any part of India and will formulate responses to terror threats.[20]

However, the body has not seen the light of the day because of the opposition of states who consider it as diluting the federal structure of the country. This is because unlike the American National Counterterrorism Center, which deals only with strategic planning and integration of intelligence, or the British Joint Terrorism Analysis Centre, which has also has a coordinating role, the NCTC has sweeping powers to conduct operations. This, the states say, goes against the constitutional provisions which place law and order under the state's list. While the government has altered the original provisions by keeping the NCTC out of IB and handing over arrested suspects to state police, but these have still not satisfied states and resultantly, the all-important terrorism fighting organization remains hanging in limbo.

The state police and its intelligence set-up: Under India's federal Constitution, the responsibility for policing and maintenance of law and order is that of the individual states. The central government in New Delhi can only give them advice, financial help, training and other assistance to strengthen their professional capabilities and share with them the intelligence collected by it. The responsibility for follow-up action lies with the state police.

The national intelligence community: This consists of the internal intelligence agency (the ministry of home affairs' Intelligence Bureau), the external intelligence agency (the Cabinet secretariat's Research and Analysis Wing), the Defence Intelligence Agency , and the intelligence directorates general of the armed forces.

The IB collects terrorism-related intelligence inside the country and RAW does it outside. The DIA and the intelligence directorates general of the armed forces essentially collect tactical intelligence during their counter-terrorism operations in areas such as Jammu and Kashmir, Nagaland, etc. where they are deployed.

Physical security agencies: These include the Central Industrial Security Force, responsible for physical security at airports and sensitive establishments; the National Security Guards, a specially trained intervention force to terminate terrorist situations such as hijacking, hostage-taking, etc; and the Special Protection Group, responsible for the security of the prime minister and former prime ministers.

Paramilitary forces: These include the Central Reserve Police Force and the Border Security Force, which assist the police in counter-terrorism operations when called upon to do so.

The Army: Their assistance is sought as a last resort when the police and paramilitary forces are not able to cope with a terrorist situation. But in view of Pakistan's large-scale infiltration in Jammu and Kashmir and the presence and activities of a large number of Pakistani mercenaries, many of them ex-servicemen, the army has a more active, permanent and leadership role in counter-terrorism operations here. What India is facing in J&K is not just terrorism, but a proxy war being waged by the Pakistani Army through its *jihadi* surrogates.[22]

WHAT NEEDS TO BE DONE?

- All cities must establish a network of mohalla committees and housing societies to monitor all suspicious movement in their own locality. Each city must have a dedicated police officer to man this 24x7. This measure will enhance both intelligence gathering as well as alert police to movement of terrorists. Police can circulate photographs and information of the fugitive suspects to these committees. In short a city wide concept of 'neighbourhood watch' needs to be implemented immediately. This will cost next to nothing,
- In many western countries the police or intelligence agencies have launched 'sting operations' to lure and nab would be terrorists before they commit an act of sabotage. It is time our security establishment did the same;
- Like guerrillas without help similarly terrorists without local help would be like fish out of water. Infringement of laws to support acts of terror either for money or due to ideology needs to be viewed seriously by both the police (and especially) the judiciary;
- There is an urgent need to create a well thought out standard operating procedure in case of a terrorist incident. Once an incident is declared as a 'terrorist incident' by the designated authority (could be the police commissioner in case of a city) then all resources civil,

military or private must come under the pre-designated commander. All agencies must be obliged to obey his orders. It is the lack of unified command and pooling of resources on 26/11 that resulted in the terrorists holding out for over 72 hours and recent Pathankot attack took almost four days.

- The judiciary must deal with terrorism related cases quickly and punish the mass murderers. It is time that the judiciary sheds its proclivity to give the benefit of doubt to the criminals while doubting the intention of the law enforcers. If not corrected in time, we may soon come to a situation where the honest policeman will prefer not to act.[23]

CONCLUSION

Indians do not believe in concept of one church, one holy book or one prophet. Pluralism and freedom of choice is the core value of Indian civilization. Pluralism of worship, thought, language, dress and aesthetics has been embedded in the Indian past for at least 5,000 years. This is the best guarantee for the religious or ethnic minorities and not merely the constitution. India has not become secular or plural because of the constitution. It is the other way round and that is because majority of Indians believe in pluralism that India enacted a constitution that does not discriminate on basis of caste or creed.

There's a connection between Modi's visit to Pakistan and the terrorist attacks, but not a fundamentally causal one. Rather, the visit was a trigger for carefully laid plans in a pre-existing terrorist playbook. The idea to attack Pathankot didn't first arise on December 25, when Modi touched down unexpectedly in Pakistan. Such attacks are months in the making. India needs to be alive to the probability that Pakistani terrorists and their ISI handlers have plans to attack every major military installation within range of Pakistan. There are also plans, surely, for assaults on Indian nuclear installations and naval bases, as well as Indian diplomatic missions. Punjab is a cesspit of corruption and drug smuggling, ruled by a venal family and party that have brought India's most dynamic province to its knees. India cannot afford such mismanagement of a strategic border state. Corruption not only distorts the local economy and politics, it destroys morale, creating the perfect conditions for terrorist infiltration and attack. Now that it's apparent that terrorists (and the ISI) have widened their incursive focus beyond Kashmir, India cannot let any of its western border states be so rotten.

NOTES

1. "Pathankot-Jammu highway sealed after terror attack", *India Today*, 2 January 2016.
2. "Pathankot terror attack strikes at heart of PM Modi's Pakistan peacemaking". *The Indian Express,* 2 January 2016.
3. "Operation enters third day, more forces rushed to airbase". *The Hindu*, 4 January 2016.
4. "Pathankot attack: How 'Operation Dhangu' was won - Times of India" *Times of India*, 7th January, 2016.
5. "Phone number of Pathankot attacker's 'ustaad' in Pakistan", *The Times of India*, Jan 8, 2016.
6. "Six IAF men killed as terrorists storm Indian air force base, Pakistan condemns attack". *The Dawn.* 2 January 2016.
7. "Pak condemns Pathankot attack, says committed to eradicate terror". *Hindustan Times.* 3 January 2016.
8. Hoffman B. (2006), *Inside Terrorism*, Columbia University Press, pp.23-30.
9. "800 Terror Cells Active in Country". *The Times of India.* 12 August 2008.
10. "Country Reports on Terrorism 2012", Department of State, United States (May 2013).

11. "Combatting Terrprism Protecting by Righteousness", Administrative Reforms Commission, Government of India (June 2008)
12. Schmid & Jongman (1988), *Political Terrorism: a new guide to actors, authors, concepts, data bases, theories and, literature.*
13. Combatting Terrprism Protecting by Righteousness", Administrative Reforms Commission, Government of India (June 2008)
14. Hoffman B. (2006), *Inside terrorism*, Columbia University Press, Columbia, pp.124-136.
15. "Helping India fight terrorism" Ministry of External Affairs, Govt of India (2012) .
16. Enders & Sandler (2011), *The political economy of terrorism,* 2nd edition, Cambridge University Press, Cambridge, pp.23-42.
17. Sharma (2013), Growing overlap between terrorism and organized crimc in India: A case study, *Security Journal*, 26(1), pp. 60-79.
18. Audrey Kurth Cronin, The Foreign Terrorist Organization List, *Foreign Affairs,* December 21, 2011.
19. Eben Kaplan, and Jayshree Bajoria "Counterterrorism in India" Council on Foreign Relations, November 27, 2008http://www.cfr.org/india/counterterrorism-india/p11170
20. "What's the fuss on NCTC". *The Sunday Guardian.* 17 February 2012.
21. *Vivek Lall "Counter Terrorism and Global Learning",* May 2012;
22. "India's counter-terrorism strategy" Rediff.com, http://www.rediff.com/news/2003/apr/05spec.htm
23. Anil Athale, "Seven simple steps to curb terrorism in India" August 06, 2012.

17

INDIA AND THE 'NEW GREAT GAME' IN CENTRAL ASIA

Central Asia and India have long traditions of social-cultural, religious, political and economic contact from ancient period. The two regions have common and contiguous borders, climatic continuity, similar geographical features and geo-cultural affinity. There has always been uninterrupted flow of people, material and the ideas between the two regions. There are extensive references to people of Central Asia in Indian literature like Atharvaveda, Vamsa Brahmana of Samveda, Aitareya Brahmana, Satapatha Brahmana, Puranas, Manusmiriti, Ramayana, Mahabharata, Raghuvamsa, Brihat-Katha -Manjari, Katha-Saritsagara, Rajaratrangini, Mudra-rakshasa, Kavymimansa and host of other old Sanskrit literature.

In the post-cold war period, the Central Asian countries have engaged themselves in nation building and consolidation of their statehoods. The pessimistic scenarios feared in the early nineties of Central Asia disintegrating have not fortunately been realized. No state has become a failing state. On the contrary, countries like Kazakhstan have made great strides. At the same time, the Central Asian countries continue to face daunting socio-economic and security problems.[1] The relations among themselves are far from smooth. Issues like environmental degradation, border disputes, migration, ethnic conflicts, energy security, and religious extremism and fundamentalism pose serious challenge to regional stability.

The past decade has seen a notable rise in India's efforts to engage with Central Asia. Analysts suggest this is driven by two primary concerns: securing and diversifying India's energy supplies in order to sustain economic growth; and keeping a check on the rise of radical Islamist groups that may pose a threat to India's security. In addition, India is keen to tap the considerable commercial potential of the Central Asian region. Meanwhile, the strategic location of Central Asia means that it is a central focus of geopolitical manoeuvring affecting India's relations with Pakistan, China, the US, and other powers in the region.

India has great interest to ensure political stability, security and prosperity in Central Asia. New Delhi has developed a strategic approach towards Central Asian countries mostly based on security and energy issues. India rented Ayni airbase in Tajikistan in 2003 "in its quest for strategic footing in Central Asia," but it lost this base to Russia in 2010 after Tajikistan declared that Moscow would be the only country to use the airbase. [2] With the aim of developing strong bilateral partnerships in the region particularly on energy supply, India signed the pacts with Uzbekistan and Kazakhstan on the import of uranium. Furthermore, India launched the *"Connect Central Asia"* policy in 2012 to establish strategic and security cooperation particularly in the field of energy development.[3]

INDIA'S 'CONNECT CENTRAL ASIA' POLICY

India's '*Connect Central Asia*' Policy is a broad-based approach, including political, security, economic and cultural connections. On 12 June 2012 India's Minister of State for External Affairs E. Ahamed gave a Keynote address at First India-

Central Asia Dialogue. He outlined some of the elements of India's 'Connect Central Asia' policy as follows:

1. India will continue to build on our strong political relations through the exchange of high level visits. Its leaders will continue to interact closely both in bilateral and multilateral fora.
2. India will strengthen its strategic and security cooperation. India already has strategic partnerships in place with some Central Asian countries. In focus will be military training, joint research, counter-terrorism coordination and close consultations on Afghanistan.
3. India will step up multilateral engagement with Central Asian partners using the synergy of joint efforts through existing fora like the Shanghai Cooperation Organisation, Eurasian Economic Community (EEC) and the Custom Union. India has already proposed a Comprehensive Economic Cooperation Agreement to integrate its markets with the unifying Eurasian space.
4. India looks to Central Asia as a long term partner in energy, and natural resources. Central Asia possesses large cultivable tracts of land and it sees potential for India to cooperate in production of profitable crops with value addition.
5. The medical field is another area that offers huge potential for cooperation. India is ready to extend cooperation by setting up civil hospitals/clinics in Central Asia.
6. India's higher education system delivers at a fraction of the fees charged by Western universities. Keeping this in mind, India would like to assist in the setting up of a Central Asian University in Bishkek that could come up as a centre of excellence to impart world class education in areas like Information Technology, management, philosophy and languages.
7. India is working on setting up a Central Asian e-network with its hub in India, to deliver, tele-education and tele-

medicine connectivity, linking all the five Central Asian States.

8. Indian companies can showcase its capability in the construction sector and build world class structures at competitive rates. Central Asian countries, especially Kazakhstan, have almost limitless reserves of iron ore and coal, as well as abundant cheap electricity. India can help set up several medium size steel rolling mills, producing its requirement of specific products.
9. As for land connectivity, India has reactivated the International North-South Transport Corridor (INSTC). India & Central Asian nations need to join our efforts to discuss ways to bridge the missing links in the Corridor at the earliest and also work on other connecting spurs along the route.
10. Absence of a viable banking infrastructure in the region is a major barrier to trade and investment. Indian banks can expand their presence if they see a favourable policy environment.
11. India will jointly work to improve air connectivity between our countries. India is one of the biggest markets for outbound travellers estimated at $ 21 billion in 2011. Many countries have opened tourist offices in India to woo Indian tourists. Central Asian countries could emerge as attractive holiday destinations for tourists and even for the Indian film industry which likes to depict exotic foreign locales in its films.
12. Connections between our peoples are the most vital linkages to sustain our deep engagement. I would particularly like to emphasise exchanges between youth and the future leaders of India and Central Asia. India already has a robust exchange of students. India will encourage regular exchanges of scholars, academics, civil society and youth delegations to gain deeper insights into each other's cultures.[4]

RUSSIA AND CHINA IN CENTRAL ASIA: WHERE DOES INDIA STAND?

China's presence and influence in Central Asia - Kazakhstan, Kyrgyzstan, Tajikistan, Turkmenistan, and Uzbekistan - have been increasing. The westward strategy articulated by Chinese President Xi Jinping in his "*New Silk Road* economic belt" highlights Central Asia's importance for Chinese economy and development. Central Asia is resource rich, and, because of its proximity to China offers a great opportunity for cheap, reliable energy imports. China has been investing billions of dollars in the energy sector which include a series of contracts with Kazakhstan worth $30 billion, 31 agreements of $15 billion value with Uzbekistan, and natural gas transactions with Turkmenistan in 2013, which reached about $16 billion. China has also provided loans and aid of $8 billion to Turkmenistan and is expected to provide at least $1 billion to Tajikistan. Last year, China upgraded relations with Kyrgyzstan to a strategic level. Perhaps more important, Beijing views Central Asian countries as important allies in the fight against Islamic extremists that foment ethnic unrest in China's west; Xinjiang is a sovereignty issue, and therefore a "core interest." Finally, as the US rebalances to East Asia, China seeks strategic space to the west.[5] In 2015, Russia's Gazprom and the China National Petroleum Corporation have signed a $400 billion contract to jointly build a gas pipeline.

If Ukraine is Russia's front yard, then Central Asia must be considered its back yard. Russia has longstanding historical, economic, and political ties to Central Asian governments. Moscow has sought to consolidate those relationships through regional integration initiatives such as the Commonwealth of Independent States, the Customs Union, and the Eurasian Economic Union. Moscow is especially keen to maintain control of Central Asian energy and resource exports to protect its own position in the market: Central Asia is a potential competitor to Russia's energy exports, the lifeblood of the Russian economy. Its ownership of the old Soviet pipeline network offers control over Central Asia energy exports. Russia is also able to enhance the quality of its own product by blending it with higher quality oil from Kazakhstan, while maintaining control over price and supply.[6]

Russia has benefited from its historical, linguistic, economic and political ties with Central Asian countries from the very beginning of their independence. After a short period of recovery, Russia reasserted its strategic ambitions in Central Asia as well as in other ex-Soviet republics by declaring its "Near Abroad Doctrine" in 1993. Central Asian states are economically and politically highly dependent on Russia. Collective Security Treaty Organization (CSTO) and Shanghai Cooperation Organization (SCO) are the main instruments for Russia to keep the Central Asian states in its own sphere of influence.[7]

After resolving border disputes among Shanghai Five's three members, Kazakhstan, Kyrgyzstan and Tajikistan, Beijing has further deepened economic, military and political cooperation with Central Asian states. China plays a pro-active role in the fields of trade, energy security, investments, combating terrorism and fundamentalism, illegal transactions, and organized crime and also aims to increase its soft power in the region.[8]

Indian leaders have acknowledged that Central Asia could be an effective catalyst in the normalization of Indo-Pak relations and the stabilization process of Afghanistan. The emergence of predominantly Muslim but, in fact, multi-ethnic and multi-religious CARs has added a new strategic dimension to the geopolitics of the whole of Asia and more so, for the countries located in its immediate neighbourhood. Central Asia lies at the strategic junction between two nuclear powers, Russia and China, and at the interface between Russia and the Islamic world. It shares borders with Afghanistan, which is a major source of spreading religious extremism in the region.

India has a vital interest in the security and political stability of this region. Obviously given the Kashmir angle, India cannot be walled off from the political developments which take place in the Central Asian region. Any advance by Islamic extremist groups in the CARs could invigorate similar elements active in Kashmir. For reasons dictated by geography, India's strategic concerns are tied up with the regions bordering its north and northwest. Pakistan in its northwest continues to be antagonistic towards India. Pakistan is already sponsoring cross-border terrorism in Kashmir. For India, the Kashmir issue pertains not to four million Muslims living in Kashmir Valley alone, but to the peace and security of 130 million Muslims elsewhere in India.[9] Therefore, for India the geostrategic importance of CARs is immense. Under no circumstance can India ignore this region.

The implementation of Turkmenistan-Afghanistan-Pakistan-India (TAPI) pipeline project which was announced in 1995 and has recently revitalized carries a considerable potential to ensure regional economic integration and to create mutual dependency between Central and South Asia.[10] The 1,735-kilometer pipeline will transport 33 billion cubic metres of gas annually to South Asia for a period of 30 years. The integration of Afghanistan to both Central and South Asia, especially through the security establishments and economic cooperation could be beneficial not only for the relatively weak and fragile states of the region, but also for the major regional players such as Russia, China, United States (U.S.) and India.[11]

India has invested US$100 million in free trade zone in Chabahar. The Chinese are also getting interested in Chabahar and have announced Euro 60 million credits to Iran to upgrade the Port. The significance of Chabahar Port is that it will facilitate a transit route to land-locked Afghanistan. Despite direct road links, Pakistan does not allow transit facility from India to Afghanistan. Therefore, connectivity through the Chabahar Port could become an important route linking India to Afghanistan and Central Asia.

In his Seven days trip to five Central Asian nations from 6 to 13 July, 2015, Indian Prime Minister Narendra Modi aimed to deepen economic and political cooperation in the region. During this visit, in Tashkent, Modi said the relationship between Central Asia and India has "ancient roots" and "now occupies a significant place in India's future." Similarly, Modi's speech in Astana promising to "write a new chapter in an ancient relationship" between India and Central Asian states was highly optimistic.[12]

WHAT NEEDS TO BE DONE BY INDIA?

Firstly, for Central Asian states, India is a balancing factor that may ensure their strategic autonomy against Chinese and Russian dominance. Central Asian states have not attempted to balance India by aligning with each other or Pakistan so far.[13]

Secondly, for energy-rich countries of Central Asia, Kazakhstan, Uzbekistan and Turkmenistan that need to diversify their economic partnerships, especially in terms of hydropower and energy export, India could be an alternative market as well as a geopolitical counterweight.

Thirdly, India as an extended neighbour of CARs has major geostrategic and economic interests in this region. The future prospects for cooperation between Central Asia and India in the field of energy security seem to be very important.

Fourthly, peace and stability in CARs and Afghanistan seem to be the most crucial factor for India's security. There is already a realisation by world powers of the danger posed by religious extremism and terrorism. In fact, the problem of terrorism is not only being addressed at the bilateral level but also in various regional forums like Shanghai Five and Conference on Interaction and Confidence-building Measures in Asia (CICA).

Fifthly, another problem related to terrorism, and one that confronts India, Russia and CARs is that of drug trafficking. A lucrative drugs trade in Central Asia poses a major threat to stability in Central Asia. Central Asia was the hardest hit by the explosion in Afghan heroin. The Russian mafia, its ties to Afghanistan established during the Soviet occupation, used their networks to move heroin through Central Asia, Russia, and the Baltics into Europe. Tajikistan and Kyrgyzstan developed important opium routes and became significant opium producers themselves. Drugs are penetrating into Russia along two main channels. First, from the "golden triangle" of Southeast Asia via the Far East; the second from Southwest Asia–mainly Afghanistan and Pakistan–via Central Asia and the South Caucasus.

Finally, Central Asian region also remains highly vulnerable to the smuggling of fissile material for WMD. This region lies between two nuclear superpowers–Russia and China and also its neighbours, the two new nuclear powers, India and Pakistan. During the Soviet period Central Asia was the raw material base for its nuclear programme. After independence, Kazakhstan has closed its nuclear test range and has committed itself to being a non-nuclear weapon state under the Nuclear Non Proliferation Treaty (NPT), but it has not lost its potential of being a nuclear power. Uzbekistan has the world's third largest uranium deposits. Tajikistan also has uranium reserves and the capability of enrichment. Kyrgyzstan, meanwhile, has a lot of nuclear waste left over as a legacy of the former Soviet Union. Thus, in this region there is a serious threat of the proliferation of Weapons of Mass Destruction (WMD) Routes, which have been created for other illegal trafficking, can also be used for transporting components of WMD.

CONCLUSION

India is now looking intently at the region through the framework of its 'Connect Central Asia' policy, which is based on pro-active political, economic and people-to-people engagement with Central Asian countries, both individually and collectively. India's active presence in the region will contribute to stability and development in the entire Central and South Asia region. In this analysis, we must factor in the regional situation and especially the challenge of rebuilding the Afghan nation. A cooperative approach for embedding Afghanistan into a more meaningful regional economic and security framework would have benefits for the entire region. One way is to work towards converting Afghanistan into a hub for trade and energy, connecting Central and South Asia. The landmark agreement for the construction of the TAPI (Turkmenistan-Afghanistan-Pakistan-India) pipeline has put the spotlight on the importance of Central Asia for India's future energy plans. It would also greatly benefit Afghanistan.

Central Asian countries could also gain from the techno-economic-potential of India, which could be accessed in cooperative, mutually beneficial partnerships. Central Asia's desire for diversifying hydro-power and energy export routes would correspond with India's quest for diversifying imports. India will be keen to invest in setting up downstream production facilities, instead of exporting raw materials out of the region through expensive pipelines. The approach could differ from those seeking exclusively to pump out Central Asia's riches.

NOTES

1. Arvind Gupta, "India and Central Asia: Need for a Pro-active Approach" *IDSA* Policy bief, October 14, 2013.

2. Jhinuk Chowdhury, "How India Lost the Game in Central Asia and Why It Is Being Welcomed Back Now,"*Swarajya*, July 17, 2015.
3. Saurav Jha, "In Central Asia, Modi Jump-Starts India's 'Look North' Strategy," *World Politics Review*, July 16, 2015.
4. "Keynote address by MOS E. Ahamed at First India-Central Asia Dialogue, India's 'Connect Central Asia' Policy," *Ministry of External Affairs*, June 12, 2012.http://www.mea.gov.in/Speeches Statements.htm?dtl/19791/Keynote+address+by+MOS+Shri+E+Ahamed+at+First+IndiaCentral+Asia+Dialogue.
5. Virginia Marantidou, Ralph A. Cossa, "China and Russia's Great Game in Central Asia" *The National Interest*, October 1, 2014.
6. Ibid.
7. Arzu Turgut, "*India Footing In Central Asia: A Regional Balancer?* The Turkish Sunday, Dec 21, 2015.
8. Pauline Jones Luong & Erika Weinthal, "New Friends, New Fears in Central Asia", *Foreign Affairs*, Vol. 81, No. 2, 2003, p. 65.
9. Meena Singh Roy, "India's Interests in Central Asia" *IDSA*, New Delhi. For detail seehttp://www.idsa-india.org/an-mar-9.01.html.
10. "TAPI gas pipeline project to start from December 13," *The Times of India*, November 25, 2015.
11. Gulshan Sachdeva, "TAPI Gas Pipeline May Become Game Changer in South Asian Geopolitics," *Hindustan Times*, December 20, 2015.
12. Catherine Putz, "A 'New Chapter' for India and Central Asia?" *The Diplomat*, July 8, 2015.
13. Barry Buzan, "The South Asian Security Complex in a Decentring World Order: Reconsidering Regions and Powers Ten Years on," *International Studies*, 48:1, 2011, p. 3.

BIBLIOGRAPHY

Ambrosio, Thomas (2005), "*Challenging America's Global Preeminence: Russia's Quest for Multipolarity*", Chippenham, Wiltshire,Antony Rose.

Amin, Saikal and William Maley (1995), "*Russia in Search of its Future*", Cambridge: Cambridge University Press.

Anderson Jennifer (1999), "*The Limits of Sino-Russian Partnership*", London: IISS.

Aron, Leon and Kenneth Jonser (1994), "*The Emergence of Russian Foreign Policy*", Washington D.C: US Institute of Peace.

Bajpai, Kanti and Mattoo, A. (1996), "*Securing India: Strategic Thought and Practice*", New Delhi: Manohar.

Black, J.L. (2004), "*Vladmir Putin and the New World Order Looking East, Looking West*", New York: Rowman and Littlefield.

Blank, Stephen J. (1997), "Russia and China in Central Asia", in Stephen J. Blank and Alvin Z. Rubinstein Durham (eds.), *Imperial Decline: Russia's Changing Role in Asia,* N.C.: Duke Univ. Press.

Blank, Stephen J. (1997), "*The Dynamics of Russian Weapons Sales to China*", Carlisle, Penna: Strategic Studies Institute, U.S. Army War College.

Boquerat, G. and Grare, Frederic (2004), "*India-China, Russia Intricacies of an Asian Triangle*", New Delhi; India Research Press.

Christopher, Bluth (2000), "*The Nuclear Challenge: US-Russian Strategic Relations After the Cold War*", Hants: Ashgate Publishing Limited.

Chufrin, G. (1999), "*Russia and Asia: The Emerging Security Agenda*", New York: Sipri OUP.

Chufrin, Gennady (1999), "Asia as a Factor in Russia's international Posture", in Gennady Chufrin (eds.), *Russia and Asia: The Emerging Security Agenda*, London: SIPRI, OUP.

Davisha, K. and Parrot B. (1994), "*Russia and New States of Eurasia: The Politics of upheaval*", Cambridge: Cambridge University Press.

Dawish, Adid and Davisha, Karen (1995), "*The Making of Foreign Policy in Russia and the New States of Eurasia*", New York: M.C. Sharpe.

Denda, Milorad (2000), "Partnership on Long Term Basis", *Review of International Affairs*, 51(1096): 2l-23.

Donaldson, R.H. and Nogee J. L. (1988), "*The Foreign Policy of Russia. Changing Systems, Enduring Interest*", New York: M. E. Sharpe.

Dutt, V.P. (2003), "Putin's Russia and India: Overview" in V.D. Chopra (eds.), *New Trends in Indo-Russian Relations*, New Delhi: Kalpaz.

Ellison, H.J. (1982), "*The Sino-Soviet Conflict*", Seattle: University of Washington Press.

Garnet, Sherman W. (1998), "*Limited Partnership*", Report of the Study Group on Russia-China Relations, Washington DC: Carnegie Endowment for International Peace.

Garnett, W.S (1998), "*Limited Partnership: Russia China Relations in a Changing Asia*", Washington: Russian and Eurasian Program Carnegie Endowment for International Peace.

Gill, G. and Slider, D. (1993), "*The Politics of Transition: Shaping a Post-Soviet Future*", Cambridge: Cambridge University Press.

Goldman, M. I. (1992), "*What Went Wrong with Perestroika*", New York: W.W. Norton.

Gorbachev, Mikhail (1987), "*Perestroika: New Thinking for our Country and the World*", London: Collins.

Grare, Frederic and Mattoo, Amitabh (2001), "*India and ASEAN' the Politics of India's Look East Policy*", New Delhi: Manohar.

Guo, Sujian and Shiping Hua, (eds.) (2008), "New Dimensions of China's Foreign Policy", Lanham, Md.: Lexington Books.

Harada, Chikahito (1997), "*Russia and North-East Asia*", Adelphi Paper 310, Oxford, U.K.: Oxford Univ. Press for the International Institute for Strategic Studies.

Harris, Stuart and Klintworth, Garry (1995), "*China as a Great Power: Myths, Realities and Challenges in Asia-Pacific Region*", Melbourne: Longman.

Huntington, S. P. (1991), "*The Third Wave: Democratization in the Late Twentieth Century*", Norman: University of Oklahoma Press.

Igor, Rogachev (1997), "Russia-China: The Principles and Parameters of Partnership", *Far Eastern Affairs*, 3: 25.

Igor, Ivanov (2002), "*The New Russian Diplomacy*", Washington D.C: The Nixon Centre and Brookings Institution Press.

Kavet, R.E. and A.V. Kozhmiakin (1997), "The Foreign Policy of the Russian Federation", London: MacMillan.

Laszek Buszynski (1992), "*Russian and Asia-Pactfic Region*", Banberra: Australian National University Press.

Lederer, Ivo (1962), "*Russian Foreign Policy: Essays in Historical Perspective*", New Haven: Yale University.

Leo, Cooper (1999), "*Russia and One World. New States of Play one International Stage*", London: Macmillan.

Levin, Michael (2008), "*The Next Great Clash: China and Russia vs. the United States*", Westport, Conn.: Praeger Security International.

Lo, Bobo (2002), "*Russian Foreign Policy in the Post-Soviet Era: Reality, Illusion and Mythmaking*", New York: Palgrave Macmillan.

Lo, Bobo (2003), "Vladmir Putin and the Evolution of Russian Foreign Policy", London: Blackwell pub.

Malik Hafeez (1997), "*Role of US, Russia and China in the world Order*", London: Macmillan.

Mathews, M. (1986), "*Poverty in the Soviet Union*", Cambridge: Cambridge University Press.

Menon, Rajan and Charles E. Ziegler (2002), "The Balance of Power and US Foreign Policy Interest in the Russian Far East" in Thorton J and Ziegler E.C. (eds.), *Russia's Far East a region at risk*, London; University of a Washington Press.

Miller, John (1993), "*Mikhail Gorbachev and End of Soviet Power*", London: Macmillan.

Mosbahi, Mohiaddin (1994), "*Russia and Third World in Post Soviet Era*", Gainesville: University of Florida Press.

Nathan, A.J. and Ross R.S. (1997), "*The Great Wall and The Empty Fortress; China's Search for Identity*", New York: W. W. Norton.

Nathan, Andrew J. and Robert S. Ross (1997), "*The Great Wall and the Empty Fortress: China's Search for Security*", New York: W. W. Norton.

Nelson, Harvey W. (1998), "*Power and Insecurity: Beijing Moscow and Washington, 1949-1988*", London: Lynne Reinner Publishers.

Pillsbury, Michael (2000), "*China and Debates the Future Security Environment*", Washington DC: National Defence University Press.

Pipe, Caroline K. (1998), "*Russia and World 1917-1991*", London: Arnold.

Qimao, Chen (1999), "Sino-Russian Relationship after the Break Up of the Soviet Union" in Chaufrin Gennady (eds.), *Russia and Asia: Emerging Security Agenda,* New York: SIPRA, OUP.

Rahr, Alexander (1994), "*Russia and Europe: An End of Confrontation?*", London: The Royal Institute of International Affairs.

Rasgotra, M. and Chopra V.D. (1997), "*Indiia's Relation with Russia and China*", New Delhi: Gyan Books.

Rasgotra, M. (1998), "*India's Relation with 'he Russia and China: A New Phase*", New Delhi: Gyan Books.

Ray, J.K. (2000), "*Asia Annual 2000* ", Delhi: Shipra.

Rodman, Peter W. (2000), "Between Friendship and Rivalry", Ted Galen Carpenter and James A. Dorn (eds.) *China's Future: Constructive Partner or Emerging Threat?* Washington, D.C.: CATO Institute.

Roger, E. Kanet (1992), "*Soviet Foreign Policy in Transition*", Cambridge: Cambridge University Press.

Sakwa, Richard (2003), "Putin's Foreign Policy: Transforming the East" in Garbriel Gorodetsky (eds.), *Russia Between East and West: Russian Foreign Policy on the Threshold of 21st Century*, London: Frankcass.

Sergounin, Alexander (1999), "*Sino-Russian Military-Technical Cooperation: Incentives, Major Programs, Security Implications*", Taipei: IPSS.

Shambaugh, David (2002), "*Annual Report on the Military Power of the People's Republic of China*", Washington, D.C.

Shambaugh, David (2003), "*Modernizing China's Military: Progress, Problems, and Prospects,* Berkeley: University of California Press.

Sherarman, Peter (1995), "*Russian Foreigr. Policy Since 1990*", San Francisco: Westview Press.

Singh, Swaran (2003), "India-China-Russia: A Strategic Triangle?", *World Focus,* 24(1): 9- 17.

Solzhenitsyn, A. (1991), "*Rebuilding Russia*", London: March.

Ted, Apopf (1999), "*Understanding of Russian Foreign Policy*", Pennsylvania: Pennsylvania State University.

Tremin, Dmitri (1999), "*Russia's China Problem*", Washington: Carnegic Endowment for International Peace.

Trenin, Dmitri (2003), "The China Factor: Challenge and Chance for Russia", in Garnett, (eds.), *Rapprochement or Rivalry,* Washington DC: Blackwell.

Trenin, Dmitri. (2002), "*The End of Eurasia: Russia on the Border between Geopolitics and Globalization*", Washington, D.C.: Carnegie Endowment for International Peace.

Tsyganov, Yuri V. (1999), "Russia and China: What is in the pipeline" in Gennady Chufrin (eds.), *Russia and Asia: The Emerging Security Agenda,* London: SIPRI, OUP.

Voskresensski, A.D. (2003), "*Russia and China: A Theory of inter-State Relation*", London and New York: Routledge Curzon.

Webber, MarK (1996), "The International Politics of Russia and the Successor States", Manchester: Manchester University Press.

White, S. (1993), "*After Gorbachev*", Cambridge: Cambridge University Press.

Wishnick, Elisabeth (2001), "*Mending Fences, The Evolution of Moscow's China Policy from Brezhnev to Yeltsin*", Seattle, Wash.: University of Washington Press.

Xuejun, Li and A. Taklev, (2001), "*Sino-Rusian Relationship: a Search at the Turn of the Century*", Beijing: China Nationality Press.

Yakovlev, A.G (2002), "Triangle: Russia-China India: Prospects and Contrast", *China Report*, 38(1): 101-113.

Yeltsin, Boris (1994), "*The View From Kretvzlin*", London: Harper Collins.

Yu, Guozheng (2000), "*The Russian Far East in Sino-Russian Relations*", Changchum, China.

Ziegler, Charles E. (1993), "*Foreign Policy and East Asia: Learning and Adaptation in the Gorbachev Era*", Cambridge Soviet Paperbacks, Cambridge: Cambridge University Press.

INDEX